# THE CHURCH OF SOUTH INDIA

---

# THE BOOK OF
# COMMON WORSHIP

THE CHURCH OF SOUTH INDIA

# THE BOOK OF
# COMMON WORSHIP

AS AUTHORISED BY
THE SYNOD 1962

LONDON
OXFORD UNIVERSITY PRESS
NEW YORK   MADRAS
1963

*Oxford University Press, Amen House, London E.C.4*

GLASGOW  NEW YORK  TORONTO  MELBOURNE  WELLINGTON
BOMBAY  CALCUTTA  MADRAS  KARACHI  LAHORE  DACCA
CAPE TOWN  SALISBURY  NAIROBI  IBADAN  ACCRA
KUALA LUMPUR  HONG KONG

*The material in this book was first published in a
series of separate booklets in the years 1950–1962.
First published in this form 1963*

PRINTED IN GREAT BRITAIN

# NOTE

*The Book of Common Worship* comprises the following, all revised by the Synod Liturgy Committee with the approval of the Executive Committee in September 1961, and authorised by the Synod for general use in January 1962.

AN ORDER FOR THE LORD'S SUPPER OR THE HOLY EUCHARIST. 1950. 2nd edition, 1954. 3rd edition, 1962.

THE PROPERS: BIBLE READINGS, COLLECTS, AND PREFACES, PROPER FOR SUNDAYS AND SPECIAL DAYS, SEASONS, AND OCCASIONS. 1962. The second edition of *Bible Readings and Collects*, 1954, and *Additional Bible Readings and Collects*, 1956

ORDERS FOR MORNING AND EVENING WORSHIP. 1962. The second edition of *An Order for Morning and Evening Prayer and a Service of Worship*, 1958

AN ORDER FOR HOLY BAPTISM. 1955. 2nd edition, 1960.

AN ORDER OF SERVICE FOR THE RECEPTION OF BAPTIZED PERSONS INTO THE FULL FELLOWSHIP OF THE CHURCH, COMMONLY CALLED CONFIRMATION. 1950. 2nd edition, 1960.

THE COVENANT SERVICE. 1962. The second edition of *Order of Service for such as would enter into or renew their COVENANT WITH GOD*, 1956.

THE MARRIAGE SERVICE. 1960. 2nd edition, 1962.

THE BURIAL SERVICE. 1960. 2nd edition, 1962.

THE ORDINAL. 1958. A revision of the orders used in 1947. 2nd edition, 1962.

A SHORT ORDER FOR THE LORD'S SUPPER. 1962.

DAILY BIBLE READINGS. 1954. 2nd edition, 1960.

# ACKNOWLEDGEMENTS

THE Synod Liturgy Committee acknowledges with grateful thanks the permission of the following to use and to adapt copyright material:

The General Synod of the Anglican Church of Canada and Cambridge University Press (from the *Draft Prayer Book, Canada*, 1955); His Grace the Archbishop of Cape Town (from *The South African Prayer Book*); C.M.S. Press, Kottayam (from *The Order of Public Worship of the Mar Thoma Syrian Church*); The Metropolitan of the Church of India, Pakistan, Burma, and Ceylon, and the S.P.C.K.-in-India (from *The C.I.P.B.C. Prayer Book*, and *The Ceylon Liturgy*); The Church of Scotland Committee on Public Worship and Aids to Devotion (from *The Book of Common Order* and *The Ordinal*); The Publication Committee of the Episcopal Church in Scotland and Cambridge University Press (from the *Scottish Prayer Book*); The Guild of Health, London (from *Dedication and Thanksgiving After Childbirth*); The Rev. Canon H. G. G. Herklots; The Rt. Rev. L. S. Hunter (from *New Every Morning*, 1936); Longmans, Green & Co. Ltd. (from *A Cambridge Bede Book*, edited by E. Milner-White); Mrs. Macnutt and A. R. Mowbray & Co. Ltd. (from *The Prayer Manual*, by F. B. Macnutt); The Methodist Publishing House (from *The Book of Offices*, 1936); Oxford University Press (from *A Book of Public Worship*, by J. Huxtable, J. Marsh, R. Micklem, and J. Todd; from *Daily Prayer*, edited by E. Milner-White and G. W. Briggs; from *Divine Service*, 1926, by W. E. Orchard); The Custodian of the *Book of Common Prayer* of the Protestant Episcopal Church in the United States of America; Mrs. Temple and Macmillan & Co., Ltd. (from *A Call to Prayer* for the Life and Liberty Movement, 1918, by William Temple); The United Basel Mission, Mangalore (from *The Liturgy of the United Basel Mission*

*Church in India*); The General Council of the United Church of Canada (from *The Book of Common Order*).

Quotations from the Bible have been taken, as a rule, from the Revised Standard Version, by permission of the National Council of Churches of Christ in the United States of America, but occasionally they have been taken from the Authorised Version, the Revised Version, and the Book of Common Prayer.

The Book of Common Prayer and the Authorised Version of the Bible are Crown copyright and extracts from them are used by permission. Extracts from the Prayer Book as Proposed in 1928 have been used by permission of the holders of the copyright.

Verse divisions, &c., in Psalms and Canticles are mostly from *The Oxford Psalter*, by permission of Oxford University Press.

# CONTENTS

# DIRECTIONS TO MINISTERS

# AN ORDER FOR THE LORD'S SUPPER OR THE HOLY EUCHARIST

1 THE CONDUCT OF THE SERVICE. The parts appointed for the deacon in reading the litany, leading the worship of the people, and assisting the presbyter in the administration of Communion, may be taken either by another presbyter or by a layman.

Throughout the service the people's part is printed in heavy type.

The paragraph sign (¶) shows that the passage so marked is an alternative.

Where there is no special difficulty or objection, the presbyter throughout the service, unless he is reading Scripture from the lectern or preaching from the pulpit, should stand or kneel behind the Holy Table, facing the people. The offertory should be brought forward by others.

Hymns or lyrics may be sung at the beginning of the service, after the reading from the Old Testament, after the creed, at the offertory, and at the close: but the hymn at the offertory at least should not be omitted.

The three lessons from Scripture may be read by one, two, or three people, lay or ordained. The Bible carried in at the beginning shall be used throughout.

The reader each time begins by naming first the book of the Bible, then the chapter, then the verse, so as to help the people in their places to read their own Bibles along with him.

2 THE USE OF THE THIRD PART ONLY. The third part of the service, the Breaking of the Bread, may be used without the first and second parts in any special service which includes the praise of God, the confession of sin and prayer for forgiveness, the reading and preaching of the word of God, and intercession.

3 A DEVOTION BEFORE THE LORD'S SUPPER may be followed on the night (or at any other convenient time during the week) before a celebration. Where it is difficult for all to gather in church, the Devotion may be conducted by church-workers in different parts of the pastorate, or in each family by the head of the household. The Devotion may instead be followed before the celebration, with an interval for silent common prayer. One at least of the passages in the Devotion should be read with every celebration, either beforehand or in the Liturgy itself, and all should be read sometimes.

4 INVITATION TO VISITORS. When visitors are present, the presbyter may invite any communicant member of any Church with which the Church of South India is in fellowship to partake of the Holy Communion with this congregation (*see* the Constitution, II. 14).

5 THE CONFESSION. The alternatives recommended are:

Psalm 51:1–3, 9–12, said or sung.

One of the Confessions in the Orders for Morning and Evening Worship.

A hymn.

Extempore prayer by the presbyter.

6 THE COLLECTION OF ALMS. The people may place their alms in vessels set at the door as they enter the church; or a collection may be made during the hymn after the creed or the offertory hymn. If it is made during the hymn after the creed, the alms are kept in some suitable place until the offertory. If it is made during the offertory hymn, the alms of the non-communicants who go out after the benediction may be received at the doors. In any case, the alms, with the bread and wine for the Communion, are brought to the Lord's Table during the offertory hymn. This may suitably be done by lay people.

7 THE PEACE. When the Peace is given, the giver places his right palm against the right palm of the receiver, and each closes his left hand over the other's right hand. The Peace is given before the offertory (see Matthew 5:23, 24) as a sign of fellowship, and the offertory sentences recall St. Augustine's teaching that the sacrifice we offer is our unity in Christ. The presbyter gives the Peace to those ministering with him, and these in turn give it to the congregation. It may be passed through the congregation either along the rows, or from those in front to those behind. Each person as he gives the Peace may say in a low voice 'The peace of God', or 'The peace of God be with you'.

8 THE EUCHARISTIC PRAYER. At the words 'took bread', the presbyter shall take the paten with the bread into his hand. At the words 'took the cup', he shall take the cup into his hand.

9 THE COMMUNION. Communion may be administered in the place and manner customary in the congregation. Communion may be given by 'tables', i.e. the people come forward to receive in front of the Holy Table, and each row remains kneeling till the presbyter dismisses them with a blessing such as 'The grace of the Lord Jesus Christ be with you all'. When this is done, it is convenient to have stewards.

A spoon may be used for administering the wine.

10 THE WORDS OF ADMINISTRATION. The following alternatives are recommended:

'The body of our Lord Jesus Christ, which was given for thee, preserve thy body and soul unto everlasting life. Take and eat this in remembrance that Christ died for thee, and feed on him in thy heart by faith with thanksgiving. 'The blood of our Lord Jesus Christ, which was shed for thee, preserve thy body and soul unto everlasting life. Drink this in remembrance that Christ's blood was shed for thee, and be thankful.'

*Or*

'The Communion of the Body of Christ.' 'The Communion of the Blood of Christ.'

*Or*

'Take ye, eat ye; this is the body of Christ which is broken for you: this do in remembrance of him.' 'This cup is the new covenant in the blood of Christ, which is shed for many unto remission of sins: drink ye all of it.'

11 EXCOMMUNICATION. Any who are excommunicate or under discipline shall leave at the end of the Ministry of the Word.

**12 The Communion of the Sick.** The presbyter shall make it known to his people that they may receive Communion in their homes if sick or disabled.

(*a*) There may be a shortened celebration in the sickroom, some members of the congregation being present if possible. The parts of the service which shall not be omitted are: the Eucharistic Prayer from 'Truly holy, truly blessed' to the end of the Lord's Prayer; the Words of Administration; and the Peace Benediction. The other parts may be included or omitted at the discretion of the minister.

(*b*) When there has been a celebration of the Lord's Supper in church, some of the bread and wine which have been set apart may be taken by a presbyter as soon as convenient to the sick in his parish, and may be administered to the sick without any further setting apart. In such a case, the parts of the Order for the Lord's Supper which shall not be omitted are: the Lord's Prayer, the Words of Administration, and the Peace Benediction. Other parts of the service may be used at the discretion of the minister, except for the Eucharistic Prayer from 'Truly holy, truly blessed' to 'world without end. **Amen.**'

The following lessons may be read: Isaiah 43:1–3a; 2 Corinthians 1:3–5; John 10:14, 15, 27–30; and Psalm 130; with the following collect:

Almighty God, Giver of life and health: Look mercifully, we beseech thee, on *this* thy *servant*, that by thy blessing upon *him* and upon those who minister to *him, he* may speedily be restored to health, if it be thy gracious will, and give thanks to thee in thy holy Church; through Jesus Christ our Lord. **Amen.**

The following collects in *The Propers* may also be found suitable: Seventh after Christmas; Twenty-fourth after Pentecost; Luke Evangelist and Physician.

**13 The Parts of the Order.** Some traditional names are added as alternatives, and parts that may be omitted, or may be used at different places, are in brackets.

(The Warrant; the Commandments or Summary; the Exhortation.)

*The Preparation.* (Collection; hymn.) The Collect for Purity; the 'Glory to God' or *Gloria in Excelsis*, the 'Holy God' or *Trisagion*, the Litany of the Lamb.

The Call to Self-examination, short silence, the Invitation, the Confession, the Gracious Word of God or the Comfortable Words, short silence, the Prayer for Forgiveness or Absolution.

*The Ministry of the Word of God.* The Greeting or Salutation; the Collect of the Day; the Old Testament Lesson, (psalm or hymn,) the Epistle, the Gospel; the Sermon; the Creed.

(Announcements; hymn; collection; biddings.)

The Intercession (First and Second Litanies), the Intercessory Collects; the First Benediction.

*The Breaking of the Bread.* The Offertory Sentences, (the Peace,) hymn, (collection,) the Offertory, the 'Holy Father' or Offertory Prayer.

The 'Be present'; the Greeting, the 'Lift up your hearts' or *Sursum Corda*, the Preface (general or proper), the Thrice Holy or Sanctus, the 'Blessed be he' or *Benedictus qui venit*; the Eucharistic Prayer: (*a*) The Words of Institution, the First Response, (*b*) the Remembering or Anamnesis, the Second Response, and (*c*) the Invocation of the Spirit or Epiclesis; the Lord's Prayer; silence; the 'We do not presume' or Prayer of Humble Access.

The Breaking of the Bread or Fraction; the Communion, the Words of Administration. (The 'Lamb of God' or *Agnus Dei*.)

The First and Second Thanksgiving Collects, the Response; the Peace Benediction. (Hymn.)

# CHRISTIAN INITIATION: 1 BAPTISM

1 PREPARATON FOR BAPTISM. Candidates able to answer for themselves must be well instructed in the Christian faith and way of life and approved by the minister and the representatives of the congregation before they are brought to baptism. At the beginning of their preparation they may be publicly received as catechumens, according to the service appointed, and commended to the prayers of the congregation.

2 PARENTS AND GODPARENTS. Only those who are baptized and in good standing may bring their children for baptism.

If, however, a husband and wife have been excommunicated, or otherwise disciplined, but still come regularly to church and show a sincere desire to bring up their children in the Christian way, the minister may, at his discretion, make an exception to the above rule and may baptize their children.

The parents or guardians of a child to be baptized must inform the minister some days beforehand that they desire to bring their child to baptism. They must also submit to him the names of the godparents, where it is customary to have them.

As soon as possible after notice has been given, full inquiry should be made and all necessary instruction and exposition of the service given by the minister or some other competent and instructed leader. For this purpose the parents or guardians should be visited in their home, or they should be asked to attend at the church at a convenient hour. Instruction should be regarded as particularly necessary in the case of a first child. If the parents or guardians cannot give the promises contained in the service, the minister may defer the baptism of the child.

The choice of godparents to make the promises at the baptism of children and to share in the responsibility of their Christian upbringing, and the choice of witnesses at the baptism of those able to answer for themselves, are ancient customs observed in many congregations of the Church of South India.

Only those who have the status of communicants are qualified to act as godparents or witnesses.

The parents of children to be baptized make the promises, and the godparents, if any, make the promises with them.

At the time of baptism one of the parents may present the child to the minister and name him, and the other may receive him back.

3 THE CONDUCT OF THE SERVICE. Baptism is as a rule administered at a public service of the church.

It is usual for the ministrant of the sacrament to be a presbyter; but deacons are authorised to baptize, and a layman or woman may do so in an emergency.

If a person or child to be baptized is too weak or ill to be brought to church, he may be baptized at home. The service may be shortened, but must include at least baptism with water in the name of the Trinity and the Lord's Prayer. When a person thus baptized has recovered from his sickness, he comes to a public service of the Church and makes his promises. The minister declares that he has been received into the Church, and the congregation welcomes him, using the forms provided at the end of the service ('The Thanksgiving'). In the case of a sick child, the parents bring him to church after recovery and make the promises for him, and the minister declares that he has been received into the Church.

Where it is the custom to administer baptism during a service of the Lord's Supper, the Order for Holy Baptism may come after the Preparation and be substituted for the Ministry of the Word.

If baptism is administered during Morning or Evening Worship, the Order for Holy Baptism may be substituted for the Ministry of the Word; or it may be added at the beginning of the Prayers (the creed in Morning or Evening Worship being omitted); or at the end of the service.

If it is uncertain whether a candidate has been baptized already or not, the following form of words is used at the baptism:

'*N*, if thou art not already baptized, I baptize thee in the name of the Father, and of the Son, and of the Holy Spirit.'

A candidate who has been converted from a faith in which idolatry is not practised (e.g. Islam) is not required to renounce idolatry.

At the discretion of the minister, the questions in the Renunciation, Profession of Faith, and the Promises, and those in the Office for the Making of Catechumens, may be put in the form of statements to be repeated after him by the candidates, or the parents (and godparents). Supplementary questions (or statements) may also be framed in accordance with the particular circumstances of the candidates.

When those able to answer for themselves are baptized together with their children, the minister reads the Order for the Baptism of those able to answer for themselves, with the addition of the promises in the Order for the Baptism of Infants. The parents (together with godparents, if any) make the promises for their children after they have made their own.

Baptisms, whether public or private, must be entered in the Baptismal Register.

For the combination of Baptism and Confirmation in one service, see the directions on the Confirmation Service.

4. ADDITIONAL CEREMONIES. In addition to the optional use of the sign of the cross, as provided for in the Order, the ceremonies of the light and of the putting on of a white garment may be performed immediately after the Reception into the Church, at the discretion of the minister and with the goodwill of the congregation.

It should be noted, however, that they in no wise add to the efficacy of baptism.

## CHRISTIAN INITIATION: 2 CONFIRMATION

1 PREPARATION FOR CONFIRMATION. The candidates are prepared by the presbyter of their own congregation, or someone appointed by him, that in the power of the Holy Spirit they may give themselves to Christ.

2 THE CONDUCT OF THE SERVICE. In the Church of South India Confirmation is administered by the bishop or a presbyter. If a presbyter conducts the service, it is desirable that he should be the presbyter responsible for that congregation, or a presbyter appointed by the bishop.

Before the service, the bishop, or the presbyter appointed by him, may meet the candidates for such examination as he thinks desirable.

The Confirmation Service may be held:

(*a*) as a separate service;

(*b*) during a celebration of the Lord's Supper (in this case the minister substitutes the Confirmation Service for The Ministry of the Word in the Order for the Lord's Supper); or

*Or*

(*c*) along with Baptism, if the candidates have been specially prepared to be baptized and confirmed at the same time. In this case the two orders may be combined in one service as follows:

*Baptism:* The Declaration of the Word.

*Confirmation:* The Vows.

*Baptism:* The Baptism, the Thanksgiving.

*Confirmation:* The Confirmation, the Reception.

This arrangement is suitable only when all candidates are being baptized and confirmed at the same time.

## CHRISTIAN INITIATION:
## 3 THE RECEPTION OF MEMBERS
## FROM OTHER CHURCHES

For those who have not been baptized or confirmed, baptism or confirmation according to the rites of the Church of South India is necessary, and is sufficient. The Church of South India recognises as true baptism the baptism of all denominations which baptize with water in the name of the Trinity.

Baptized and communicant members in good standing of Churches in communion with the Church of South India who desire for good reasons to be received into the Church of South India shall if possible bring letters of recommendation from some responsible member of their former Church. The minister, after inquiry, shall read out their names during public worship, preferably at a celebration of the Lord's Supper after the First Benediction. He bids them stand up in their places, and says: 'We bid you welcome to the fellowship of this Church, in the name of the Father, and of the Son, and of the Holy Spirit.' Persons thus received shall be given a membership card.

If the persons who desire to be received into the Church of South India are baptized and communicant members of a Church not in communion with the Church of South India, the presbyter shall satisfy himself as to their motives, and shall ascertain that there is no impediment to their reception. He shall report the matter to the Pastorate Committee and to the bishop. If there is no impediment, he shall receive them during public worship, preferably at a celebration of the Lord's Supper, after the First Benediction, in the following form:

*The presbyter stands; the person(s) to be received come(s) forward, and the presbyter says:*

BELOVED, we are now, in the sight of God and of this congregation, to receive *this person* who *desires* full fellowship in the Church of South India. Let us first pray God to bless this work of ours, that it may bear the fruit of love.

### Let us pray

Go before us, O Lord, in all our doings with thy most gracious favour, and further us with thy continual help; that in all our works begun, continued, and ended in thee, we may glorify thy holy name, and finally by thy mercy obtain everlasting life; through Jesus Christ our Lord. **Amen.**

*Then the presbyter asks:*

Do you desire to be admitted into the Church of South India as a communicant member?
*Answer:* I do.

*Q.*—Do you accept the teachings and discipline of the Church of South India as being in accordance with the word of God?
*A.*—I do.

*Q.*—Will you remain faithful to that teaching and submit *yourself* willingly to that discipline, seeking only the ministrations of this Church and the Churches which are in fellowship with it?
*A.*—I will.[1]

*Then the person(s) to be received kneel(s), and the presbyter, still standing, says:*

Lord, have mercy upon us.
**Christ, have mercy upon us.**
Lord, have mercy upon us.

**Our Father . . .**

### Let us pray

ALMIGHTY and everlasting God, the Father of our Lord Jesus Christ, we give thee hearty thanks that

---

[1] *Questions may be added according to particular needs, e.g.* 'Do you renounce all such teaching as is contrary to God's holy word?'

thou hast called us to the knowledge of thy grace and to faith in thee; increase this knowledge and confirm this faith in us evermore. Grant to thy *servant* the continued aid of thy Holy Spirit, that abiding with us in the fellowship of thy holy Church, *he* may remain faithful in thy service and obtain thy promises, through the same our Lord Jesus Christ, who liveth and reigneth with thee and the same Spirit, ever one God, world without end. **Amen.**

*Then the presbyter, giving the right hand of fellowship, says:*

We admit you into the fellowship of the Church of South India, in the name of the Father, and of the Son, and of the Holy Spirit. **Amen.**

MAY God, the Giver of all grace, who has called you to share his eternal glory through Christ, make you perfect, stablish and strengthen you. **Amen.**

# THE COVENANT SERVICE

Besides the solemn act of dedication which is its central purpose, the Covenant Service contains the main elements of the Preparation and the Ministry of the Word in the Order for the Lord's Supper: adoration, confession, absolution, plentiful use of Scripture and exhortation based upon it, and repeated declaration of Christian faith. There is thus no need for a creed or a sermon. It may therefore be used as an alternative for the first and second parts of the Liturgy, and should be completed, wherever possible, by the Breaking of the Bread, beginning at the offertory sentences. An additional sentence has been included to provide a fitting transition. The service will thus be incorporated into the central act of Christian worship. The time taken by this arrangement will be found to be about the same as for the normal service of the Liturgy.

## THE MARRIAGE SERVICE

1 THE BANNS OF MARRIAGE. The banns of those who are to be married shall be published in the church on Sundays as required by the Synod, the minister saying:

I publish the banns of marriage between *N*, son of . . ., a member of the . . . Church in . . ., and *M*, daughter of . . ., a member of the . . . Church in . . . .

If any of you know just cause why these two persons should not be joined together in marriage, you are to declare it in writing to the presbyter in charge of this congregation.

This is the first [*or* second *or* third] time of asking.

*The Minister then says:*

Let us pray for *N* and *M*.

O GOD our Father, we ask for thy blessing upon these thy servants, who seek to be joined together in marriage. Prepare them, we beseech thee, for this sacred union, and be thou their Guide all the days of their life; through Jesus Christ our Lord. **Amen.**

2 COMMUNION. It is desirable that the man and his wife should receive the Lord's Supper, either as part of the Marriage Service, or as soon as convenient thereafter.

For other conditions to be fulfilled, see *Guidance concerning Marriage Law . . . of the Church of South India* (C.L.S., Madras, 1959).

## A DEVOTION BEFORE THE LORD'S SUPPER

*As often as possible, a special service is held the night before the celebration of the Lord's Supper, or at some other convenient time. Or it may be held before the celebration on the same day, with an interval for silent common prayer. Such a service may include, besides the praise of God and the confession of sin and the reading and preaching of God's word:*

1 *The reading of 1 Corinthians 11:23–29;*

2 *The reading, with responses, of the Ten Commandments or of our Lord's Summary of the Law and the Prophets;*

3 *An Exhortation.*

### THE TEN COMMANDMENTS

GOD spoke all these words, saying:

I I am the Lord your God. You shall have no other gods before me.

*After each commandment except the last the people say:*

**Lord, have mercy upon us, and incline our hearts to keep this law.**

II You shall not make for yourself a graven image, or any likeness of anything that is in heaven above, or that is in the earth beneath, or that is in the water under the earth; you shall not bow down to them or serve them.

III You shall not take the name of the Lord your God in vain.

IV Remember the sabbath day, to keep it holy. Six days you shall labour, and do all your work; but the seventh day is a sabbath to the Lord your God.

V Honour your father and your mother.

VI You shall not kill.

VII You shall not commit adultery.

VIII You shall not steal.

## THE ORDINAL

1 The ordination of deacons and presbyters should ordinarily take place at separate services.

If, however, it is thought necessary to ordain them together, the order of service should be as follows:

Presentation of those to be ordained deacons.
Presentation of those to be ordained presbyters.
Collect and lessons, the latter to be chosen by the bishop.
Sermon, creed, hymn.
Examination of those to be ordained deacons.
Examination of those to be ordained presbyters.
Ordination of deacons.
Ordination of presbyters.
The first of the additional suffrages in the litany:
'For the servants of God now ordained deacons and presbyters . . .'
The Proper Preface, as appointed for the Ordination of Presbyters.

2 When an ordination is in an Indian language, a hymn of prayer for the coming of the Holy Spirit which is composed in an Indian metre and set to an Indian tune should be chosen.

3 The wife of a newly ordained minister should receive communion together with her husband immediately after the bishop and his assistants.

4 Other lessons may be chosen at the discretion of the bishop instead of the lessons prescribed.

5 Before any ordination, full notice shall be given during public worship both in the church in which the service is to be held and in the churches in which the candidates for ordination are best known; and it shall be said that if anyone knows of any objection he is required to make it known in writing immediately to the bishop. Also, the people shall be asked to pray for the candidates.

Rules for the election of bishops are laid down in the Constitution, Chapter IV.

## A SHORT ORDER FOR THE
## LORD'S SUPPER

THIS Short Order is intended for use when there is a celebration on a week-day, but may also be used on Sundays and on Special Days when the full Order is found to be too long. The full Order, however, is normal, and shall be used wherever possible.

The following passages may also be omitted if desired:

The Gracious Word of God;
The First Lesson;
The Sermon (if there is another service with a sermon the same week);
The Creed;
The Prayer 'We do not presume';
Hymns, except at the offertory.

On the other hand, any passage in the full Order may be added.

# AN ORDER FOR
# THE LORD'S SUPPER
## OR THE HOLY EUCHARIST

IX You shall not bear false witness.

X You shall not covet.                                    Exod. 20

**Lord, have mercy upon us, and write all these thy laws in our hearts, we beseech thee.**

## OUR LORD'S SUMMARY OF THE LAW AND THE PROPHETS

OUR Lord Jesus Christ said: Hear, O Israel: The Lord our God, the Lord is one; and you shall love the Lord your God with all your heart, and with all your soul, and with all your mind, and with all your strength. This is the great and first commandment. And a second is like it, You shall love your neighbour as yourself. There is no other commandment greater than these. On these two commandments depend all the law and the prophets.                Mark 12 and Matt. 22

**Lord, have mercy upon us, and incline our hearts to keep this law.**

## AN EXHORTATION

DEARLY beloved, it is right that we who would come to the Lord's Table should take to heart the mystery of this sacrament. The mystery is this: that Christ truly gives unto us his body and blood as food and drink of everlasting life. The Good Shepherd has laid down his life for the sheep; he who was without guile has died for sinners, the Head for his members, the Bridegroom for his bride the Church; in obedience to the Father's will and in infinite love to us, the High Priest has offered himself as the perfect sacrifice. By his death he has done away with all that stood in the way of our fellowship with God the Father, that we may assuredly be his children, be upheld by his love, be guided by him all the days of our life, and rejoice in the hope of his glory. In the fellowship of his sufferings he calls us to crucify the old man with his lusts, and to bear trials and tribulations patiently, to the glory of his name. In the power of his resurrection he calls us to newness of life. In the fellowship of his Spirit he joins us together, and seeks to change us into his image. By the same Spirit he pours his love into our hearts, so that we may love one another, and our enemies for his sake.

If any man will not lay this to heart, but is minded to continue in sin and unrighteousness, let him not approach the

Table of the Lord. Let a man examine himself and so let him eat of that bread and drink of that cup. The worthiness which the Lord requires from us is that we be truly sorry for our sins and find our joy and salvation in him. For we come to this supper not as righteous in ourselves, but trusting in the righteousness of Christ our Saviour. He invites us to partake of this holy meal.

# THE LORD'S SUPPER

## THE PREPARATION

*A hymn or psalm may be sung or said.*

*As the ministers come to the Lord's Table, the people stand.
The presbyter, or one of those with him, carries in both hands
the Bible from which the lessons are to be read, and places it
on the Table or on a lectern. The presbyter may stand behind
the Table, facing the people.*

*The presbyter says, the people standing:*

### Let us pray

ALMIGHTY God, unto whom all hearts be open, all
desires known, and from whom no secrets are hid:
Cleanse the thoughts of our hearts by the inspiration of thy Holy Spirit, that we may perfectly love
thee, and worthily magnify thy holy name; through
Christ our Lord. **Amen.**

*Then all sing or say:*

**Glory to God in the highest, and on earth peace
among men in whom he is well pleased. We praise
thee, we bless thee, we worship thee, we glorify thee,
we give thanks to thee for thy great glory, O Lord
God, Heavenly King, God the Father almighty.**

**O Lord, the only-begotten Son Jesus Christ, O
Lord God, Lamb of God, Son of the Father, that
takest away the sin of the world, have mercy upon us;
thou that takest away the sin of the world, receive
our prayer. Thou that sittest at the right hand of God
the Father, have mercy upon us.**

**For thou only art holy, thou only art Lord, thou
only art most high, O Jesus Christ, with the Holy
Spirit, in the glory of God the Father. Amen.**

¶ *Or this ancient hymn, thrice repeated:*

Holy God:
**Holy and mighty, holy and immortal, have mercy
on us.**

¶ *Or this litany, the deacon leading the responses:*

WORTHY is the Lamb that hath been slain to
receive the power, and riches, and wisdom, and
might, and honour, and glory, and blessing.

**Unto the Lamb be glory!**

Unto him that sitteth on the throne, and unto the
Lamb, be the blessing, and the honour, and the
glory, and the dominion, for ever and ever.

**Unto the Lamb be glory!**

Worthy art thou, for thou wast slain, and didst
purchase unto God with thy blood men of every
tribe, and tongue, and people, and nation.

**Unto the Lamb be glory! Salvation unto our God
which sitteth on the throne, and unto the Lamb.
Blessing, and glory, and wisdom, and thanksgiving,
and honour, and power, and might, be unto our God
for ever and ever. Amen.**                    Rev. 5 and 7

¶ *Or another hymn may be sung.*

---

*If there has been no special service before the celebration,
one or more of the passages set for the 'Devotion before the
Lord's Supper' may be read here.*

*Then the presbyter says:*

BRETHREN, we have come together to hear God's most holy word, and to receive the body and blood of the Lord. Let us therefore kneel and examine ourselves in silence, seeking God's grace that we may draw near to him with repentance and faith.

*All kneel. After a short silence the presbyter says:*

YE that do truly and earnestly repent you of your sins, and are in love and charity with your neighbours, and intend to live a new life, following the commandments of God and walking from henceforth in his holy ways, make your humble confession to almighty God, that you may be reconciled anew to him through our Lord Jesus Christ.

*The deacon leading, all say together:*

**Heavenly Father, we confess that we have sinned against thee and our neighbour. We have walked in darkness rather than in light; we have named the name of Christ, but have not departed from iniquity. Have mercy upon us, we beseech thee; for the sake of Jesus Christ forgive us all our sins; cleanse us by thy Holy Spirit; quicken our consciences; and enable us to forgive others; that we may henceforth serve thee in newness of life, to the glory of thy holy name. Amen.**

¶ *Or the presbyter may use certain other forms.*

*Then the presbyter stands and says:*

HEAR the gracious word of God to all who truly turn to him through Jesus Christ.

Come unto me, all ye that labour and are heavy laden, and I will give you rest.

Matt. 11:28

God so loved the world, that he gave his only-begotten Son, that whosoever believeth on him should not perish, but have eternal life.

John 3:16

Faithful is the saying, and worthy of all acceptation, that Christ Jesus came into the world to save sinners.

1 Tim. 1:15

If any man sin, we have an Advocate with the Father, Jesus Christ the righteous: and he is the propitiation for our sins.

1 John 2:1, 2

*After a short silence, the presbyter says:*

ALMIGHTY God, our heavenly Father, who of his great mercy has promised forgiveness of sins to all who forgive their brethren and with hearty repentance and true faith turn unto him: Have mercy upon you; pardon and deliver you from all your sins; confirm and strengthen you in all goodness; and bring you to eternal life; through Jesus Christ our Lord.

**Amen. Thanks be to God.**

*The presbyter may say* us *and* our *for* you *and* your; *if so, the prayer precedes the reading of the Gracious Word of God.*

# THE MINISTRY OF THE WORD OF GOD

The Lord be with you:
**And with thy spirit.**

## Let us pray

*The Collect of the Day, or another short prayer, is said.*

*The people may stand for the reading of Scripture, or at least for
the reading of the Gospel. Before each lesson the reader says:*
Hear the word of God, as it is written in [*the name of the
Book*], in the . . . chapter, beginning at the . . . verse; *and after it he says:* Here ends the lesson.

*The lesson from the Old Testament is read, and after it the
people say:*
**Thanks be to thee, O God.**

*A psalm or hymn may be sung.*

*The Epistle is read, and the people say:*
**Thanks be to thee, O God.**

*The Gospel is read, and the people say:*
**Praise be to thee, O Christ.**

*The Sermon is preached, the people sitting.*

*The Nicene Creed is said or sung by all, standing.*

**I believe in one God the Father almighty, Maker
of heaven and earth, And of all things visible and
invisible :
And in one Lord Jesus Christ, the only-begotten
Son of God, Begotten of his Father before all worlds,
God of God, Light of Light, Very God of very God,
Begotten, not made, Being of one substance with the
Father, By whom all things were made : Who for us
men, and for our salvation, came down from heaven,
And was incarnate by the Holy Spirit of the Virgin**

Mary, And was made man, And was crucified also for us under Pontius Pilate. He suffered and was buried, And the third day he rose again according to the Scriptures, And ascended into heaven, And sitteth on the right hand of the Father. And he shall come again with glory to judge both the quick and the dead: Whose kingdom shall have no end.

And I believe in the Holy Spirit, The Lord, the Giver of life, Who proceedeth from the Father and the Son, Who with the Father and the Son together is worshipped and glorified, Who spake by the Prophets.

And I believe One, Holy, Catholic, and Apostolic Church. I acknowledge one Baptism for the remission of sins. And I look for the Resurrection of the dead, And the Life of the world to come. Amen.

¶ *Or the Apostles' Creed may be said or sung.*

*Announcements may be made here, and the collection may be taken. A hymn may also be sung.*

*Biddings for prayer may be made, and then, all kneeling, one of these litanies is said or sung, the deacon leading; or the presbyter offers intercession in his own words for the Church and the world.*

### Let us pray

ALMIGHTY God, who hast taught us to make prayers and supplications, and to give thanks, for all men; hear us when we pray: That it may please thee to inspire continually the universal Church with the spirit of truth, unity, and concord:

**Hear us, we beseech thee, O Lord** (*and so after each petition*).

That it may please thee to grant that all they that do confess thy holy name may agree in the truth of thy holy word, and bear witness to it with courage and fidelity:

That it may please thee to lead the nations in the paths of righteousness and peace:

That it may please thee to guide with thy pure and peaceable wisdom those who bear authority in the affairs of men, especially the President of the Indian Republic . . . . . . . . and those who rule over us; that we and all men may be godly and quietly governed:

That it may please thee to give grace to all bishops, presbyters, and deacons, especially thy servants . . . . . . . ., our Moderator, and . . . . . . . ., our Bishop, that by their life and doctrine they may set forth thy true and living word, and rightly and duly administer thy holy sacraments:

That it may please thee to guide and prosper those who are labouring for the spread of thy gospel among the nations, and to enlighten with thy Spirit all places of education, learning, and healing:

That it may please thee that through thy heavenly benediction we may be saved from dearth and famine, and may with thankful hearts enjoy the fruits of the earth in their season:

That it may please thee to give thy heavenly grace to all thy people in their several callings, and especially to this congregation here present; that, with meek heart and due reverence, they may hear, and receive, thy holy word; truly serving thee in holiness and righteousness all the days of their life:

That it may please thee of thy goodness, O Lord, to comfort and succour all them, who in this transitory life are in trouble, sorrow, need, sickness, or any other adversity:

And we praise thee for all thy servants departed this life in thy faith and fear, beseeching thee to give us grace that we may follow their good examples, and with them be made partakers of thy heavenly kingdom:

---

¶ *The second litany:*

FOR the peace that is from above, and for the salvation of our souls, let us pray to the Lord.

**Lord, have mercy** (*and so after each bidding*).

For the peace of the whole world, for the welfare of God's holy Churches, and for the union of all, let us pray to the Lord.

For our bishops and all other ministers, especially . . . . . . . . ., our Moderator, and . . . . . . . . ., our Bishop, that with a good heart and a pure conscience they may accomplish their ministry, let us pray to the Lord.

For the rulers of our country and all in authority, let us pray to the Lord.

For the sick, the suffering, the sorrowful, and the dying, let us pray to the Lord.

For the poor, the hungry, orphans and widows, and them that suffer persecution, let us pray to the Lord.

For ourselves and all who confess the name of Christ, that we may show forth the excellencies of him who called us out of darkness into his marvellous light, let us pray to the Lord.

That, with all his servants who have served him here and are now at rest, we may enter into the fullness of his unending joy, let us pray to the Lord.

---

*After either litany the presbyter says:*

## Let us pray

ALMIGHTY God, the Fountain of all wisdom, who knowest our necessities before we ask, and our ignorance in asking: We beseech thee to have compassion upon our infirmities; and those things, which for our unworthiness we dare not, and for our blindness we cannot ask, vouchsafe to give us, for the worthiness of thy Son Jesus Christ our Lord. **Amen.**

¶ *Or this:*

ALMIGHTY and everlasting God, by whose Spirit the whole body of the Church is governed and sanctified: Receive our supplications and prayers, which we offer before thee for all estates of men in thy holy Church, that every member of the same, in his vocation and ministry, may truly and godly serve thee; through our Lord and Saviour Jesus Christ. **Amen.**

*The presbyter then gives the First Benediction:*

THE grace of the Lord Jesus Christ, and the love of God, and the fellowship of the Holy Spirit, be with you all. **Amen.**

*He may say* us *instead of* you.

*Those who leave shall leave now.*

# THE BREAKING OF THE BREAD

*All stand, and the presbyter says:*

BEHOLD, how good and joyful a thing it is, brethren, to dwell together in unity.　　　Ps. 133:1

We, who are many, are one bread, one body, for we all partake of the one bread.　　　1 Cor. 10:17

**I will offer in his dwelling an oblation with great gladness, I will sing and speak praises unto the Lord.**
Ps. 27:6

*The Peace may be given here.*

*A hymn is sung, and the bread and wine for the Communion, together with the alms of the people, are brought forward and placed on the Table. Those who bear the offertory stand before the Table during the following prayer.*

*All standing, the presbyter says:*

HOLY Father, who through the blood of thy dear Son hast consecrated for us a new and living way to thy throne of grace, we come to thee through him, unworthy as we are, and we humbly beseech thee to accept and use us and these our gifts for thy glory. All that is in heaven and earth is thine, and of thine own do we give to thee. **Amen.**

*The bearers of the offertory return to their places.*

*The presbyter and people kneel, and say together:*

**Be present, be present, O Jesus, thou good High Priest, as thou wast in the midst of thy disciples, and make thyself known to us in the breaking of the bread, who livest and reignest with the Father and the Holy Spirit, one God, world without end. Amen.**

*The presbyter stands.*

The Lord be with you:
**And with thy spirit.**

Lift up your hearts:
**We lift them up unto the Lord.**

Let us give thanks unto our Lord God:
**It is meet and right so to do.**

IT is verily meet, right, and our bounden duty, that we should at all times, and in all places, give thanks unto thee, O Lord, Holy Father, almighty and everlasting God;

[1]Through Jesus Christ thy Son our Lord, through whom thou didst create the heavens and the earth and all that in them is, and didst make man in thine own image, and when he had fallen into sin didst redeem him to be the firstfruits of a new creation.

**Therefore with angels and archangels and with all the company of heaven, we laud and magnify thy glorious name; evermore praising thee, and saying, Holy, Holy, Holy, Lord God of hosts, heaven and earth are full of thy glory. Glory be to thee, O Lord most high.**

**Blessed be he that hath come and is to come in the name of the Lord, Hosanna in the highest.**

---

[1] *Instead of the words* Through Jesus Christ . . . a new creation, *another Preface proper to the season of the Christian Year or to the occasion may be said.* (*See pp. 69–72.*)

Truly holy, truly blessed art thou, O heavenly Father, who of thy tender love towards mankind didst give thine only Son Jesus Christ to take our nature upon him and to suffer death upon the cross for our redemption; who made there, by his one oblation of himself once offered, a full, perfect, and sufficient sacrifice, oblation, and satisfaction, for the sins of the whole world; and did institute, and in his holy gospel command us to continue, a perpetual memory of that his precious death, until his coming again: Who, in the same night that he was betrayed, took bread, and when he had given thanks, he brake it, and gave it to his disciples, saying, Take, eat, this is my body which is given for you: do this in remembrance of me. Likewise after supper he took the cup, and, when he had given thanks, he gave it to them, saying, Drink ye all of this; for this is my blood of the new covenant, which is shed for you and for many for the remission of sins: do this, as oft as ye shall drink it, in remembrance of me.

**Amen. Thy death, O Lord, we commemorate, thy resurrection we confess, and thy second coming we await. Glory be to thee, O Christ.**

Wherefore, O Father, having in remembrance the precious death and passion, and glorious resurrection and ascension, of thy Son our Lord, we thy servants do this in remembrance of him, as he hath commanded, until his coming again, giving thanks to thee for the perfect redemption which thou hast wrought for us in him.

**We give thanks to thee, we praise thee, we glorify thee, O Lord our God.**

And we most humbly beseech thee, O merciful Father, to sanctify with thy Holy Spirit us and these thine own gifts of bread and wine, that the bread which we break may be the communion of the body of Christ, and the cup which we bless the communion of the blood of Christ. Grant that, being joined together in him, we may all attain to the unity of the faith, and may grow up in all things unto him who is the Head, even Christ, our Lord, by whom and with whom, in the unity of the Holy Spirit, all honour and glory be unto thee, O Father almighty, world without end. **Amen.**

*Here the presbyter may kneel.*

As our Saviour Christ hath commanded and taught us, we are bold to say:

**Our Father, who art in heaven, Hallowed be thy name. Thy kingdom come; Thy will be done; In earth as it is in heaven. Give us this day our daily bread; And forgive us our trespasses, As we forgive them that trespass against us; And lead us not into temptation, But deliver us from evil. For thine is the kingdom, The power and the glory, For ever and ever. Amen.**

*Silence is kept for a space, all kneeling.*

**We do not presume to come to this thy Table, O merciful Lord, trusting in our own righteousness, but in thy manifold and great mercies. We are not worthy so much as to gather up the crumbs under thy Table. But thou art the same Lord, whose property is always to have mercy: Grant us therefore, gracious Lord, so to eat the Flesh of thy dear Son Jesus Christ, and to drink his Blood, that our sinful bodies and souls may be made clean by his most precious Body and Blood, and that we may evermore dwell in him, and he in us. Amen.**

*The presbyter rises, and breaks the bread, saying:*

THE bread which we break, is it not a communion in the body of Christ?  1 Cor. 10:16

¶ *Or this:*

THE things of God for the people of God.

¶ *Or he may break the bread in silence.*

*The ministers and people receive the bread and wine.*

*The following words of administration may be used:*

THE body of our Lord Jesus Christ, the Bread of life. The blood of our Lord Jesus Christ, the true Vine.

¶ *Or certain other words may be used.*

*During this time these words may be said or sung:*

**O Lamb of God, that takest away the sin of the world, have mercy upon us.**

**O Lamb of God, that takest away the sin of the world, have mercy upon us.**

**O Lamb of God, that takest away the sin of the world, grant us thy peace.**

¶ *Or some other hymn may be sung.*

*When all have partaken, the presbyter says:*

HAVING now by faith received the sacrament of the Body and the Blood of Christ, let us give thanks.

*One of the following prayers is said or sung by the presbyter alone, or by all together:*

O ALMIGHTY God, our heavenly Father, who hast accepted us as thy children in thy beloved Son Jesus Christ our Lord, and hast fed us with the spiritual food of his most precious Body and Blood, giving us the forgiveness of our sins and the promise of everlasting life: We thank and praise thee for these inestimable benefits, and we offer and present unto

thee ourselves, our souls and bodies, to be a holy
and living sacrifice, which is our reasonable service.
Grant us grace not to be conformed to this world,
but to be transformed by the renewing of our minds,
that we may learn what is thy good and perfect will,
and so obey thee here on earth, that we may at the
last rejoice with all thy saints in thy heavenly kingdom; through Jesus Christ our Lord, who liveth
and reigneth with thee and the Holy Spirit, one
God, for ever.

¶ *Or this:*

ALMIGHTY and everlasting God, we most heartily
thank thee, for that thou dost vouchsafe to feed us,
who have duly received these holy mysteries, with
the spiritual food of the most precious Body and
Blood of thy Son our Saviour Jesus Christ; and dost
assure us thereby of thy favour and goodness towards us; and that we are very members incorporate
in the mystical body of thy Son, which is the blessed
company of all faithful people; and are also heirs
through hope of thine everlasting kingdom, by the
merits of the most precious death and passion of
thy dear Son. And we most humbly beseech thee,
O heavenly Father, so to assist us with thy grace,
that we may continue in that holy fellowship, and
do all such good works as thou hast prepared for us
to walk in. And here we offer and present unto thee
ourselves, our souls and bodies, to be a reasonable,
holy, and living sacrifice unto thee, through Jesus
Christ our Lord, to whom with thee and the Holy
Spirit be all honour and glory, world without end.

**Amen. Blessing, and glory, and wisdom, and
thanksgiving, and honour, and power, and might, be
unto our God for ever and ever. Amen.**

*The presbyter gives the Second Benediction:*

THE peace of God, which passeth all understanding, keep your hearts and minds in the knowledge and love of God, and of his Son Jesus Christ our Lord: and the blessing of God almighty, the Father, the Son, and the Holy Spirit, be amongst you and remain with you always. **Amen.**

*The presbyter may say* our *and* us *instead of* your *and* you.

*A hymn of praise and thanksgiving, or a part of Psalm 103, or the Song of Simeon* (Nunc Dimittis), *may be sung after the benediction.*

*After the benediction the ministers go out, carrying with them the Bible, the gifts of the people, and the vessels used for the Communion. Any bread or wine set apart in the service which remains over is carried out to the vestry, and there is reverently consumed.*

*The Lord's Prayer may be said before the Thanksgiving, and the* Glory to God *after it, instead of at the usual places.*

*If the bread or wine set apart be insufficient, the presbyter, taking more, may say:*

OBEYING the command of our Lord Jesus Christ, we take this bread [wine] to be set apart for this holy use, in the name of the Father and of the Son and of the Holy Spirit. Amen.

¶ *Or the words of the Institution may be repeated.*

# THE PROPERS

## BIBLE READINGS, COLLECTS, AND PREFACES, PROPER FOR SUNDAYS AND SPECIAL DAYS, SEASONS, AND OCCASIONS

## TABLE I
## SUNDAYS AND OTHER SPECIAL DAYS OF THE CHRISTIAN YEAR

### BEFORE CHRISTMAS

4 The Coming of the Lord
3 Christ in the Old Testament

2 The Fore-runner
1 God at Hand

### CHRISTMAS EVE AND CHRISTMAS DAY

### AFTER CHRISTMAS

1 Mankind restored
2 The Wise Men
3 The Presentation of Christ
4 The Baptism of Jesus

5 The First Disciples
6 The First Sign
7 The New Blessedness

### BEFORE EASTER

9 The Creation
8 The Fall
7 Redemption
   *Ash Wednesday*
6 Temptation

5 Repentance
4 Forgiving one another
3 The Transfiguration
2 The Cross

PALM SUNDAY, HOLY WEEK, AND EASTER

AFTER EASTER

1 'My Lord and my God'
2 The Good Shepherd
3 The Light of the World
4 Way, Truth, and Life

5 Going to the Father
  *Ascension Day*
6 Christ the High Priest

PENTECOST AND TRINITY SUNDAY

AFTER PENTECOST: THE CHRISTIAN LIFE
GOD'S CALL

2 The Call of God
3 Man's Choice

4 Faith
5 The Freedom of the Spirit

BIBLE, CHURCH, AND SACRAMENTS

6 The Bible
7 The Church
8 The Sacraments
9 The Unity of the Church

10 The Witness of the Church
11 The Ordained Ministry

THE LIFE OF DEVOTION

12 Love towards God
13 Prayer
14 Joy

15 Enduring to the End
16 Self-denial
17 The Lord's Day

LIFE IN THE WORLD

18 Love towards Neighbour
19 The Family
20 The Church in the World

21 Daily Work
22 The State
23 Christian Giving

THE END

24 The Christian Hope
25 The Two Worlds

26 The Two Ways
27 The Day of the Lord

SUNDAY NEXT BEFORE ADVENT

FOURTH SUNDAY BEFORE CHRISTMAS
THE BEGINNING OF ADVENT

*The Coming of the Lord*

ALMIGHTY God, give us grace that we may cast away the works of darkness, and put upon us the armour of light, now in the time of this mortal life, in which thy Son Jesus Christ came to visit us in great humility; that in the last day, when he shall come again in his glorious majesty to judge both the quick and the dead, we may rise to the life immortal; through him who liveth and reigneth with thee and the Holy Spirit, now and ever. **Amen.**

*This collect may be said after the Collect of the Day every day until Christmas Eve.*

Morning

| | |
|---|---|
| Isaiah 40:1–5 | The Way of the Lord |
| ¹Psalm 96 | 'O sing to the Lord' |
| Romans 13:11–14 | Time to wake up |
| John 3:16–21 | Darkness and Light |

Evening

| | |
|---|---|
| Isaiah 26:1–9 | The Strong City |
| John 3:1–15 | The New Birth |

THIRD BEFORE CHRISTMAS
SECOND IN ADVENT

*Christ in the Old Testament*

ALMIGHTY God, who in many and various ways didst speak to thy chosen people by the prophets, and hast given us, in thy Son our Saviour Jesus Christ, the fulfilment of the hope of Israel: Hasten, we beseech thee, the coming of the day when all things shall be subject to him, who liveth and reigneth with thee and the Holy Spirit, ever one God, world without end. **Amen.**

¹ *The Psalms are said or sung after the reading of the Old Testament or at the beginning of the service.*

*Where the third Sunday before Christmas is kept as Bible Sunday, the collect appointed for the sixth Sunday after Pentecost may be said after the Collect of the Day.*

| | |
|---|---|
| Isaiah 11:1–10 | An Ensign to the Peoples |
| Psalm 40:1–8 | 'I waited patiently' |
| Romans 15:4–13 | Christ and the Promise |
| Luke 24:13–27 | Christ the Interpreter |
| Deuteronomy 18:9–19 | The Prophet to come |
| Acts 8:26–40 | The Ethiopian Minister |

### SECOND BEFORE CHRISTMAS
### THIRD IN ADVENT
*The Fore-runner*

O LORD Jesus Christ, who at thy first coming didst send thy messenger to prepare thy way before thee: Grant that we, paying urgent heed to the message of repentance, may with hearts prepared await thy final coming to judge the world; who with the Father and the Holy Spirit ever livest and reignest, one God, world without end. **Amen.**

| | |
|---|---|
| Malachi 3:1–5 | The Messenger of the Covenant |
| Luke 1:68–79 (*for Psalm*) | 'Blessed be the Lord' |
| Revelation 3:14–22 | Christ at the Door |
| Luke 3:2–17 | Fruits of Repentance |
| Isaiah 40:6–11 | Good Tidings for Zion |
| Matthew 11:2–15 | More than a Prophet |

### NEXT BEFORE CHRISTMAS
### FOURTH IN ADVENT
*God at Hand*

O LORD, raise up, we pray thee, thy power, and come among us, and with great might succour us; that whereas, through our sins and wickedness, we are sorely hindered in running the race that is set before us, thy bountiful grace and mercy may speedily help and deliver us; through Jesus Christ thy Son our Lord, to whom, with thee and the Holy Spirit, be honour and glory, world without end. **Amen.**

| Zechariah 2:10–13 | 'The Lord has roused himself' |
| Psalm 50:1–6 | 'The Mighty One' |
| Philippians 4:4–7 | 'Rejoice in the Lord' |
| Luke 15:1–10 | Seeking the lost |
| Isaiah 64:1–8 | 'Come down' |
| Revelation 1:1–8 | Alpha and Omega |

*When this Sunday falls on Christmas Eve, the Propers for the Sunday are read in the morning, and the Propers for Christmas Eve are read in the evening.*

## CHRISTMAS EVE

O GOD, who makest us glad with the yearly remembrance of the birth of thy only Son, Jesus Christ: Grant that as we joyfully receive him for our Redeemer, so we may with sure confidence behold him, when he shall come to be our Judge; who liveth and reigneth with thee and the Holy Spirit, one God, world without end. **Amen.**

O GOD, who before all others didst call shepherds to the cradle of thy Son: Grant that by the preaching of the gospel the poor, the humble, and the forgotten, may know that they are at home with thee; through Jesus Christ our Lord. **Amen.**

| Micah 5:2–4 | Little Bethlehem |
| Psalm 19 | 'The heavens are telling' |
| Titus 3:3–7 | Saved by God's Mercy |
| Luke 2:1–20 | The Birth of Jesus |

## CHRISTMAS DAY

ALMIGHTY God, who hast given us thine only-begotten Son to take our nature upon him and to be born of a pure virgin: Grant that we, being born again, and made thy children by adoption and grace, may daily be renewed by thy Holy Spirit; through the same our Lord Jesus Christ, who liveth and reigneth with thee and the same Spirit, ever one God, world without end. **Amen.**

| Isaiah 9:2–7 | A great Light |
| Psalm 85:8–13 | 'Let me hear' |
| Hebrews 1:1–12 | These last Days |
| John 1:1–14 | The Word made Flesh |
| Isaiah 7:10–14 | Immanuel |
| Matthew 1:18–25 | The Spirit |

## NEXT AFTER CHRISTMAS

### Mankind restored

ALMIGHTY God, who didst wonderfully create man in thine own image, and didst yet more wonderfully restore him: Grant, we beseech thee, that as thy Son our Lord Jesus Christ was made in the likeness of men, so we may be made partakers of the divine nature; through the same thy Son, who with thee and the Holy Spirit liveth and reigneth, one God, world without end. **Amen.**

| Jeremiah 31:10–13 | The Ransom of Jacob |
| Psalm 8 | 'O Lord, our Lord' |
| Hebrews 2:10–18 | Jesus the Deliverer |
| John 1:14–18 | The Glory of the Son |
| Isaiah 45:18–25 | God and Saviour |
| Romans 11:25–36 | Mercy on all |

## SECOND AFTER CHRISTMAS

### The Wise Men

O GOD, who by a star didst guide the Wise Men to the worship of thy Son: Lead, we pray thee, to thyself the wise and the great in every land, that unto thee every knee may bow, and every thought be brought into captivity; through Jesus Christ our Lord. **Amen.**

| Isaiah 60:1–7 | 'Nations shall come' |
| Psalm 72:1–19 | 'Give the king' |
| Revelation 21:22—22:2 | The Glory of the Nations |
| Matthew 2:1–12 | The Wise Men |

Job 28                              The Beginning of Wisdom
1 Corinthians 1:18–25                     The Wisdom of God

*These Propers may be followed also on the traditional date for
the Epiphany, January 6.*

### THIRD AFTER CHRISTMAS

*The Presentation of Christ*

O LORD Jesus Christ, who as a child wast presented
in the temple and received with joy by Simeon and
Anna as the Redeemer of Israel: Mercifully grant
that we, like them, may be guided by the Holy
Spirit to acknowledge and love thee unto our lives'
end; who with God the Father, in the unity of the
Holy Spirit, livest and reignest God, world without
end. **Amen.**

1 Samuel 1:20–28                      Hannah and Samuel
Psalm 118:19–26                            'Open to me'
Romans 11:33—12:2                      The Ways of God
Luke 2:22–40                          The Presentation

Micah 4:1–5                            The Lord's House
Luke 2:41–52                             The Boy Jesus

*These Propers may be followed also on the traditional date,
February 2.*

### FOURTH AFTER CHRISTMAS

*The Baptism of Jesus*

O LORD Jesus Christ, who didst humble thyself to
take the baptism of sinful men, and wast forthwith
declared to be the Son of God: Grant that we who
have been baptized into thee may rejoice to be the
sons of God, and servants of all; for thy name's
sake, who with the Father and the Holy Spirit livest
and reignest ever one God, world without end.
**Amen.**

| Isaiah 42:1–7 | The Chosen Servant |
| Psalm 2 | 'Why do the nations...' |
| Galatians 3:23–29 | God's Promise |
| Mark 1:1–11 | The Baptism of Jesus |

| Isaiah 49:1–6 | A Light to the Nations |
| Colossians 2:8–15 | Buried and raised with Him |

*The series of Propers for Sundays after Christmas is followed only until the ninth Sunday before Easter.*

FIFTH AFTER CHRISTMAS

*The First Disciples*

ALMIGHTY God, whose blessed Son did call the apostles and send them forth to preach his name in all the world: Grant us like grace, that obeying his call we may be faithful disciples and witnesses to him, who with thee and the Holy Spirit liveth and reigneth, ever one God, world without end. **Amen.**

| Isaiah 8:11–18 | Isaiah's Disciples |
| Psalm 119:33–40 | 'Teach me, O Lord' |
| Philippians 2:12–18 | Lights in the World |
| Mark 1:16–20 | The First Disciples |

| Jeremiah 1:4–10 | The Call of Jeremiah |
| Matthew 10:1–16 | The Mission of the Twelve |

SIXTH AFTER CHRISTMAS

*The First Sign*

ALMIGHTY God, the Giver of strength and joy: Change, we beseech thee, our bondage into liberty, and the poverty of our nature into the riches of thy grace; that by the transformation of our lives thy glory may be revealed; through Jesus Christ, our Lord. **Amen.**

| 1 Kings 17:8–16 | The Widow's Cruse |
| Psalm 111 | 'I will give thanks' |

| 2 Peter 1:3–8 | The Love that abounds |
| John 2:1–11 | Water turned into Wine |

| Ezekiel 47:1–12 | Healing Waters |
| 1 Corinthians 15:35–45 | A life-giving Spirit |

SEVENTH AFTER CHRISTMAS

*The New Blessedness*

ALMIGHTY and everlasting God, who art always
more ready to hear than we to pray, and art wont to
give more than either we desire, or deserve: Pour
down upon us the abundance of thy mercy, forgiving us those things whereof our conscience is
afraid, and giving us those good things which we
are not worthy to ask, but through the merits and
mediation of Jesus Christ, thy Son, our Lord.
**Amen.**

| Isaiah 61:1–4 | A Garland for Ashes |
| Psalm 103:1–5, 19–22 | 'Bless the Lord' |
| 1 Peter 3:8–18 | Blessing and blessed |
| Matthew 5:1–12 | The Beatitudes |

| Deuteronomy 11:26–32 | Blessing or Curse |
| Luke 10:17–24 | 'Blessed are your eyes' |

NINTH BEFORE EASTER

*The Creation*

O ALMIGHTY God, who hast created the heavens
and the earth, and hast made man in thine own
image: Give us grace so to meditate on thy power,
wisdom, and love, that we may glorify thee in thy
works; through Jesus Christ our Lord. **Amen.**

| Genesis 1:1–5, 26–31 | The Creation |
| Psalm 8 | 'O Lord, our Lord' |
| Revelation 21:1–7 | The new Creation |
| John 5:1–18 | The Father's Work and the Son's |

Job 38:1–11          The Foundations
Colossians 1:9–20          Christ in Creation

### EIGHTH BEFORE EASTER

*The Fall*

O GOD of love, who in a world estranged from thee didst send forth thy Son to turn mankind from darkness to light, and from the power of Satan to thyself the living God: Overcome in us, we pray thee, all pride and self-will, and remake us a people in whom thou art well pleased; through Jesus Christ our Lord. **Amen.**

Genesis 3:1–19          The Fall
Psalm 14          'The fool says'
Romans 5:12–19          The First Adam and the Second
John 8:39–47          The Father of Lies

Jeremiah 17:9–17          The Deceitful Heart
Romans 3:21–30          'All come short'

### SEVENTH BEFORE EASTER

*Redemption*

O GOD, the Strength of all them that put their trust in thee: Mercifully accept our prayers; and because through the weakness of our mortal nature we can do no good thing without thee, grant us the help of thy grace, that in keeping of thy commandments we may please thee, both in will and deed; through Jesus Christ our Lord. **Amen.**

Exodus 6:2–9          God and Moses
Psalm 115:1–11          'Not to us'
Titus 2:11–14          The Appearing of the Glory
Luke 19:1–10          Salvation to the House of Zacchaeus

Isaiah 44:21–28          God the Redeemer
Romans 8:26–39          'God is for us'

## ASH WEDNESDAY

ALMIGHTY and everlasting God, who hatest nothing that thou hast made, and dost forgive the sins of all them that are penitent: Create and make in us new and contrite hearts, that we, worthily lamenting our sins, and acknowledging our wretchedness, may obtain of thee, the God of all mercy, perfect remission and forgiveness; through Jesus Christ our Lord. **Amen.**

*This collect may be said, after the Collect of the Day, every day till the day before Palm Sunday.*

| | |
|---|---|
| Isaiah 58:1–8 | True Fasting |
| Psalm 51:6–12 | 'Behold, thou desirest truth' |
| 2 Corinthians 7:2–10 | Godly Sorrow |
| Matthew 6:16–21 | 'Not as the hypocrites' |
| | |
| Joel 2:12–17 | 'Rend your hearts' |
| 1 Corinthians 9:19–27 | Paul the Athlete |

## SIXTH BEFORE EASTER: FIRST IN LENT

*Temptation*

O ALMIGHTY God, who alone canst order the unruly wills and affections of sinful men: Grant unto thy people, that they may love the thing which thou commandest, and desire that which thou dost promise; that so, among the sundry and manifold changes of the world, our hearts may surely there be fixed, where true joys are to be found; through Jesus Christ our Lord. **Amen.**

| | |
|---|---|
| Exodus 17:1–7 | The People at Rephidim |
| Psalm 95 | 'O come, let us sing' |
| James 1:12–18 | Enduring Trial |
| Matthew 4:1–11 | The Temptation of Jesus |
| | |
| Exodus 32:1–14 | The Golden Calf |
| 1 Corinthians 10:1–13 | The Way out of Temptation |

### FIFTH BEFORE EASTER: SECOND IN LENT

*Repentance*

GRANT, we beseech thee, merciful Lord, to thy faithful people pardon and peace, that they may be cleansed from all their sins, and serve thee with a quiet mind; through Jesus Christ our Lord. **Amen.**

| | |
|---|---|
| 2 Samuel 12:1–13 | Nathan and David |
| Psalm 32 | 'Blessed is he' |
| 1 John 1:5—2:2 | The Advocate |
| Luke 15:11–32 | The Prodigal Son |
| Jeremiah 7:1–15 | Lying Words |
| Luke 11:24–36 | The Example of Nineveh |

### FOURTH BEFORE EASTER: THIRD IN LENT

*Forgiving one another*

GRANT, O Lord, that as thy Son our Saviour Jesus Christ prayed for his enemies on the cross, so we may have grace to forgive those that wrongfully or scornfully use us; that we ourselves may be able to receive thy forgiveness; through the same Jesus Christ our Lord. **Amen.**

| | |
|---|---|
| Genesis 50:15–21 | Joseph and his Brothers |
| Psalm 15 | 'O Lord, who shall sojourn...?' |
| Colossians 3:12–17 | Love the Bond of Perfectness |
| Matthew 18:21–35 | The Two Debtors |
| 1 Samuel 24 | The Forbearance of David |
| Mark 11:19–26 | Forgiving and forgiven |

### THIRD BEFORE EASTER: FOURTH IN LENT

*The Transfiguration of Jesus*

O ALMIGHTY and everlasting God, whose blessed Son revealed himself to his chosen apostles when he was transfigured on the holy mount, and amidst the excellent glory spake with Moses and Elijah of his departure which he should accomplish at Jerusalem: Grant to us thy servants, that, beholding the brightness of his countenance, we may be strengthened to bear the cross, and be changed into his likeness from glory to glory; through the same Jesus Christ our Lord. **Amen.**

| | |
|---|---|
| Exodus 24:12–18 | Moses on the Mountain |
| Psalm 27 | 'The Lord is my light' |
| 2 Peter 1:16–19 | A Lamp in a dark Place |
| Luke 9:28–36 | The Transfiguration |
| Exodus 34:29–35 | Moses' Face |
| 2 Corinthians 3:4–18 | The new Glory |

*These Propers may be followed also on August 6, the traditional day of the Transfiguration.*

## SECOND BEFORE EASTER: PASSION SUNDAY

*The Cross*

O BLESSED Saviour, who by thy cross and passion didst give life to the world: We pray thee to enlighten, visit, and comfort, all thy servants who bear the cross and glory in thy name; whom with the Father and the Holy Spirit we worship and glorify, one God, for ever and ever. **Amen.**

| | |
|---|---|
| Job 19:21–27 | The living Redeemer |
| Psalm 130 | 'Out of the depths' |
| Hebrews 9:11–15 | The redeeming Death |
| Mark 10:35–45 | A Ransom for many |
| Isaiah 44:1–8 | Redeemer and Rock |
| Matthew 11:20–30 | The Invitation of Jesus |

## NEXT BEFORE EASTER: PALM SUNDAY

*This collect may be said daily until Thursday evening:*

ALMIGHTY and everlasting God, who, of thy tender love towards mankind, hast sent thy Son, our

C 1163                    C

Saviour Jesus Christ, to take upon him our flesh, and to suffer death upon the cross, that all mankind should follow the example of his great humility: Mercifully grant that we may both follow the example of his patience, and also be made partakers of his resurrection; through the same Jesus Christ our Lord. **Amen.**

*This collect may be said on Palm Sunday only:*

O CHRIST, the King of glory, who didst enter the holy city in meekness to be made perfect through the suffering of death: Give us grace, we beseech thee, in all our life here to take up our cross daily and follow thee, that hereafter we may rejoice with thee in thy heavenly kingdom; who livest and reignest with the Father and the Holy Spirit, God, world without end. **Amen.**

| | |
|---|---|
| Zechariah 9:9–12 | 'Your king comes' |
| Psalm 118:19–26 | 'Open to me' |
| Philippians 2:5–11 | 'He emptied himself' |
| Mark 15 | Trial, Death, and Burial |
| *or* John 12:12–19 | The Triumphal Entry |
| | |
| Genesis 22:1–14 | Abraham and Isaac |
| Mark 11:1–11 | The Triumphal Entry |

MONDAY

| | |
|---|---|
| Isaiah 42:1–9 | 'My servant' |
| Psalm 13 | 'How long, O Lord?' |
| Ephesians 2:11–22 | Christ our Peace |
| Mark 11:12–19 | The Temple cleansed |
| | |
| Ezekiel 36:22–28 | God's Promises |
| Hebrews 10:19–25 | 'Be therefore bold' |

TUESDAY

| | |
|---|---|
| Isaiah 49:1–13 | A Light to the Gentiles |
| Psalm 31:1–5 | 'In thee, O Lord' |

| Romans 5:6–11 | Reconciled |
| Mark 11:20—12:44 | Questions |

| Isaiah 5:1–7 | God's Vineyard |
| 1 Peter 2:18–25 | Christ's Example |

WEDNESDAY

| Isaiah 50:4–9 | 'He is near' |
| Psalm 43 | 'Vindicate me, O God' |
| Hebrews 5:5–10 | Made perfect |
| Mark 14:1–11 | Anointed and sold |

| Numbers 21:4–9 | The brass Serpent |
| John 3:11–21 | Lifted up |

THURSDAY

O LORD Jesus Christ, who hast ordained this holy
sacrament to be a pledge of thy love, and a continual remembrance of thy passion: Grant that we,
who partake thereof by faith with thanksgiving,
may grow up into thee in all things, until we come
to thine eternal joy; who with the Father and the
Holy Spirit livest and reignest, one God, world
without end. **Amen.**

| Jeremiah 31:31–34 | The new Covenant |
| Psalm 63:1–4 | 'O God, thou art my God' |
| Hebrews 8:1–6 | A better Covenant |
| Mark 14:12–72 | The Upper Room and the Garden |

| Isaiah 63:7–9 | 'He was afflicted' |
| John 13 | Jesus and his Disciples |

GOOD FRIDAY

ALMIGHTY God, we beseech thee graciously to
behold this thy family, for which our Lord Jesus
Christ was contented to be betrayed, and given up
into the hands of wicked men, and to suffer death
upon the cross; who now liveth and reigneth with
thee and the Holy Spirit, ever one God, world without end. **Amen.**

O MERCIFUL God, who hast made all men, and hatest nothing that thou hast made: Have mercy upon thine ancient people the Jews, and upon all who have not known thee, or deny the faith of Christ crucified; take, we beseech thee, from every nation all ignorance, hardness of heart, and contempt of thy word; and so fetch them home, blessed Lord, to thy fold, that they may be one flock under one Shepherd, Jesus Christ our Lord; who liveth and reigneth with thee and the Holy Spirit, one God, world without end. **Amen.**

| Isaiah 52:13—53:12 | A Ransom for many |
| Psalm 22 | 'My God, my God' |
| Hebrews 10:4–18 | The true Sacrifice |
| John 18:1—19:16 | Arrest and Trials |

| Lamentations 1:7–12 | 'Is it nothing?' |
| John 19:17–42 | Friday Evening |

### SATURDAY

O LORD Jesus Christ, who after thy death on the cross wast laid in the tomb: Grant that we, having been buried with thee by baptism into thy death, may also be made partakers of thy resurrection; so that, serving thee here in newness of life, we may finally inherit thine everlasting kingdom; who livest and reignest with the Father and the Holy Spirit, ever one God, world without end. **Amen.**

| Daniel 12:1–4 | The Resurrection |
| Psalm 16 | 'Preserve me, O God' |
| 1 Peter 3:17–22 | Spirits in Prison |
| Matthew 27:57–66 | Burial; the Guard |

| Ezekiel 37:1–14 | The Valley of Dry Bones |
| Romans 6:1–11 | Buried with Him |

EASTER DAY

ALMIGHTY God, who through thine only-begotten Son Jesus Christ hast overcome death, and opened unto us the gate of everlasting life: Grant us so to die daily unto sin, that we may evermore live with him in the joy of his resurrection; through the same Jesus Christ our Lord. **Amen.**

| | |
|---|---|
| Exodus 15:1–11 | 'Doing wonders' |
| Psalm 118:14–17 | 'The Lord is my strength' |
| Colossians 3:1–4 | Life hid with Christ |
| John 20:1–18 | Jesus and Mary |
| | |
| Isaiah 12 | Wells of Salvation |
| Luke 24:13–35 | The Walk to Emmaus |

NEXT AFTER EASTER

*'My Lord and my God'*

ALMIGHTY Father, who hast given thine only Son to die for our sins, and to rise again for our justification: Grant us so perfectly, and without all doubt, to believe in his resurrection, that in thy sight our faith may never be reproved; through the same Jesus Christ our Lord. **Amen.**

| | |
|---|---|
| Zephaniah 3:14–20 | Bringing Israel home |
| Psalm 93 | 'The Lord reigns' |
| 1 John 5:1–12 | The World overcome |
| John 20:19–31 | The Risen Lord |
| | |
| 2 Kings 6:8–23 | 'Open his eyes' |
| John 11:17–44 | The Raising of Lazarus |

SECOND AFTER EASTER

*The Good Shepherd*

ALMIGHTY God, who hast given thine only Son to be unto us both a sacrifice for sin, and also an example of godly life: Give us grace that we may always most thankfully receive that his inestimable benefit, and also daily endeavour ourselves to follow the blessed steps of his most holy life; through the same Jesus Christ our Lord.  **Amen.**

| | |
|---|---|
| Ezekiel 34:11–16 | God the Shepherd |
| Psalm 23 | 'The Lord is my shepherd' |
| 1 Peter 2:18–25 | Shepherd and Bishop |
| John 10:7–18 | The Good Shepherd |
| Jeremiah 23:1–8 | Gathering the Flock |
| Luke 15:1–7 | The Lost Sheep |

### THIRD AFTER EASTER
*The Light of the World*

O THOU who art the Light of the minds that know thee, the Life of the souls that love thee, and the Strength of the wills that serve thee: Help us so to know thee that we may truly love thee, so to love thee that we may fully serve thee, whose service is perfect freedom; through Jesus Christ our Lord.
**Amen.**

| | |
|---|---|
| Isaiah 60:15–19 | The Lord our Light |
| Psalm 36:5–9 | 'Thy steadfast love' |
| 2 Corinthians 4:1–6 | The Light of Christ |
| John 9:1–11 | The Light of the World |
| Zechariah 14:1–7 | Light at Evening |
| Acts 26:1–20 | Light for Paul |

### FOURTH AFTER EASTER
*The Way, the Truth, and the Life*

O LORD Jesus Christ, who art the Way, the Truth, and the Life: Suffer us not, we pray thee, to wander from thee, who art the Way; nor to distrust thee, who art the Truth; nor to look for strength any-where but in thee, who art the Life; ever living and

reigning with the Father and the Holy Spirit, one
God, world without end. **Amen.**

| Proverbs 4:10–18 | The Way of Wisdom |
| Psalm 119:9–16 | 'How can a young man...?' |
| 1 John 1:1–4 | The Life made manifest |
| John 14:1–11 | The Way, the Truth, and the Life |
| Isaiah 30:19–26 | 'This is the way' |
| John 16:1–15 | The Spirit of Truth |

## FIFTH AFTER EASTER

*Going to the Father*

O LORD Jesus Christ, who hast gone to the Father
to prepare a place for us: Grant us so to live in
communion with thee here on earth, that hereafter
we may enjoy the fullness of thy presence; who
livest and reignest with the Father and the Holy
Spirit, ever one God, world without end. **Amen.**

| Daniel 7:9–14 | Ancient of Days and Son of Man |
| Psalm 67 | 'May God be gracious' |
| Ephesians 4:1–10 | Ascending and descending |
| John 16:25–33 | Going to the Father |
| Genesis 28:10–22 | Jacob's Dream |
| Mark 14:55–62 | At the Right Hand |

## ASCENSION DAY

GRANT, we beseech thee, almighty God, that like
as we do believe thine only-begotten Son our Lord
Jesus Christ to have ascended into the heavens, so
we may also in heart and mind thither ascend, and
with him continually dwell, who liveth and reigneth
with thee, O Father, and the Holy Spirit, one God,
world without end. **Amen.**

| 2 Kings 2:1–15 | The Ascension of Elijah |
| Psalm 47 | 'Clap your hands' |

Acts 1:1–11      The Ascension of Jesus
Luke 24:44–53      God's Promise

Isaiah 65:17–25      New Heavens and a new Earth
Acts 1:12–26      After the Ascension

## SIXTH AFTER EASTER
## SUNDAY AFTER ASCENSION

### *Christ the High Priest*

O GOD, whose blessed Son, our great High Priest, has entered once for all into the holy place, and ever liveth to intercede on our behalf: Grant that we, sanctified by the offering of his body, may draw near with full assurance of faith by the way which he has dedicated for us, and evermore serve thee, the living God; through the same thy Son our Lord Jesus Christ, who liveth and reigneth with thee, O Father, and the Holy Spirit, one God, world without end. **Amen.**

Genesis 14:14–20      Melchizedek
Psalm 110      'The Lord says to my lord'
Hebrews 4:14–16      A great High Priest
John 12:20–33      'I will draw all men'

Exodus 28:1–6, 15–30      Aaron's Robes
John 17:1–19      The High Priest's Prayer

## PENTECOST

O GOD, who according to thy promise hast given thy Holy Spirit to us thy people, that we might know the freedom of thy children and taste on earth our heavenly inheritance: Grant that we may ever hold fast the unity which he gives, and, living in his power, may be thy witnesses to all men; through Jesus Christ our Lord. **Amen.**

Joel 2:28–32      The Promise
Psalm 29      'Ascribe to the Lord'

| | |
|---|---|
| Acts 2:1–12 | Pentecost |
| John 14:15–26 | The Paraclete |
| | |
| Numbers 11:16, 24–29 | Moses and the Spirit |
| 1 Corinthians 12:1–13 | Many Gifts, one Spirit |

## NEXT AFTER PENTECOST: TRINITY SUNDAY

ALMIGHTY and everlasting God, who hast revealed thyself as Father, Son, and Holy Spirit, and dost ever live and reign in the perfect unity of love: Grant that we may always hold firmly and joyfully to this faith, and, living in praise of thy divine majesty, may finally be one in thee; who art three Persons in one God, world without end.

**Amen.**

| | |
|---|---|
| Isaiah 6:1–8 | A Vision of God |
| Psalm 97 | 'The Lord reigns' |
| Revelation 4 | The Throne in Heaven |
| Matthew 28:16–20 | The Name of God |
| | |
| Ezekiel 1:15—2:2 | The Likeness of a Throne |
| Ephesians 1:3–14 | The Summing up |

## SECOND AFTER PENTECOST

*The Call of God*

REMEMBER, O Lord, what thou hast wrought in us, and not what we deserve; and as thou hast called us to thy service, make us worthy of our calling; through Jesus Christ our Lord. **Amen.**

| | |
|---|---|
| Exodus 3:1–15 | The Call of Moses |
| Psalm 135:1–6 | 'Praise the name' |
| 1 Corinthians 1:26–31 | God's Choice |
| Luke 5:1–11 | The Catch of Fish |
| | |
| Judges 6:1, 11–24 | The Call of Gideon |
| Luke 14:15–24 | The Great Supper |

THIRD AFTER PENTECOST

*Man's Choice*

GRANT to us, Lord, we beseech thee, the spirit to think and do always such things as be rightful; that we, who cannot do anything that is good without thee, may by thee be enabled to live according to thy will; through Jesus Christ our Lord. **Amen.**

| | |
|---|---|
| Joshua 24:14–24 | The last Words of Joshua |
| Psalm 62 | 'For God alone' |
| Hebrews 4:1–13 | The Word of God |
| John 6:53–69 | 'To whom shall we go?' |
| Exodus 32:15–29 | The Lord's Side |
| Acts 4:5–22 | The Boldness of Peter and John |

FOURTH AFTER PENTECOST

*Faith*

O GOD, who, calling Abraham to go forth to a country which thou wouldest show him, didst promise that in him all the families of the earth would be blessed: Fulfil thy promise in us, we pray thee, giving us such faith in thee as thou shalt count unto us for righteousness; that in us and through us thy purpose may be fulfilled; through Jesus Christ our Lord. **Amen.**

| | |
|---|---|
| Genesis 12:1–9 | Abraham's Faith |
| Psalm 91 | 'He who dwells' |
| Hebrews 11:1–16 | The Work of Faith |
| Luke 7:1–10 | The Centurion and his Servant |
| Isaiah 30:8–18 | Quietness and Confidence |
| Luke 18:9–14 | The Pharisee and the Tax-collector |

FIFTH AFTER PENTECOST

*The Freedom of the Spirit*

O GOD, forasmuch as without thee we are not able to please thee: Mercifully grant, that thy Holy

Spirit may in all things direct and rule our hearts; through Jesus Christ our Lord. **Amen.**

| | |
|---|---|
| Exodus 12:51—13:10 | Out of Bondage |
| Psalm 31:1–8 | 'In thee, O Lord' |
| Galatians 5:1–15 | Christian Freedom |
| John 8:31–38 | Truth and Freedom |
| Micah 6:1–8 | What the Lord requires |
| Romans 8:12–27 | Spirit of Sonship |

## SIXTH AFTER PENTECOST

### The Bible

BLESSED Lord, who hast caused all Holy Scriptures to be written for our learning: Grant that we may in such wise hear them, read, mark, learn, and inwardly digest them, that by patience, and comfort of thy holy word, we may embrace and ever hold fast the blessed hope of everlasting life, which thou hast given us in our Saviour Jesus Christ. **Amen.**

*This collect may be said also on the third Sunday before Christmas*

| | |
|---|---|
| Deuteronomy 6:1–9 | 'Hear, O Israel' |
| Psalm 119:105–112 | 'Thy word is a lamp' |
| Romans 10:1–13 | The Calling of God |
| Mark 12:18–27 | A Lesson from Scripture |
| Jeremiah 23:23–32 | The Word like Fire |
| Luke 4:16–30 | Jesus in the Synagogue |

## SEVENTH AFTER PENTECOST

### The Church

O ALMIGHTY God, who hast built thy Church upon the foundation of the apostles and prophets, Jesus Christ himself being the head Corner-stone: Grant us so to be joined together in the unity of the Spirit by their doctrine, that we with all the saints may be made a holy temple acceptable unto thee; through Jesus Christ our Lord. **Amen.**

| Exodus 19:1–8 | A holy Nation |
| Psalm 87 | 'On the holy mount' |
| 1 Peter 2:1–10 | God's own People |
| Matthew 16:13–19 | Founded on a Rock |

| Isaiah 43:8–13 | God's Witnesses |
| Matthew 18:1–20 | Little Ones and Brothers |

EIGHTH AFTER PENTECOST

*The Sacraments*

O LORD Jesus Christ, who hast ordained the signs whereby we are assured of thy gracious work in us: Grant that, being born anew of water and the Spirit, we may by faith receive thy precious Body and Blood, and, in union with thee, offer ourselves a living sacrifice, holy and acceptable to the Father; who liveth and reigneth with thee and the Holy Spirit, ever one God, world without end. **Amen.**

| Exodus 16:11–15 | Bread from Heaven |
| Psalm 105:37–45 | 'He led forth' |
| Romans 6:1–11 | Life from Death |
| John 6:47–58 | The Bread of Life |

| Ezekiel 36:22–28 | 'I will cleanse you' |
| Mark 6:30–44 | Feeding the Crowd |

NINTH AFTER PENTECOST

*The Unity of the Church*

O GOD, the Creator and Father of all mankind, who by thy Holy Spirit hast made a diversity of peoples one in the confession of thy name: Lead them, we beseech thee, by the same Spirit to display to the whole earth one mind in belief and one passion for righteousness; through Jesus Christ our Lord. **Amen.**

| | |
|---|---|
| 2 Chronicles 30:1–9 | All Israel |
| Psalm 133 | 'Behold, how good' |
| Ephesians 2:11–22 | One new Man |
| John 17:20–26 | 'That they may all be one' |
| Ezekiel 37:15–28 | One Shepherd |
| 1 Corinthians 3 | God's Building |

## TENTH AFTER PENTECOST
### *The Witness of the Church*

O LORD, who hast called us to be thy witnesses to all the nations: Have mercy upon us, who have known thy will but have failed to do it. Cleanse us from unbelief and sloth, and fill us with hope and zeal, that we may do thy work, and bear thy cross, and bide thy time, and see thy glory; who with the Father and the Holy Spirit art one God, world without end. **Amen.**

| | |
|---|---|
| Isaiah 52:7–10 | Good Tidings |
| Psalm 150 | 'Praise the Lord' |
| Romans 10:11–17 | Preaching Christ |
| Matthew 10:24–33 | Acknowledging Jesus |
| Isaiah 55:1–5 | A Witness to the Peoples |
| Acts 10:34–43 | Witnesses of the Resurrection |

## ELEVENTH AFTER PENTECOST
### *The Ordained Ministry*

ALMIGHTY God, Giver of all good things, who by thy one Spirit hast appointed a diversity of ministrations in thy Church: Mercifully behold thy servants who are called to the ministry, and so fill them with thy Holy Spirit, that, both by word and good example, they may faithfully and joyfully serve thee, to the glory of thy name and the building up of thy Church; through Jesus Christ our Lord.
**Amen.**

| Ezekiel 33:1-6 | The Duty of the Watchman |
| Psalm 99 | 'The Lord reigns' |
| 2 Corinthians 5:11-21 | Ambassadors for Christ |
| John 21:15-19 | 'Feed my sheep' |

| Ezekiel 2:3—3:3 | Ezekiel's Commission |
| 1 Corinthians 4 | Stewards of the Mysteries |

## TWELFTH AFTER PENTECOST

*Love towards God*

O GOD, who hast prepared for them that love thee such good things as pass man's understanding: Pour into our hearts such love toward thee, that we, loving thee in all and above all, may obtain thy promises, which exceed all that we can desire; through Jesus Christ our Lord. **Amen.**

| Deuteronomy 26:1-11 | Offering Firstfruits |
| Psalm 116 | 'I love the Lord' |
| 1 John 4:7-21 | 'God is love' |
| Mark 12:28-34 | The Great Commandment |

| Deuteronomy 10:12-22 | 'He is thy praise' |
| Luke 17:11-19 | The ten Lepers |

## THIRTEENTH AFTER PENTECOST

*Prayer*

LOOK graciously upon us, O Holy Spirit, and give us for our hallowing thoughts that pass into prayer, prayers that pass into love, and love that passeth into life with thee for ever. **Amen.**

| 1 Kings 18:36-39 | A Prayer of Elijah |
| Psalm 42 | 'As a hart longs' |
| Ephesians 3:14-21 | A Prayer of Paul |
| Matthew 6:5-15 | Jesus on Prayer |

| Genesis 32:22-32 | Jacob at Jabbok |
| Revelation 8:1-5 | The Prayers of the Saints |

FOURTEENTH AFTER PENTECOST

*Joy*

O LORD, who hast promised that thy joy would be
in us, so that our joy might be full: Grant that,
living close to thee, we may learn to rejoice and
give thanks in all things; for thy loving mercy's
sake. **Amen.**

| | |
|---|---|
| Isaiah 35 | Everlasting Joy |
| Psalm 100 | 'Make a joyful noise' |
| Galatians 5:16–25 | The Fruit of the Spirit |
| John 15:1–11 | 'That your joy may be full' |
| | |
| Nehemiah 8:1–3, 5–12 | The Joy of the Lord |
| John 16:16–24 | Sorrow turned into Joy |

FIFTEENTH AFTER PENTECOST

*Enduring to the End*

GO before us, O Lord, in all our doings with thy
most gracious favour, and further us with thy continual help; that in all our works, begun, continued,
and ended, in thee, we may glorify thy holy name,
and finally by thy mercy obtain everlasting life;
through Jesus Christ our Lord. **Amen.**

| | |
|---|---|
| Ruth 1:8–18 | The Faithfulness of Ruth |
| Psalm 125 | 'Those who trust' |
| Hebrews 11:32—12:2 | Heroes of Faith |
| Mark 13:3–13 | Enduring to the End |
| | |
| Hosea 2:16–23 | Betrothed in Faithfulness |
| Revelation 2:1–11 | The Crown of Life |

SIXTEENTH AFTER PENTECOST

*Self-denial*

ALMIGHTY God, whose gracious will it was that
thy Son should empty himself and become like us:
Grant that we, with the example of his earthly life

continually before us, and with the Holy Spirit
working in our hearts, may be changed into his
likeness; through the same Jesus Christ our Lord.
**Amen.**

| | |
|---|---|
| Jeremiah 45 | Jeremiah to Baruch |
| Psalm 132:1–10 | 'Remember, O Lord' |
| Galatians 2:15–20 | Crucified with Christ |
| Mark 8:27–38 | The Cross of the Disciple |
| Nehemiah 5:1–13 | Selfishness rebuked |
| Philippians 3:3–11 | Everything as Loss |

## SEVENTEENTH AFTER PENTECOST
### *The Lord's Day*

ALMIGHTY God, who hast given a day of rest to
thy people, and, through thy Spirit in the Church,
hast consecrated the first day of the week to be
a perpetual memorial of thy Son's resurrection:
Grant that we may so use thy gift that, refreshed
and strengthened in soul and body, we may serve
thee faithfully all the days of our life; through the
same Jesus Christ our Lord. **Amen.**

| | |
|---|---|
| Genesis 1:31—2:3 | The Day of Rest |
| Psalm 24 | 'The earth is the Lord's' |
| Revelation 1:9–18 | Worship on the Lord's Day |
| John 20:19–23 | Jesus in the Midst |
| Deuteronomy 5:12–15 | The Purpose of the Sabbath |
| Mark 2:23—3:6 | Lord of the Sabbath |

## EIGHTEENTH AFTER PENTECOST
### *Love towards Neighbour*

O LORD, who hast taught us that all our doings
without charity are nothing worth: Send thy Holy
Spirit, and pour into our hearts that most excellent
gift of charity, the very bond of peace and of all
virtues; without which whosoever liveth is counted

dead before thee: Grant this for thine only Son
Jesus Christ's sake. **Amen.**

| | |
|---|---|
| Leviticus 19:9–18 | 'I am the Lord' |
| Psalm 15 | 'O Lord, who shall sojourn...?' |
| 1 Corinthians 13 | Love |
| Luke 10:25–37 | The Good Samaritan |
| Exodus 23:1–12 | Consideration for Others |
| Romans 12:9–21 | Overcoming Evil |

NINETEENTH AFTER PENTECOST

*The Family*

ALMIGHTY God and heavenly Father, whose Son
Jesus Christ shared in Nazareth the life of an
earthly home: Send down thy blessing, we beseech
thee, upon all Christian families, that parents by the
spirit of understanding and wisdom, and children
by the spirit of obedience and reverence, may be
bound each to each by mutual love; through him
who became a child, and learned obedience to thy
will, even Jesus Christ our Lord. **Amen.**

| | |
|---|---|
| Proverbs 4:1–9 | Father and Son |
| Psalm 127 | 'Unless the Lord builds' |
| Ephesians 5:21—6:4 | Family Life |
| Mark 10:1–16 | Marriage; Children |
| 2 Samuel 18:24–33 | David and Absalom |
| 1 Peter 3:1–9 | Husbands and Wives |

TWENTIETH AFTER PENTECOST

*The Church in the World*

ALMIGHTY God, who hast manifested thy Son
Jesus Christ to be a light to mankind: Grant that
we thy people, being nourished by thy word and
sacraments, may be strengthened to show forth to
all men the unsearchable riches of Christ, so that he
may be known, adored, and obeyed, to the ends of

the earth; who liveth and reigneth with thee and the Holy Spirit, one God, world without end. **Amen.**

| | |
|---|---|
| Zechariah 8:16–23 | Many Nations seeking God |
| Psalm 82 | 'God has taken his place' |
| Colossians 4:2–6 | Consideration for those outside |
| Matthew 25:31–46 | Sheep and Goats |
| Job 31:13–22 | A Good Neighbour |
| Philippians 1:3–11 | Partakers in Grace |

## TWENTY-FIRST AFTER PENTECOST
### Daily Work

O GOD, who movest in love unceasing, and dost give to each man his appointed work: Help us steadfastly, and as in thy sight, to fulfil the duties of our calling; that when our Lord shall take account of us, we may be found faithful in that which is least, and enter into his eternal joy. **Amen.**

| | |
|---|---|
| Exodus 35:30—36:1 | Bezalel |
| Psalm 104:14–24 | 'Thou dost cause' |
| 2 Thessalonians 3:6–13 | Daily Work |
| Matthew 25:14–30 | The Talents |
| Nehemiah 4 | Building the Wall |
| 1 Thessalonians 5:12–24 | Spirit, Soul, and Body |

## TWENTY-SECOND AFTER PENTECOST
### The State

O GOD the Redeemer, who didst send thy servant Moses to lead thy people out of bondage and affliction: Give to us and to all nations leaders obedient to thee, to teach us to know and to keep thy laws, and to bring us on our way to that country which thou hast prepared for us; through Jesus Christ our Lord. **Amen.**

| | |
|---|---|
| Exodus 18:13–27 | Sharing the Burden |
| Psalm 72:1–14 | 'Give the king thy justice' |

| 1 Peter 2:11–17 | Authority |
| Mark 12:13–17 | The Things that are Caesar's |

| Amos 5:1–15 | Justice |
| Romans 13:1–7 | Authority |

## TWENTY-THIRD AFTER PENTECOST

### Christian Giving

LORD Jesus, who for our sake didst become poor, that by thy poverty we might become rich: Grant to thy people so to give of their substance as to acknowledge that they belong wholly to thee; for thine own sake. **Amen.**

| 1 Chronicles 29:1–9 | The Free-will Offering |
| Psalm 112 | 'Blessed is the man' |
| 2 Corinthians 8:1–9 | 'First giving themselves' |
| Luke 20:45—21:4 | The Widow's Mite |

| 1 Chronicles 29:10–20 | 'All is thine' |
| Acts 20:17–35 | The Blessedness of giving |

## TWENTY-FOURTH AFTER PENTECOST

### The Christian Hope

O GOD, the Protector of all that trust in thee, without whom nothing is strong, nothing is holy: Increase and multiply upon us thy mercy; that, thou being our ruler and guide, we may so pass through things temporal, that we finally lose not the things eternal; grant this, O heavenly Father, for Jesus Christ's sake our Lord. **Amen.**

| Habakkuk 2:1–4 | The Watchman on his Tower |
| Psalm 31:19–24 | 'O how abundant' |
| 1 Corinthians 15:50–58 | Victory in Christ |
| Luke 12:22–34 | The Father's good Pleasure |

| Isaiah 55:6–13 | His Ways and ours |
| Hebrews 6:9–20 | Hope the Anchor |

*The series of Propers for Sundays after Pentecost is followed only until the Sunday next before Advent.*

TWENTY-FIFTH AFTER PENTECOST

*The Two Worlds*

ALMIGHTY and merciful God, of whose only gift it cometh that thy faithful people do unto thee true and laudable service: Grant, we beseech thee, that we may so faithfully serve thee in this life, that we fail not finally to attain thy heavenly promises; through the merits of Jesus Christ our Lord. **Amen.**

| | |
|---|---|
| Daniel 3:1–18 | The golden Image |
| Psalm 9:1–11 | 'I will give thanks' |
| Philippians 3:17—4:1 | Citizenship in Heaven |
| John 15:18–27 | Jesus and the World |
| | |
| Daniel 3:19–30 | The Furnace |
| Hebrews 13:7–16 | Outside the Camp |

TWENTY-SIXTH AFTER PENTECOST

*The Two Ways*

O GOD, whose blessed Son was manifested that he might destroy the works of the Devil, and make us the sons of God, and heirs of eternal life: Grant us, we beseech thee, that, having this hope, we may purify ourselves, even as he is pure; that, when he shall appear again with power and great glory, we may be made like unto him in his eternal and glorious kingdom; where with thee, O Father, and thee, O Holy Spirit, he liveth and reigneth, ever one God, world without end. **Amen.**

| | |
|---|---|
| Deuteronomy 30:15–20 | Life or Death |
| Psalm 1 | 'Blessed is the man' |
| James 1:19–27 | Doers of the Word |
| Matthew 7:13–20 | The easy Way and the hard |
| | |
| Jeremiah 6:16–21 | The Good Way |
| Romans 6:15–23 | Wages or Gift |

TWENTY-SEVENTH AFTER PENTECOST

*The Day of the Lord*

O CHRIST our God, who wilt come to judge the
world in the manhood which thou hast assumed:
We pray thee to sanctify us wholly, that in the day
of thy coming we may be raised up to live and
reign with thee for ever. **Amen.**

| | |
|---|---|
| Zephaniah 1:14–18 | The Day of Wrath |
| Psalm 76 | 'In Judah God is known' |
| 1 Thessalonians 4:13–18 | The Dead in Christ |
| Mark 13:14–27 | The Coming |
| | |
| Amos 5:18–24 | The Day of the Lord |
| Matthew 25:1–13 | Waiting for the Bridegroom |

NEXT BEFORE ADVENT

*Preparedness*

MAKE us, we beseech thee, O Lord our God,
watchful in awaiting the coming of thy Son, Christ
our Lord; that when he shall come and knock, he
may find us not sleeping in sin, but awake, and
rejoicing in his praises; through the same Jesus
Christ our Lord. **Amen.**

| | |
|---|---|
| Malachi 3:13—4:2 | The Sun of Righteousness |
| Psalm 98 | 'O sing to the Lord' |
| 1 Thessalonians 5:1–11 | The Second Coming |
| Mark 13:28–37 | 'Watch!' |
| | |
| Amos 4:6–13 | God's Warnings |
| Luke 21:25–36 | 'Your redemption' |

# TABLE II

## SPECIAL DAYS ON FIXED DATES
## (OTHER THAN CHRISTMAS DAY)

The Propers in Tables II and III may be followed at any service on the date specified or on any of the seven days following.

When a Special Day in Table II or Table III falls on a Sunday or any other Special Day in Table I:

(1) The Beginning of Advent, Ash Wednesday, Ascension Day, Pentecost, and Trinity Sunday take precedence over any other day. A Special Day which falls on one of these days may be observed on any day of the week following.

(2) If a Special Day (e.g. the Annunciation or Mark the Evangelist) falls on any day from Palm Sunday to the Sunday next after Easter, it is transferred to the Tuesday or any other day of the week following the Sunday next after Easter. Similarly, if a Special Day falls during the week of Pentecost, it is transferred to the Tuesday or any other day of the following week.

(3) When a Special Day falls on any other Sunday, the collects for both days and the lessons for either day may be read.

(4) The Propers for September 27 may be read even when September 27 falls on a Sunday.

---

| Nov. | 30 | Andrew | June | 11 | Barnabas |
|------|----|--------|------|----|----------|
| [Dec. | 26 | Stephen] | | 24 | John the Baptist |
| Jan. | 1 | Covenant | | 29 | Peter |
| | 25 | Paul | July | 22 | Mary Magdalene |
| | 26 | Republic Day | | 25 | James |
| [Feb. | 2 | The Presentation] | [Aug. | 6 | The Transfiguration] |
| Feb. | 15 | Stephen | Aug. | 15 | Independence Day |
| Mar. | 25 | The Annunciation | Sept. | 21 | Matthew |
| Apr. | 25 | Mark | | 27 | Inauguration of CSI |
| May | 6 | John the Apostle | | 29 | Michael |

| Oct. | 6 Thomas | — | Harvest Festival |
|------|----------|---|------------------|
|      | 18 Luke  | — | Meetings of Synod |
| Nov. | 1 All Saints | — | Dedication of a Church |

---

*November 30*   ANDREW THE APOSTLE

ALMIGHTY God, who didst give such grace unto thy holy apostle Saint Andrew, that he readily obeyed the calling of thy Son Jesus Christ, and brought others with him: Grant unto us all, that we, being called by thy holy word, may be faithful disciples and witnesses of our Saviour Jesus Christ.
**Amen.**

Amos 7:10–15         Philippians 1:3–11
Psalm 147:1–11       John 1:35–42

*[December 26*   STEPHEN THE MARTYR]

*Stephen may be commemorated on some more suitable date, for example February 15. The Propers will be found there.*

*January 1*   THE DAY OF THE COVENANT

O GOD, who hast appointed our Lord Jesus Christ as Mediator of a new covenant, grant us grace, we beseech thee, to draw near with fullness of faith and join ourselves in a perpetual covenant to thee; through the same Jesus Christ our Lord. **Amen.**

Genesis 17:1–8        Colossians 2:8–15
Psalm 25:1–10         Mark 14:22–26

*These Propers are followed only if there is no Covenant Service.*

*January 25*   THE CONVERSION OF PAUL

O GOD, who didst call Saul, the persecutor of the Church, to be the apostle Paul, and to proclaim the gospel of thy Son Jesus Christ to the Gentiles: Grant that, as thou hast called us also, we may be true to our calling, and count everything loss for the gain of knowing Christ Jesus as our Lord and Saviour; to whom with thee and the Holy Spirit be all honour and glory, world without end. **Amen.**

Jeremiah 1:4–10            Acts 9:1–19
Psalm 67                   Matthew 19:27–30

*January 26*   REPUBLIC DAY

O GOD, who art the Ruler and the Judge of all nations, look mercifully on our land. Sanctify all that is rich and noble in our traditions. Grant that our ideals and aspirations may be in accordance with thy will. Take away pride and false pretence from our midst; give us humility in our relations with others and sobriety in our dealings at home. Bless our leaders and the people, in our several efforts to make this land happy and prosperous. Help us to discipline ourselves so that our national freedom may be used for the common good, and may bring us all to the knowledge of him whose service is perfect freedom, even Jesus Christ our Lord and Saviour. **Amen.**

Isaiah 32:1–8             1 Timothy 2:1–6
Psalm 144:9–15            Matthew 6:19–34

[*February 2*   THE PRESENTATION OF CHRIST]
*The Propers are given at the third Sunday after Christmas.*

*February 15*   STEPHEN THE MARTYR

GRANT, O Lord, that in all our sufferings here upon earth for the testimony of thy truth, we may steadfastly look up to heaven, and by faith behold the glory that shall be revealed; and, being filled with the Holy Spirit, may learn to love and bless our persecutors by the example of thy first martyr

Saint Stephen, who prayed for his murderers to thee,
O blessed Jesus, who standest at the right hand of
God to succour all those that suffer for thee, our
only Mediator and Advocate. **Amen.**

2 Chronicles 24:20–22     Acts 7:55–60
Psalm 73:24–28            Matthew 23:34–39

*The traditional day for commemorating Stephen is December 26.*

## *March 25*   THE ANNUNCIATION

WE beseech thee, O God, pour thy grace into our
hearts; that as, at the message of an angel, Mary
was overshadowed by the Holy Spirit, and became
the mother of the Lord and the most blessed among
women, so we, believing thy word, may receive
Christ to dwell in our hearts, and by our life make
manifest the mystery of his incarnation; who hath
exalted our manhood into the glory of his Godhead, even Jesus Christ our Lord. **Amen.**

Genesis 18:1–14          Galatians 4:1–7
Psalm 89:1–18            Luke 1:26–38

## *April 25*   MARK THE EVANGELIST

O ALMIGHTY God, who hast instructed thy holy
Church with the heavenly doctrine of Mark the
Evangelist: Give us grace, that we may be estab-
lished in the truth of thy holy gospel, and faithful
servants of the same; through Jesus Christ our
Lord. **Amen.**

Hosea 6:1–6              2 Timothy 4:1–11
Psalm 119:1–8           Mark 14:43–52

## *May 6*   JOHN THE APOSTLE AND EVANGELIST

MERCIFUL Lord, we beseech thee to cast thy
bright beams of light upon thy Church, that it, being

enlightened by the doctrine of thy blessed Apostle and Evangelist Saint John, may so walk in the light of thy truth, that it may at length attain to the light of everlasting life; through Jesus Christ our Lord. **Amen.**

| Exodus 33:7–23 | 1 John 1 |
| Psalm 27 | John 21:15–25 |

## *June 11*   BARNABAS THE APOSTLE

O LORD God almighty, who didst endue thy holy Apostle Barnabas with singular gifts of the Holy Spirit: Leave us not, we beseech thee, destitute of thy manifold gifts, nor yet of grace to use them alway to thy honour and glory; through Jesus Christ our Lord. **Amen.**

| Job 29:11–16 | Acts 11:22–30 |
| Psalm 34 | Matthew 5:13–16 |

## *June 24*   JOHN THE BAPTIST

ALMIGHTY God, by whose providence thy servant John Baptist was wonderfully born, and sent to prepare the way of thy Son our Saviour, by preaching of repentance: Make us so to follow his doctrine and holy life, that we may truly repent according to his preaching; and after his example constantly speak the truth, boldly rebuke vice, and patiently suffer for the truth's sake; through Jesus Christ our Lord. **Amen.**

| Malachi 3:1–6 | Galatians 4:28—5:1 |
| Psalm 3:1–6 | Luke 3:7–20 |

## *June 29*   PETER THE APOSTLE

O ALMIGHTY God, who by thy Son Jesus Christ didst give to thine Apostle Saint Peter many excellent gifts, and commandedst him earnestly to feed thy flock: Grant that thy Church may be ordered and guided by faithful and true pastors, and obediently walk according to thy will; through the same Jesus Christ our Lord. **Amen.**

Ezekiel 3:4–11          Acts 11:1–18
Psalm 48                   Matthew 16:13–19

*July 22*   MARY MAGDALENE

O ALMIGHTY God, whose blessed Son did sanctify Mary Magdalene, and called her to be a witness to his resurrection: Mercifully grant that by thy grace we may be healed of all our infirmities, and alway serve thee in the power of his endless life, who with thee and the Holy Spirit liveth and reigneth, one God, world without end. **Amen.**

Zephaniah 3:14–20      2 Corinthians 5:14–17
Psalm 116:1–16           John 20:11–18

*July 25*   JAMES THE APOSTLE

GRANT, O merciful God, that as thine holy Apostle Saint James, leaving his father and all that he had, without delay was obedient unto the calling of thy Son Jesus Christ, and followed him; so we, forsaking all worldly affections, may be evermore ready to follow thy holy commandments; through Jesus Christ our Lord. **Amen.**

1 Kings 19:19–21        Acts 11:27—12:3
Psalm 16                    Mark 10:35–45

[*August 6*   THE TRANSFIGURATION OF CHRIST]

*The Propers are in Table I, at the third Sunday before Easter.*

*August 15* INDEPENDENCE DAY

O GOD of all nations, look in mercy, we beseech thee, on our land. Give wisdom and understanding to the President, the Prime Minister, and all her rulers, and to her people unity and concord. Guide their policies by the light of thy life-giving Spirit, that she may go forward in justice and liberty, prosperity and peace; and in thy good time grant that she may bring her glory and honour into the kingdom of thy blessed Son, Jesus Christ our Lord.
**Amen.**

1 Kings 3:5–14      Romans 13:1–10
Psalm 33:12–22      Mark 12:13–17

*September 21* MATTHEW THE APOSTLE AND EVANGELIST

O ALMIGHTY God, who by thy blessed Son didst call Matthew from the receipt of custom to be an apostle and evangelist: Grant us grace to forsake all covetous desires, and inordinate love of riches, and to follow the same thy Son Jesus Christ, who liveth and reigneth with thee and the Holy Spirit, one God, world without end. **Amen.**

Proverbs 3:13–17      2 Corinthians 4:1–6
Psalm 146      Matthew 9:9–13

*September 27* THE INAUGURATION OF THE CHURCH OF SOUTH INDIA

O GOD, who to an expectant and united Church didst grant at Pentecost the gift of the Holy Spirit, and hast wonderfully brought into one fold those who now worship thee here: Grant, we beseech thee, the help of the same Spirit in all our life and worship, that we may expect great things from thee, and attempt great things for thee, and being one

in thee may show to the world that thou didst send
Jesus Christ our Lord, to whom, with thee and the
Holy Spirit, be all honour and glory, world without
end. **Amen.**

Ezekiel 37:15–22          Ephesians 4:1–16
Psalm 122                John 17:20–26

*September 29*  MICHAEL AND ALL ANGELS

O EVERLASTING God, who hast ordained and
constituted the service of angels and men in a
wonderful order: Mercifully grant that, as thy
holy angels alway do thee service in heaven, so by
thy appointment they may succour and defend us on
earth; through Jesus Christ our Lord. **Amen.**

Daniel 12:1–3            Revelation 12:7–11
Psalm 103:15–22          Matthew 18:1–10

*October 6*  THOMAS THE APOSTLE

ALMIGHTY God, who to thy holy Apostle Thomas
didst reveal thine incarnate Son in his risen glory:
Draw, we beseech thee, the people of our land to
know and confess him as their Lord and God, that
coming to thee by him they may believe and have
life in thy name; through the same Jesus Christ our
Lord and Saviour. **Amen.**

Job 42:1–6              Hebrews 13:13–21
Psalm 66                John 20:24–29

*October 18*  LUKE THE EVANGELIST AND
             PHYSICIAN

ALMIGHTY God, who didst inspire thy servant
Luke the physician to set forth in the Gospel the
love and healing power of thy Son: Manifest in thy
Church the like power and love, to the healing of

our bodies and our souls; through the same thy
Son Jesus Christ our Lord. **Amen.**

Isaiah 35:3–6  Acts 16:6–12
*or* Ecclesiasticus 38:1–14  Luke 1:1–4
Psalm 78:1–7

*November 1* ALL SAINTS

O ALMIGHTY God, who hast knit together thine
elect in one communion and fellowship, in the
mystical body of thy Son Jesus Christ our Lord:
Grant us grace so to follow thy blessed saints in all
virtuous and godly living, that we may come to
those unspeakable joys which thou hast prepared
for them that unfeignedly love thee; through Jesus
Christ our Lord. **Amen.**

Daniel 7:27  Revelation 7:9–17
*or* Wisdom 5:15,16  Matthew 5:1–12
Psalm 145:1–13a

THANKSGIVING FOR HARVEST

O ALMIGHTY and everlasting God, who hast given
unto us the fruits of the earth in their season:
Grant us grace to use the same to thy glory, the
relief of those that need, and our own comfort,
through Jesus Christ, who is the living Bread which
cometh down from heaven and giveth life unto the
world; to whom, with thee and the Holy Spirit, be
all honour and glory, world without end. **Amen.**

Deuteronomy 26:1–11  2 Corinthians 9:6–15
Psalm 65  John 6:26–35

MEETINGS OF SYNOD, DIOCESAN COUNCILS, ETC.

O GOD, by whom the meek are guided in judgement, and light riseth up in darkness for the godly:

Grant us, in all our doubts and uncertainties, the grace to ask what thou wouldst have us to do; that the Spirit of wisdom may save us from all false choices, and that in thy light we may see light, and in thy straight path may not stumble; through Jesus Christ our Lord. **Amen.**

| Micah 6:6–8 | Philippians 2:1–11 |
| Psalm 97 | John 15:1–8 |

## DEDICATION OF A CHURCH OR ANNIVERSARY

O ALMIGHTY God, whose blessed Son by his presence hallowed the feast of the dedication of the temple at Jerusalem: Send down upon us thy heavenly blessing; and because holiness becometh thine house for ever, sanctify us, we beseech thee, that we may be living temples, holy and acceptable unto thee; through the same Jesus Christ thy Son our Lord. **Amen.**

| 1 Kings 8:22–30 | 1 Corinthians 3:9–17 |
| Psalm 84 | Matthew 21:12–16 |

## TABLE III

### COMMON FORMS FOR COMMEMORATIONS

The Common Forms are provided for the commemoration of persons not included in Table I or Table II.

Unless the Synod shall authorise a list of persons who may be commemorated in the public worship of the Church, each diocese may make its own rules.

---

| | | | |
|---|---|---|---|
| 1 | Apostles | 7 | Doctors of the Church |
| 2 | Martyrs | 8 | Healers of the Sick |
| 3 | Faithful Women | 9 | Prophets and Reformers |
| 4 | Preachers of the Gospel | 10 | Pioneers and Builders |
| 5 | Pastors | 11 | Servants of the Church |
| 6 | Teachers | | |

---

## 1 APOSTLES

O ALMIGHTY God, who hast built thy Church upon the foundation of the apostles and prophets, Jesus Christ himself being the head Corner-stone: Grant us so to be joined together in the unity of the Spirit by their doctrine, that we with all the saints may be a holy temple acceptable unto thee; through Jesus Christ our Lord. **Amen.**

*Or*

O ALMIGHTY God, whom truly to know is ever-lasting life: Grant us perfectly to know thy Son Jesus Christ to be the Way, the Truth, and the Life, that, following the steps of the holy apostles, we may steadfastly walk in the way that leadeth to eternal life; through the same thy Son, Jesus Christ our Lord. **Amen.**

| | |
|---|---|
| Joshua 1:1–9 | 1 Corinthians 12:14–28 |
| Psalm 44:1–8 | Mark 3:13–19 |

## 2 MARTYRS

GRANT, O Lord, that as we commemorate *N*, thy witness, thy faithful one, so we may overcome the prince of this world by the blood of the Lamb and by the word of our testimony; and finally obtain the crown of righteousness which is laid up for all who love the appearing of thy Son, our Saviour, Jesus Christ. **Amen.**

| | |
|---|---|
| Daniel 3:14–25 | Revelation 7:13–17 |
| *or* Wisdom 3:1–9 | Matthew 10:24–33 |
| Psalm 69:29–36 | |

## 3 FAITHFUL WOMEN

O GOD, who hast built up thy Church through the divers gifts and graces of thy saints: We give thee humble thanks for thy servant *N*, whom we commemorate this day. Help us, we beseech thee, to follow in her steps, and fill our hearts with love of thee, and of others for thy sake; through Jesus Christ our Lord. **Amen.**

| | |
|---|---|
| 2 Kings 5:1–5a | Acts 9:36–42 |
| Psalm 68:19, 20, 24–26 | Mark 14:3–9 |

## 4 PREACHERS OF THE GOSPEL

Remembering this day *N*, let us pray for all preachers of the gospel.

ALMIGHTY and everlasting God, we thank thee for thy servant *N*, whom thou didst call to preach the gospel *to the people of* . . . ; and humbly pray thee to raise up among us those who shall be heralds and evangelists of thy kingdom, and shall build up thy Church in this and every land; through Jesus Christ our Lord. **Amen.**

*Or*

RAISE up among us, O Lord, prophets and teachers; and when the Holy Spirit shall command us to separate any to the work whereto thou dost call them, grant that we may hear and obey, so that the senders and the sent alike may do thy will, and bide thy time, and see thy glory; through Jesus Christ our Lord. **Amen.**

Isaiah 52:1–10          Acts 13:1–3
Psalm 96               Luke 10:1–20

## 5  PASTORS

Remembering this day *N*, let us pray for all bishops and pastors.

O GOD, who art the Light of thy faithful people and Shepherd of our souls, and didst choose thy blessed servant *N* to be a faithful steward of thy mysteries: We beseech thee so to work in us that we, being instructed by his words and godly life, may grow up to the fullness of Jesus Christ our Lord, who with thee, O Father, and the Holy Spirit, liveth and reigneth, ever one God, world without end. **Amen.**

Ezekiel 34:11–16          1 Peter 5:1–5
Psalm 80                 Luke 12:35–40

## 6  TEACHERS

Remembering this day *N*, let us pray for all teachers of the young.

O LORD Jesus Christ, who art the Life and Light of all thy servants: We beseech thee to help and inspire all who teach, and those also who prepare them for their work. Pour out upon them the spirit of unceasing prayer and faithful service; encourage them with good success; strengthen their faith and purpose when they are weary and disheartened; and fortify them with thy assurance that they are fellow-workers together with thee; for thy name's sake. **Amen.**

Proverbs 3:11–20   James 3:1, 13–18
Psalm 119:9–16     Mark 10:13–16

## 7 DOCTORS OF THE CHURCH

GRANT, we beseech thee, almighty God, that following the teaching of *N*, we may know thee the only true God and Jesus Christ whom thou hast sent, that we may be counted worthy ever to be numbered among the sheep who hear his voice; through the same Jesus Christ our Lord. **Amen.**

Nehemiah 8:1–8      1 Corinthians 2:6–16
*or* Wisdom 7:7–14   Matthew 13:51, 52
Psalm 119:97–104

## 8 HEALERS OF THE SICK

Remembering this day *N*, let us pray for the sick and for those who minister to them.

O GOD, who hast sent thy Son Jesus Christ to be the great Physician of our bodies: Bless, we beseech thee, all whom thou hast called to share in thy work of giving health to men, and enable us to learn and obey thy laws; so that our spirits, minds, and bodies, may be presented before thee without blemish, to the praise and glory of thy name; through the same thy Son Jesus Christ our Lord. **Amen.**

2 Kings 5:9–14          Acts 3:1–10
*or* Ecclesiasticus 38:1–14   Mark 1:40–45
Psalm 103:1–5

## 9 PROPHETS AND REFORMERS

O GOD, the King of righteousness, lead us, we pray thee, in the ways of justice and peace; inspire us to break down all tyranny and oppression, to gain for every man his due reward and from every man his due service, all living under thy rule and all guided by thy love; in the name of Jesus Christ we ask it. **Amen.**

Isaiah 1:16–20        Hebrews 12:22–29
Psalm 147:1–6        John 2:13–22

## 10 PIONEERS AND BUILDERS

O THOU who art the Light of the minds that know thee, the Life of the souls that love thee, and the Strength of the wills that serve thee: Help us so to know thee that we may truly love thee, so to love thee that we may fully serve thee, whose service is perfect freedom; through Jesus Christ our Lord. **Amen.**

Exodus 3:1–15        1 Corinthians 3:1–9
Psalm 33:1–9        Matthew 7:24–27

## 11 SERVANTS OF THE CHURCH

Remembering on this day *N*, let us pray for all who serve the Church in any way.

O ALMIGHTY God, who willest to be glorified in thy saints, and didst raise up thy servant *N* to shine as a light in the world: Shine, we pray thee, in our hearts, that we also in our generation may show forth thy praises, who hast called us out of darkness into thy marvellous light; through Jesus Christ our Lord. **Amen.**

Nehemiah 4:1–6        1 Corinthians 1:26–31
*or* Ecclesiasticus 44:1–15   Mark 12:41–44
Psalm 113        *or* Matthew 5:13–16

## TABLE IV

## PROPER PREFACES

### ADVENT

*On the fourth Sunday before Christmas, and until Christmas Eve:*

THROUGH Jesus Christ thy Son our Saviour, by whom thou hast sent a new light to shine upon the world, that we who rejoice in that light may be found cleansed from our sins and without fear when he shall come again to judge the world in righteousness.

### CHRISTMAS

*On Christmas Day, and until the Epiphany or second Sunday after Christmas:*

ESPECIALLY at this time we praise thee, because thou didst give Jesus Christ thine only Son to be born for us of Mary, that through him we might have power to become the sons of God.

### EPIPHANY

*On January 6, or the second Sunday after Christmas, and for seven days after:*

THROUGH Jesus Christ our Lord, who in the likeness of men manifested forth thy glory, that he might bring all men out of darkness into his marvellous light.

### LENT

*On Ash Wednesday, and until the second Sunday before Easter:*

THROUGH Jesus Christ our Lord, who was in all points tempted like as we are, yet without sin; by whose grace we are enabled to subdue all sinful desires and live no longer unto ourselves, but unto him who died for us and rose again.

PASSIONTIDE

*On the second Sunday before Easter (Passion Sunday), and until the Wednesday before Easter, except for Palm Sunday:*

THROUGH Jesus Christ our Lord, who, being found in fashion as a man, humbled himself, and became obedient unto death, even the death of the cross; that, being lifted up from the earth, he might draw all men unto himself.

*On the Sunday next before Easter (Palm Sunday):*

THROUGH Jesus Christ our Lord, who by thy grace fulfilled all the prophecies about him in Holy Scripture, from his birth in Bethlehem till his entry into Jerusalem, whom also we now bless with those who met him with palms and with Hosannas.

*On the Thursday before Easter:*

THROUGH Jesus Christ our Lord; who, having loved his own which were in the world, loved them unto the end, and on the night before he suffered did institute these holy mysteries, that we, receiving the benefits of his passion, and being quickened by his resurrection, might be made partakers of his divine nature, and be filled with all the fullness of God.

EASTER

*On Easter Day, and until the Ascension:*

BUT chiefly we are bound to praise thee for the glorious resurrection of thy Son Jesus Christ our Lord, who by his death has destroyed death, and by his resurrection has restored life to us.

ASCENSION

*On Ascension Day, and until Pentecost:*

BUT chiefly we are bound to praise thee for Jesus Christ our Lord, who ascended up on high, the one Mediator between God and man; who abideth for ever in that glory which he had with thee, and in that nature which he took of us, that he might bring us to the fellowship of his Godhead.

PENTECOST

*On the day of Pentecost, and until Trinity Sunday; and also at meetings of the Synod and the Diocesan Councils:*

THROUGH Jesus Christ our Lord; according to whose promise the Holy Spirit came down from heaven, lighting upon the disciples to teach them, and to lead them into all truth; giving them both the gift of tongues, and also boldness with fervent zeal constantly to preach the Gospel unto all nations.

TRINITY SUNDAY

THROUGH Jesus Christ our Lord, who, with thee and the Holy Spirit, is one God, the same in substance, equal in power and glory.

SAINTS

*On November 1, or on any day appointed for the commemoration of a saint, and for seven days after:*

WHO in the righteousness of thy saints hast given us an example of godly living, and in their blessedness a glorious pledge of the hope of our calling, that, being compassed about with so great a cloud of witnesses, we may run with patience the race that is set before us, and with them receive the crown of glory that fadeth not away.

## THE DEDICATION OF A CHURCH

*At the dedication of a church, or on its anniversary:*

WHO, though the heaven of heavens cannot contain thee, and thy glory fills all the world, dost deign to hallow places for thy worship, and in them dost pour forth gifts of grace upon thy faithful people.

## ORDINATION

*At the ordination of a deacon:*

THROUGH Jesus Christ our Lord, who came not to be ministered unto, but to minister, and to give his life a ransom for many.

*At the ordination of a presbyter or the consecration of a bishop:*

THROUGH Jesus Christ our Lord, who gave authority to his disciples, saying, As the Father hath sent me, even so send I you.

# ORDERS FOR MORNING AND EVENING WORSHIP

## FIRST ORDER OF SERVICE

*When there is no celebration of the Lord's Supper, the first two parts of the Order for the Lord's Supper, the Preparation and the Ministry of the Word, may be used by themselves. In this case (a) in the Invitation to Confession the words* and to receive the body and blood of the Lord *are omitted; (b) if there is a collection this is solemnly dedicated, together with offerings in kind, if any, after the Intercession, and a prayer of offering is said. The service ends with a hymn and a grace or benediction.*

## SECOND ORDER OF SERVICE

### PRAISE

*All stand, and the minister says:*

Let us worship God.

*The minister may read one or more sentences from the Bible, such as the following:*

GOD is spirit, and those who worship him must worship in spirit and truth. John 4:24

Grace to you and peace from God our Father and the Lord Jesus Christ. Rom. 1:7

This is the day which the Lord has made; let us rejoice and be glad in it. Ps. 118:24

*Evening.* From the rising of the sun to its setting the name of the Lord is to be praised. Ps. 113:3

God is light and in him is no darkness at all. If we walk in the light, as he is in the light, we have fellowship with one another, and the blood of Jesus his Son cleanses us from all sin.            1 John 1:5, 7

*Advent.* The Lord is at hand. Have no anxiety about anything, but in everything by prayer and supplication with thanksgiving let your requests be made known to God.            Phil. 4:5, 6

Blessed are those servants whom the master finds awake when he comes.            Luke 12:37

*Christmas.* Behold, I bring you good news of a great joy which will come to all the people; for to you is born this day in the city of David a Saviour, who is Christ the Lord.            Luke 2:10, 11

*Epiphany.* From the rising of the sun to its setting my name is great among the nations, and in every place incense is offered to my name, and a pure offering; for my name is great among the nations, says the Lord of hosts.            Mal. 1:11

*Lent.* Rend your hearts and not your garments. Return to the Lord, your God, for he is gracious and merciful, slow to anger, and abounding in steadfast love, and repents of evil.            Joel 2:13

Jesus said, 'If any man would come after me, let him deny himself and take up his cross and follow me'.            Mark 8:34

*Passiontide.* He himself bore our sins in his body on the tree, that we might die to sin and live to righteousness. By his wounds you have been healed.            1 Pet. 2:24

*Palm Sunday.* Say to the daughter of Zion, 'Behold, your salvation comes; behold, his reward is with him, and his recompense before him'. Isa. 62:11

*Good Friday.* The Son of man came not to be served but to serve, and to give his life as a ransom for many. Mark 10:45

*Easter.* Blessed be the God and Father of our Lord Jesus Christ. By his great mercy we have been born anew to a living hope through the resurrection of Jesus Christ from the dead. 1 Pet. 1:3

'I am the first and the last, and the living one,' says the Lord; 'I died, and behold I am alive for evermore, and I have the keys of Death and Hades.' Rev. 1:17, 18

*Ascension.* Since we have a great high priest who has passed through the heavens, Jesus, the Son of God, let us hold fast our confession. Let us then with confidence draw near to the throne of grace, that we may receive mercy and find grace to help in time of need. Heb. 4:14, 16

*Pentecost.* God's love has been poured into our hearts through the Holy Spirit which has been given to us. Rom. 5:5

*Trinity Sunday.* O the depth of the riches and wisdom and knowledge of God! How unsearchable are his judgements and how inscrutable his ways! For from him and through him and to him are all things. To him be glory for ever. Amen. Rom. 11:33, 36

*All Saints' Day.* I heard what seemed to be the voice of a great multitude, like the sound of many waters and like the sound of mighty thunderpeals, crying, 'Hallelujah! For the Lord our God the Almighty reigns. Let us rejoice and exult and give him the glory.'                                    Rev. 19:6, 7

*Any Saint.* Since we are surrounded by so great a cloud of witnesses, let us also lay aside every weight, and sin which clings so closely, and let us run with perseverance the race that is set before us, looking to Jesus the pioneer and perfecter of our faith, who for the joy that was set before him endured the cross, despising the shame, and is seated at the right hand of the throne of God.

Heb. 12:1, 2

*The Inauguration of the Church of South India.* Jesus said, 'The glory which thou hast given me I have given to them, that they may be one even as we are one, I in them and thou in me, that they may become perfectly one, so that the world may know that thou hast sent me and hast loved them even as thou hast loved me'.                           John 17:22, 23

*The New Year or any Anniversary.* They who wait for the Lord shall renew their strength, they shall mount up with wings like eagles, they shall run and not be weary, they shall walk and not faint.

Isa. 40:31

*Harvest.* The earth is the Lord's and the fullness thereof, the world and those who dwell therein.

Ps. 24:1

*Time of Trouble.* God is our refuge and strength, a very present help in trouble.          Ps. 46:1

*National.* Let the nations be glad and sing for joy, for thou dost judge the peoples with equity and guide the nations upon earth.          Ps. 67:4

*He then says:*

O Lord, open thou our lips:
**And our mouth shall show forth thy praise.**

Glory be to the Father: and to the Son, and to the Holy Spirit;
**As it was in the beginning, is now, and ever shall be: world without end. Amen.**

---

\* *One of the following may be said or sung. Or a hymn or lyric of praise may be sung.*

(i)

### ADORATION OF THE TRINITY

*Minister:* Holy, Holy, Holy, Lord God of hosts: heaven and earth are full of thy glory: Glory be to thee, O Lord most high.

*People:* **Blessed be he that hath come and is to come in the name of the Lord: Hosanna in the highest.**

*Minister:* Holy art thou, O God:
*People on left:* **Holy art thou, O God:**
*People on right:* **Holy art thou, O God.**

*Minister:* Holy art thou, O Almighty:
*People on left:* **Holy art thou, O Almighty:**
*People on right:* **Holy art thou, O Almighty.**

*Minister:* Holy art thou, O Immortal:
*People on left:* **Holy art thou, O Immortal:**
*People on right:* **Holy art thou, O Immortal.**

\* *Passages thus marked may be omitted at the discretion of the minister.*

*Minister:* O Lord, our Redeemer, who wast crucified for us, have mercy upon us:

*People on left:* **O Lord, our Redeemer, who wast crucified for us, have mercy upon us:**

*People on right:* **O Lord, our Redeemer, who wast crucified for us, have mercy upon us.**

*Minister:* O Lord the Holy Spirit, have mercy upon us:

*People on left:* **O Lord the Holy Spirit, have mercy upon us:**

*People on right:* **O Lord the Holy Spirit, have mercy upon us.**

*Minister:* O Lord, accept our prayers and praises and have mercy upon us:

*All:* **O Lord, have compassion and mercy upon us.**

(ii)

*The minister may say:*

PRAISE be to thee, O God the Father, who didst create all things by thy power and wisdom, and didst so love the world as to give thy Son to be our Saviour. Praise be to thee, O God the Son, who wast made man like unto us in all things, sin except, and wast delivered for our offences and raised again for our justification. Praise be to thee, O God the Holy Spirit, who dost lead us into all truth, and dost shed abroad the love of God in our hearts. All praise and glory be to thee, O God, Father, Son, and Holy Spirit, for ever and ever. **Amen.**

---

## CONFESSION

*The minister may read one or more sentences from the Bible, such as the following:*

IF we say we have no sin, we deceive ourselves, and

the truth is not in us. If we confess our sins, he is faithful and just, and will forgive our sins and cleanse us from all unrighteousness.    1 John 1:8, 9

I will arise and go to my father, and I will say to him, 'Father, I have sinned against heaven and before you; I am no longer worthy to be called your son'.    Luke 15:18, 19

The kingdom of God is at hand; repent, and believe in the gospel.    Mark 1:15

We have not a high priest who is unable to sympathize with our weaknesses, but one who in every respect has been tempted as we are, yet without sinning.    Heb. 4:15

*He then says:*

Let us kneel and examine ourselves in silence.

*All kneel and are silent for a space. After this the minister says:*

Let us humbly confess our sins to almighty God.

*All say one of the following:*

(i)

Almighty and most merciful Father; We have erred, and strayed from thy ways like lost sheep. We have followed too much the devices and desires of our own hearts. We have offended against thy holy laws. We have left undone those things which we ought to have done; And we have done those things which we ought not to have done; And there is no health in us. But thou, O Lord, have mercy upon us, miserable offenders. Spare thou them, O God, who confess their faults. Restore thou them that are penitent; According to thy promises declared unto mankind in Christ Jesus our Lord. And grant, O most merciful Father, for his sake; That we may hereafter live a godly, righteous, and sober life, To the glory of thy holy name. Amen.

(ii)

O God, our Father, We have sinned against thee in thought, word, and deed: We have not loved thee with all our heart; We have not loved our neighbours as ourselves. Have mercy upon us, we beseech thee; Cleanse us from our sins; And help us to overcome our faults; Through Jesus Christ our Lord. Amen.

*The minister says:*

MAY the almighty and merciful Lord grant unto us pardon and remission of all our sins, time for amendment of life, and the grace and comfort of the Holy Spirit. Amen.

*Or he may say* you *and* your *instead of* us *and* our.

## THE MINISTRY OF THE WORD OF GOD

*All stand. The minister says:*

Praise ye the Lord:
The Lord's name be praised.

---

\* *One of the following may be said or sung:*

(i)

### Psalm 95

O COME, let us sing unto the Lord : let us heartily rejoice in the strength of our salvation.

Let us come before his presence with thanksgiving : and show ourselves glad in him with psalms.

For the Lord is a great God : and a great King above all gods.

In his hand are all the corners of the earth : and the strength of the hills is his also.

The sea is his, and he made it : and his hands prepared the dry land.

O come, let us worship, and fall down : and kneel before the Lord our Maker.

For he is the Lord our God : and we are the people of his pasture, and the sheep of his hand.

[Today if ye will hear his voice, harden not your hearts : as in the provocation, and as in the day of temptation in the wilderness;

When your fathers tempted me : proved me, and saw my works.

Forty years long was I grieved with this generation, and said : It is a people that do err in their hearts, for they have not known my ways;

Unto whom I sware in my wrath : that they should not enter into my rest.]

Glory be to the Father : and to the Son, and to the Holy Spirit;

As it was in the beginning, is now, and ever shall be : world without end.  Amen.

(ii)

## Psalm 100

O BE joyful in the Lord, all ye lands : serve the Lord with gladness, and come before his presence with a song.

Be ye sure that the Lord he is God : it is he that hath made us, and not we ourselves; we are his people and the sheep of his pasture.

O go your way into his gates with thanksgiving, and into his courts with praise : be thankful unto him and speak good of his name.

For the Lord is gracious, his mercy is everlasting : and his truth endureth from generation to generation.

Glory be to the Father : and to the Son, and to the Holy Spirit;

As it was in the beginning, is now, and ever shall be : world without end. Amen.

*The Psalm or Psalms appointed for the day are said or sung. (For the Psalms for Sundays and Special Days see the Propers; for the daily reading of the Psalms see the Appendix to Morning and Evening Worship.) The minister and people may stand or sit for any of the Psalms and Songs.*

### THE FIRST LESSON

*The First Lesson is read from the Old Testament or Apocrypha.*

*One of the following is said or sung:*

### (i)

### THE SONG OF ZECHARIAH

### OR *BENEDICTUS*

### Luke 1:68–79

BLESSED be the Lord God of Israel : for he hath visited, and redeemed his people;

And hath raised up a mighty salvation for us : in the house of his servant David;

As he spake by the mouth of his holy prophets : who have been since the world began;

That we should be saved from our enemies : and from the hands of all that hate us;

To perform the mercy promised to our forefathers : and to remember his holy covenant;

To perform the oath : which he sware to our forefather Abraham;

That he would give us, that we being delivered out of the hand of our enemies : might serve him without fear;

In holiness and righteousness before him : all the days of our life.

And thou, child, shalt be called the Prophet of the Highest : for thou shalt go before the face of the Lord to prepare his ways;

To give knowledge of salvation unto his people :
for the remission of their sins,

Through the tender mercy of our God : whereby
the day-spring from on high hath visited us;

To give light to them that sit in darkness, and in
the shadow of death : and to guide our feet into the
ways of peace.

Glory be to the Father : and to the Son, and to
the Holy Spirit;

As it was in the beginning, is now, and ever shall
be : world without end. Amen.

### (ii)

### THE SONG OF THE THREE YOUNG MEN

#### OR *BENEDICITE*

At Daniel 3:23 (in the Apocrypha)

O ALL ye works of the Lord, bless ye the Lord :
praise him, and magnify him for ever.

O ye angels of the Lord, bless ye the Lord :
praise him, and magnify him for ever.

O ye heavens, bless ye the Lord : O ye waters that
be above the firmament, bless ye the Lord.

O all ye powers of the Lord, bless ye the Lord : O
ye sun and moon, bless ye the Lord.

O ye stars of heaven, bless ye the Lord : O ye
showers and dew, bless ye the Lord.

O ye winds of God, bless ye the Lord : O ye fire
and heat, bless ye the Lord.

O ye winter and summer, bless ye the Lord : O ye
dews and frosts, bless ye the Lord.

O ye frost and cold, bless ye the Lord : O ye ice
and snow, bless ye the Lord.

O ye nights and days, bless ye the Lord : O ye
light and darkness, bless ye the Lord.

O ye lightnings and clouds, bless ye the Lord : praise him, and magnify him for ever.

O let the earth bless the Lord : yea, let it praise him, and magnify him for ever.

O ye mountains and hills, bless ye the Lord : O all ye green things upon the earth, bless ye the Lord.

O ye wells, bless ye the Lord : O ye seas and floods, bless ye the Lord.

O ye whales, and all that move in the waters, bless ye the Lord : O all ye fowls of the air, bless ye the Lord.

O all ye beasts and cattle, bless ye the Lord : O ye children of men, bless ye the Lord.

O let Israel bless the Lord : praise him, and magnify him for ever.

O ye priests of the Lord, bless ye the Lord : O ye servants of the Lord, bless ye the Lord.

O ye spirits and souls of the righteous, bless ye the Lord : O ye holy and humble men of heart, bless ye the Lord.

O Ananias, Azarias, and Misael, bless ye the Lord : praise him and magnify him for ever.

Let us bless the Father, and the Son, and the Holy Spirit : let us praise and magnify him for ever.

Blessed art thou, O Lord, in the firmament of heaven : praised and exalted above all for ever.

## (iii)

### THE SONG OF THE VIRGIN MARY
### OR *MAGNIFICAT*

Luke 1:46–55

MY soul doth magnify the Lord : and my spirit hath rejoiced in God my Saviour.

For he hath regarded : the lowliness of his hand-maiden.

For behold from henceforth : all generations shall call me blessed.

For he that is mighty hath magnified me : and holy is his name.

And his mercy is on them that fear him : throughout all generations.

He hath showed strength with his arm : he hath scattered the proud in the imagination of their hearts.

He hath put down the mighty from their seat : and hath exalted the humble and meek.

He hath filled the hungry with good things : and the rich he hath sent empty away.

He remembering his mercy hath holpen his servant Israel : as he promised to our forefathers, Abraham and his seed, for ever.

Glory be to the Father : and to the Son, and to the Holy Spirit;

As it was in the beginning, is now, and ever shall be : world without end. Amen.

### THE SECOND LESSON

*The Second Lesson is read from the New Testament; or two lessons may be read, one from the Epistles or other books and one from the Gospels.*

*One of the following is said or sung:*

### (i)

### THE SONG OF THE CHURCH

#### OR *TE DEUM*

WE praise thee, O God : we acknowledge thee to be the Lord.

All the earth doth worship thee : the Father everlasting.

To thee all angels cry aloud : the heavens and all the powers therein.

To thee, cherubim and seraphim : continually do cry,

Holy, Holy, Holy : Lord God of Sabaoth;

Heaven and earth are full : of the majesty of thy glory.

The glorious company of the apostles : praise thee.

The goodly fellowship of the prophets : praise thee.

The white-robed army of martyrs : praise thee.

The holy Church throughout all the world : doth acknowledge thee,

The Father, of an infinite majesty : thine adorable true and only Son;

Also the Holy Spirit : the Comforter.

THOU art the King of glory, O Christ : thou art the everlasting Son of the Father.

When thou becamest man to deliver mankind : thou didst humble thyself to be born of a virgin.

When thou hadst overcome the sharpness of death : thou didst open the kingdom of heaven to all believers.

Thou sittest at the right hand of God : in the glory of the Father.

We believe that thou : shalt come to be our Judge.

We therefore pray thee, help thy servants : whom thou hast redeemed with thy precious blood.

Make them to be numbered with thy saints : in glory everlasting.

O LORD, save thy people, and bless thine heritage : govern them, and lift them up for ever.

Day by day we magnify thee : and we worship thy name ever world without end.

Vouchsafe, O Lord, to keep us this day without sin : O Lord, have mercy upon us, have mercy upon us.

O Lord, let thy mercy lighten upon us : as our trust is in thee.

O Lord, in thee is my hope : let me never be confounded.

### (ii)

#### THE SONG OF SIMEON

#### OR *NUNC DIMITTIS*

#### Luke 2:29–32

LORD, now lettest thou thy servant depart in peace : according to thy word.

For mine eyes have seen thy salvation : which thou hast prepared before the face of all people,

To be a light to lighten the Gentiles : and to be the glory of thy people Israel.

Glory be to the Father : and to the Son, and to the Holy Spirit;

As it was in the beginning, is now, and ever shall be : world without end. Amen.

#### THE SERMON AND CREED

*A sermon may be preached.*

*All stand and say or sing the Apostles' Creed:*

I believe in God the Father almighty, Maker of heaven and earth :

And in Jesus Christ his only Son our Lord, Who was conceived by the Holy Spirit, Born of the Virgin Mary, Suffered under Pontius Pilate, Was crucified, dead, and buried, He descended into hell; The third day he rose again from the dead, He ascended into heaven, And sitteth on the right hand of God the

Father almighty; From thence he shall come to judge the quick and the dead.

I believe in the Holy Spirit; The holy catholic Church; The Communion of Saints: The Forgiveness of sins; The Resurrection of the body; And the Life everlasting. Amen.

## THE PRAYERS

The Lord be with you:
**And with thy spirit.**

### Let us pray

Lord, have mercy upon us.
**Christ, have mercy upon us.**
Lord, have mercy upon us.

**Our Father, who art in heaven, Hallowed be thy name. Thy kingdom come; Thy will be done; In earth as it is in heaven. Give us this day our daily bread; And forgive us our trespasses, As we forgive them that trespass against us; And lead us not into temptation, But deliver us from evil. For thine is the kingdom, The power and the glory, For ever and ever. Amen.**

---

\* *The minister and people may say or sing the following versicles and responses:*

O Lord, show thy mercy upon us:
**And grant us thy salvation.**

O Lord, guide our rulers:
**And give them wisdom from above.**

Endue thy ministers with righteousness:
**And make thy chosen people joyful.**

O Lord, save thy people:
**And bless thine inheritance.**

Give peace in our time, O Lord:
**Because there is none other that ruleth the world, but only thou, O God.**

O God, make clean our hearts within us:
**And take not thy Holy Spirit from us.**

---

*The minister says the Collect or Collects of the Day, and then one of the following:*

### THE COLLECT FOR PEACE

(i)

O GOD, who art the Author of peace and Lover of concord, in knowledge of whom standeth our eternal life, whose service is perfect freedom: Defend us thy humble servants in all assaults of our enemies; that we, surely trusting in thy defence, may not fear the power of any adversaries; through the might of Jesus Christ our Lord. **Amen.**

(ii)

O GOD, from whom all holy desires, all good counsels, and all just works do proceed: Give unto thy servants that peace which the world cannot give; that both our hearts may be set to obey thy commandments, and also that by thee we being defended from the fear of our enemies may pass our time in rest and quietness; through the merits of Jesus Christ our Saviour. **Amen.**

*and at Morning Worship one of the following:*

### THE COLLECT FOR GRACE

(i)

O LORD our heavenly Father, almighty and ever-lasting God, who hast safely brought us to the beginning of this day: Defend us in the same with thy mighty power; and grant that this day we fall into no sin, neither run into any kind of danger; but that all our doings may be ordered by thy gover-nance, to do always that is righteous in thy sight; through Jesus Christ our Lord. **Amen.**

(ii)

O ALMIGHTY Lord, and everlasting God, vouch-safe, we beseech thee, to direct, sanctify, and govern, both our hearts and bodies in the ways of thy laws, and in the works of thy commandments; that through thy most mighty protection, both here and ever, we may be preserved in body and soul; through our Lord and Saviour Jesus Christ. **Amen.**

(iii)

LORD of all power and might, who art the Author and Giver of all good things: Graft in our hearts the love of thy name, increase in us true devotion, nourish us with all goodness, and of thy great mercy keep us in the same; through Jesus Christ our Lord. **Amen.**

*and at Evening Worship one of the following:*

### THE COLLECT FOR AID AGAINST ALL PERILS

(i)

LIGHTEN our darkness, we beseech thee, O Lord; and by thy great mercy defend us from all perils and dangers of this night; for the love of thine only Son, our Saviour, Jesus Christ. **Amen.**

### (ii)

BE present, O merciful God, and protect us through the silent hours of this night, so that we who are wearied by the changes and chances of this fleeting world, may repose upon thine eternal changelessness; through Jesus Christ our Lord. **Amen.**

*A hymn or anthem may be sung.*

*Then follow occasional prayers and thanksgivings, liturgical or extempore, which shall always include a prayer for the nation and its rulers. For example, one of the litanies from the* Order *for the Lord's Supper may be said or sung.*

---

*\* The thanksgivings may include the General Thanksgiving:*

**Almighty God, Father of all mercies, We thine unworthy servants do give thee most humble and hearty thanks For all thy goodness and lovingkindness to us, and to all men. We bless thee for our creation, preservation, and all the blessings of this life; But above all, for thine inestimable love In the redemption of the world by our Lord Jesus Christ; For the means of grace, And for the hope of glory. And, we beseech thee, give us that due sense of all thy mercies, That our hearts may be unfeignedly thankful, And that we show forth thy praise, Not only with our lips, but in our lives; By giving up ourselves to thy service, And by walking before thee in holiness and righteousness all our days; through Jesus Christ our Lord, to whom with thee and the Holy Spirit be all honour and glory, world without end. Amen.**

---

*\* The prayers and thanksgivings may conclude with one of the following:*

ALMIGHTY God, who hast given us grace at this

time with one accord to make our common supplications unto thee; and dost promise, that when
two or three are gathered together in thy name thou
wilt grant their requests: Fulfil now, O Lord, the
desires and petitions of thy servants, as may be
most expedient for them; granting us in this world
knowledge of thy truth, and in the world to come
life everlasting. **Amen.**

(ii)

O LORD, we beseech thee mercifully to receive the
prayers of thy people who call upon thee; and grant
that they may both perceive and know what things
they ought to do, and also may have grace and
power faithfully to fulfil the same; through Jesus
Christ our Lord. **Amen.**

---

*The announcements may be made, and a hymn may be sung.*
*If there is an offering of gifts, these may be collected either*
*before the service begins, or now. The minister receives them*
*and offers them to God with prayer in the name of the people,*
*after which he dismisses the people with one of the following:*

THE grace of our Lord Jesus Christ, and the love of
God, and the fellowship of the Holy Spirit, be with
you all. **Amen.**

Unto God's gracious mercy and protection we
commit you. The blessing of God almighty, the
Father, the Son, and the Holy Spirit, be amongst
you and remain with you always. **Amen.**

The Lord bless you and keep you: the Lord make
his face to shine upon you, and be gracious unto
you: the Lord lift up his countenance upon you, and
give you peace. **Amen.**

*The minister may say* us *or* ourselves *instead of* you.

*Or one of these:*

To God the Father, who has made us and all the world; to God the Son, who has redeemed us and all mankind; to God the Holy Spirit, who sanctifies us, and all the elect people of God, be all the glory for ever and ever. **Amen.**

Now to him who by the power at work within us is able to do far more abundantly than all that we ask or think, to him be glory in the Church and in Christ Jesus to all generations, for ever and ever.
**Amen.**
Eph. 3:20, 21

# THIRD ORDER OF SERVICE

## PRAISE

*All stand, and the minister says:*

Let us worship God.

*A hymn or lyric is sung.*

(i)

*Minister:* Enter his gates with thanksgiving, and his courts with praise. Give thanks to him, bless his name.

*People:* **For the Lord is good; his steadfast love endures for ever, and his faithfulness to all generations.**
Ps. 100:4, 5

*Minister:* O come, let us worship and bow down, let us kneel before the Lord, our Maker.

*People:* **For he is our God, and we are the people of his pasture, and the sheep of his hand.** Ps. 95:6, 7

*Minister:* Who shall ascend the hill of the Lord? And who shall stand in his holy place?

*People:* **He who has clean hands and a pure heart, who does not lift up his soul to what is false, and does not swear deceitfully.**                      Ps. 24:3, 4

*Minister:* To the Lord our God belong mercy and forgiveness; because we have rebelled against him, and have not obeyed the voice of the Lord our God by following his laws, which he set before us.

Dan. 9:9, 10

*People:* **The sacrifice acceptable to God is a broken spirit; a broken and contrite heart, O God, thou wilt not despise.**                      Ps. 51:17

*Minister:* Jesus said, 'Come to me, all who labour and are heavy laden, and I will give you rest'.

Matt. 11:28

*People:* **I will arise and go to my father, and I will say to him, 'Father, I have sinned against heaven and before you'.**                      Luke 15:18

*Minister and People:* **Let the words of my mouth and the meditation of my heart be acceptable in thy sight, O Lord, my rock and my redeemer.**  Ps. 19:14

### *Or* (ii)

*Minister:* The Lord is in his holy temple; let all the earth keep silence before him.      Hab. 2:20

*People:* **Honour and majesty are before him; strength and beauty are in his sanctuary.**   Ps. 96:6

*Minister:* I through the abundance of thy stead-fast love will enter thy house,

*People:* **I will worship toward thy holy temple in the fear of thee.**                      Ps. 5:7

*Minister:* The Lord is my light and my salvation; whom shall I fear?

*People:* **The Lord is the stronghold of my life; of whom shall I be afraid?** Ps. 27:1

*Minister:* He does not deal with us according to our sins, nor requite us according to our iniquities.

*People:* **For as the heavens are high above the earth, so great is his steadfast love toward those who fear him.** Ps. 103:10, 11

*Minister:* What shall I render to the Lord for all his bounty to me?

*People:* **I will lift up the cup of salvation and call on the name of the Lord.** Ps. 116:12, 13

*Minister and People:* **Let the words of my mouth and the meditation of my heart be acceptable in thy sight, O Lord, my rock and my redeemer.** Ps. 19:14

### *Or* (iii)

*The minister reads a sentence or sentences from the Bible, such as those given at the beginning of the Second Order.*

*The minister says:*

### Let us pray

*The minister prays in his own words, or he may say:*

### (i)

ALMIGHTY God, we are come into thy presence to offer unto thee, through our Lord Jesus Christ, our worship and thanksgiving. Help us to make a true confession of our sins, and to pray for others as well as for ourselves. Grant that by our listening to thy holy word we may know more truly the greatness of thy love, and show forth in our lives the fruits of thy grace, through Jesus Christ, our Lord. **Amen.**

*Or* (ii)

ALMIGHTY God, our heavenly Father, in whom alone our hearts find rest and peace: We beseech thee to reveal thyself to us in this hour of worship; pour down upon us thy spiritual gifts; and grant that this season of holy quiet may be profitable to us in heavenly things, and refresh and strengthen us to finish the work which thou hast given us to do; through Jesus Christ our Lord. **Amen.**

## CONFESSION

*The minister may read one or two sentences from the Bible, such as those given in the Second Order.*

*He then says:*

Let us confess our sins in silence.

*All are silent for a space. After this, all say:*

(i)

**Have mercy on me, O God, according to thy steadfast love; according to thy abundant mercy blot out my transgressions. Wash me thoroughly from my iniquity, and cleanse me from my sin. For I know my transgressions, and my sin is ever before me. Against thee, thee only, have I sinned, and done that which is evil in thy sight. Create in me a clean heart, O God, and put a new and right spirit within me. Restore to me the joy of thy salvation, and uphold me with a willing spirit.** Ps. 51:1–4, 10, 12

*Or* (ii)

**We confess to God almighty, the Father, the Son, and the Holy Spirit, that we have sinned in thought, word, and deed, through our grievous fault. Therefore we pray God to have mercy upon us.**

**Almighty God, have mercy upon us, forgive us all our sins, and deliver us from all evil, confirm and strengthen us in all goodness, and bring us to life everlasting; through Jesus Christ our Lord. Amen.**

*The minister says a prayer for pardon in his own words, or he may say:*

(i)

GRANT, we beseech thee, merciful Lord, to thy faithful people pardon and peace, that they may be cleansed from all their sins, and serve thee with a quiet mind; through Jesus Christ our Lord. **Amen.**

*Or* (ii)

O GOD, whose nature and property is ever to have mercy and to forgive: Receive our humble petitions; and though we be tied and bound with the chain of our sins, yet let the pitifulness of thy great mercy loose us; for the honour of Jesus Christ, our Mediator and Advocate. **Amen.**

*The minister and people may say together the General Thanksgiving (see the Second Order), or he may say another prayer of thanksgiving.*

## THE MINISTRY OF THE WORD OF GOD

*A hymn or lyric may be sung.*

*The First Lesson is read from the Old Testament or Apocrypha.*

*The Psalm or Psalms for the Day may be said or sung.*

*The Second Lesson is read from the New Testament.*

*One of the Songs from the Second Order may be said or sung. Or another hymn or lyric may be sung.*

*A children's address may be given here, or a sermon may be preached.*

*The Apostles' Creed may be said:*

I believe in God the Father almighty, Maker of heaven and earth:

And in Jesus Christ his only Son our Lord, Who was conceived by the Holy Spirit, Born of the Virgin Mary, Suffered under Pontius Pilate, Was crucified, dead, and buried, He descended into hell; The third day he rose again from the dead, He ascended into heaven, And sitteth on the right hand of God the Father almighty; From thence he shall come to judge the quick and the dead.

I believe in the Holy Spirit; The holy catholic Church; The Communion of Saints; The Forgiveness of sins; The Resurrection of the body; And the Life everlasting. Amen.

## THE PRAYERS

*Intercessions and thanksgivings for the Church and the world follow. At the end of these, minister and people say together:*

Our Father, who art in heaven, Hallowed be thy name. Thy kingdom come; Thy will be done; In earth as it is in heaven. Give us this day our daily bread; And forgive us our trespasses, As we forgive them that trespass against us; And lead us not into temptation, But deliver us from evil. For thine is the kingdom, The power, and the glory, For ever and ever. Amen.

*A hymn or lyric is sung.*

*The Sermon may be preached, if there has been no sermon after the Lessons.*

*A hymn or lyric is sung. During the singing, or directly afterwards, the offerings of the people are collected.*

*The minister may dedicate the offerings in his own words, or he may say·*

(i)

O GOD, the Giver of all good gifts, we beseech thee graciously to accept this offering of thy people, and so to bless it and them that peace and goodwill may abound throughout the world; through Jesus Christ our Lord. **Amen.**

*Or* (ii)

ALMIGHTY God, our heavenly Father, who hast not spared thine own Son, but delivered him up for us all, and who, with him, hast freely given us all things: Receive these offerings which we bring and dedicate to thee; and enable us, with all our gifts, so to yield ourselves to thee, that with body, soul, and spirit, we may truly and freely serve thee, and in thy service find our deepest joy; through Jesus Christ our Lord. **Amen.**

*The minister dismisses the people with a blessing.*

*A hymn or lyric may be sung.*

# APPENDIX

## A. PSALMS FOR DAILY READING

|    | Jan., March, May, July, Sept., Nov. | | Feb., April, June, Aug., Oct., Dec. | |
|----|------------------|------------------|------------------|------------------|
|    | *Morning*        | *Evening*        | *Morning*        | *Evening*        |
| 1  | 1; 5             | 3; 4             | 79:1–5, 8–13     | 80               |
| 2  | 8; 9             | 6; 7             | 81               | 82               |
| 3  | 10; 11           | 12; 13; 14       | 84               | 85               |
| 4  | 15; 16           | 17               | 86               | 87; 88           |
| 5  | 18:1–24          | 18:25–50         | 89:1–18          | 89:19–52         |
| 6  | 19               | 20; 21           | 90               | 91               |
| 7  | 22               | 23; 24           | 92; 93           | 94               |
| 8  | 25; 26           | 27; 28           | 95               | 96               |
| 9  | 29; 30           | 31               | 97               | 98; 99           |
| 10 | 33               | 32               | 100; 101         | 102              |
| 11 | 34               | 35               | 103              | 104:1–23         |
| 12 | 36; 37:1–11      | 37:12–40         | 104:24–35        | 105:1–22         |
| 13 | 38               | 39               | 105:23–45        | 106:1–18, 42–48  |
| 14 | 40               | 41               | 106:19–48        | 107:1–22         |
| 15 | 44               | 42; 43           | 107:23–43        | 108              |
| 16 | 45               | 46               | 109:1–5, 21–31   | 2; 110           |
| 17 | 47; 48           | 49               | 111; 112         | 113; 114         |
| 18 | 50               | 51               | 116; 117         | 115              |
| 19 | 52; 53           | 54               | 118              | 119:1–24         |
| 20 | 55               | 56               | 119:25–48        | 119:49–72        |
| 21 | 57               | 59:1–4, 9–17     | 119:73–96        | 119:97–120       |
| 22 | 60; 61           | 119:161–176      | 119:121–144      | 119:145–160      |
| 23 | 62; 63           | 64; 65           | 120; 121; 122    | 123; 124; 125    |
| 24 | 66               | 67               | 126; 127; 128    | 129; 130; 131    |
| 25 | 68:1–20, 24–35   | 69:1–21, 29–36   | 132; 133; 134    | 135              |
| 26 | 70; 71:1–16      | 71:17–24         | 136              | 137:1–6; 138     |
| 27 | 72               | 73               | 139              | 140:1–8, 12 f; 141 |
| 28 | 74               | 75               | 142; 143         | 144              |
| 29 | 76               | 77               | 145              | 146              |
| 30 | 78:1–16          | 78:17–39         | 147              | 148              |
| 31 | 78:40–55         | 78:56–72         | 149              | 150              |

*In a month with thirty days, all the Psalms provided for the 30th are read on the morning of the 30th, and those provided for the 31st in the evening.*

## B. ALTERNATIVE SHORTER TABLE

| | Jan., March, May, July, Sept., Nov. | | Feb., April, June, Aug., Oct., Dec. | |
|---|---|---|---|---|
| | Morning | Evening | Morning | Evening |
| 1 | 1 | 2 | 76 | 77:1f, 11–20 |
| 2 | 8 | 4 | 80 | 81:1–10 |
| 3 | 9:1–14 | 13 | 82 | 84 |
| 4 | 14 | 15 | 85 | 86:1–13 |
| 5 | 16 | 18:1–19 | 87 | 89:5–18 |
| 6 | 18:25–35 | 19 | 90 | 91 |
| 7 | 20 | 21:1–7 | 93 | 95 |
| 8 | 22:1–11 | 22:12–31 | 96 | 97 |
| 9 | 23 | 24 | 98 | 99 |
| 10 | 25:1–10 | 25:11–18 | 100 | 102:1–17 |
| 11 | 26 | 27 | 102:18–28 | 103 |
| 12 | 28 | 29 | 104:1–24 | 104:24–35 |
| 13 | 30 | 31:1–5 | 105:1–11 | 106:1–12 |
| 14 | 31:19–24 | 32 | 107:1–16 | 107:23–43 |
| 15 | 33:1–9 | 33:10–22 | 110 | 111 |
| 16 | 34:1–10 | 34:11–22 | 112 | 113 |
| 17 | 36:1–9 | 37:1–9 | 114 | 115:1–11 |
| 18 | 38:9–22 | 39 | 116 | 118:1–9 |
| 19 | 40:1–10 | 41 | 118:15–24 | 119:1–16 |
| 20 | 42; 43 | 44:1–8 | 119:41–56 | 119:97–112 |
| 21 | 45 | 46 | 121 | 122 |
| 22 | 47 | 48 | 124 | 125 |
| 23 | 50:1–15 | 51:1–17 | 126 | 127; 128 |
| 24 | 56 | 57 | 130; 131 | 135:1–14 |
| 25 | 61 | 62 | 136:1–9, 23–26 | 137:1–6 |
| 26 | 63 : 1–8 | 65 | 138 | 139:1–18, 23f |
| 27 | 66:1–14 | 67 | 142 | 143:1–8 |
| 28 | 68:1–10 | 69:1–15 | 145:1–9 | 145:10–21 |
| 29 | 71:12–22 | 72:1–19 | 146 | 147:1–11 |
| 30 | 73:1–3, 10–26 | 75 | 148 | 150 |
| 31 | 119:33–40 | 119:89–96 | 119:137–152 | 119:161–176 |

# HOLY BAPTISM

## I

## THE BAPTISM OF PERSONS ABLE TO ANSWER FOR THEMSELVES

---

### THE OFFICE FOR MAKING A CATECHUMEN

*The admission of a person as a catechumen should normally be at a service of public worship, and may take place after the Lessons. Suitable lessons may be read.*

*After the Lessons the candidate is led forward by his sponsors, and the presbyter says:*

*N,* who *is* present here, *desires* to be received as *a catechumen. He* has promised to undergo regular instruction. Let us therefore pray for *him* and welcome *him* with brotherly love.

#### Let us pray

ALMIGHTY and most merciful God, we pray thee to look favourably upon *this person* who *desires* to be brought out of darkness into the clear light of thy truth and the glorious liberty of thy children. Grant that *he* may now make a sincere profession of *his* purpose, and may receive of thee grace to continue steadfast in the path *he has* chosen, through Jesus Christ our Lord. **Amen.**

*He then asks:* N, what do you desire?
   *Answer:* I ask of you Christian teaching and Holy Baptism.

   Do you accept Jesus Christ as Lord and Saviour?
   *Answer:* I do.

Are you willing to place yourself under our guidance and instruction, that you may be prepared for admission into the Church by baptism?

*Answer:* I am willing.

Do you renounce all those customs and practices and teachings which you know to be contrary to Christ's will?

*Answer:* I do.

Do you promise to be diligent in prayer, regular at public worship of the Church, faithful in receiving instruction and in witnessing to others?

*Answer:* I promise.

*The people stand. The presbyter greets the candidate(s) according to the custom of the place, and says:*

We receive you as *a catechumen* of the Church of Christ, in the name of the Father, and of the Son, and of the Holy Spirit. May almighty God, who has put these good desires into your *heart*, bring the same to good effect. **Amen.**

Let us pray

*All kneel.*

¶ ALMIGHTY God, the Father of our Lord Jesus Christ, look upon *this* thy *servant*, the *catechumen*; give *him* a new heart and renew within *him* a right spirit to know and to do thy will with a ready heart and willing soul. Make *him* worthy of the holy initiation of baptism, unite *him* to thy holy Church, and give *him* a share in thy divine mysteries, through Jesus Christ our Hope. **Amen.**

*Or*

¶ O LORD Jesus Christ, Good Shepherd, who didst lay down thy life for the sheep; mercifully receive *this brother* into thy fold. Join *him* with thine own flock, and lead *him* to the pleasant pastures of everlasting life; for thy mercy's sake. **Amen.**

*Or*

¶ *The minister may pray extempore.*

## THE BAPTISM

*The minister ascertains beforehand that the candidates have not already been baptized.*

### THE DECLARATION OF THE WORD

*When the people are gathered at, or proceeding to, the place of baptism, a hymn may be sung, after which the minister says:*

Our help is in the name of the Lord:
**Who hath made heaven and earth.**

---

*Let us pray

*ALMIGHTY God, thou Shepherd of Israel, who didst deliver thy chosen people from the bondage of Egypt, and didst establish with them a sure covenant: Have mercy, we beseech thee, on thy flock, and grant that *these persons*, who are by baptism to be received into thy heritage, may be delivered from the bondage of sin through thy covenant of grace, and attain the promise of eternal life which thou hast given us in thy Son our Saviour Jesus Christ; who liveth and reigneth with thee and the Holy Spirit, ever one God, world without end.
**Amen.**

---

*The people may sit.*

Dearly beloved, we are met together to administer holy baptism to *these persons*, that according to Christ's command *they* may be sealed as *members* of Christ, *children* of God, and *heirs* of the kingdom of heaven.

* *Passages so marked may be omitted.*

Hear therefore the words of our Lord and Saviour Jesus Christ:

Go and make disciples of all nations, baptizing them in the name of the Father and of the Son and of the Holy Spirit.                    Matt. 28:19

Truly, truly, I say to you, unless one is born of water and the Spirit, he cannot enter the kingdom of God.                                    John 3:5

Hear also the word of God declared by the Apostles concerning baptism:

Repent, and be baptized every one of you in the name of Jesus Christ for the forgiveness of your sins; and you shall receive the gift of the Holy Spirit.                                   Acts 2:38

All of us who have been baptized into Christ Jesus were baptized into his death. We were buried therefore with him by baptism into death, so that as Christ was raised from the dead by the glory of the Father, we too might walk in newness of life.
                                        Rom. 6:3, 4

By one Spirit we were all baptized into one body —Jews or Greeks, slaves or free—and all were made to drink of one Spirit.            1 Cor. 12:13

*The minister expounds the teaching of Scripture concerning baptism in his own words.*

¶ *Or he says:*

You have heard the call to repent and believe in Jesus Christ. Profess therefore your faith and be baptized in Christ's name; for God is faithful who calls you and, having begun a good work in you, he will bring it to completion at the day of Jesus Christ.

## THE RENUNCIATION

*All stand, and the minister says to the candidates:*

You have presented yourselves here for baptism. You must therefore answer sincerely before God and his Church the questions which I now put to you.

Do you renounce [idolatry and] all the works of the devil?

*Answer:* I renounce them.

Do you renounce the pride and vanity of this world?

*Answer:* I renounce them.

Do you renounce impurity, strife, covetousness, and all other works of the flesh?

*Answer:* I renounce them.

## THE PROFESSION OF FAITH

Do you believe in one God, the Father, the Son, and the Holy Spirit?

*Answer:* I believe.

Let us therefore profess our faith.

*The Apostles' Creed is said or sung by all:*

**I believe in God the Father almighty, Maker of heaven and earth:**

**And in Jesus Christ his only Son our Lord, Who was conceived by the Holy Spirit, Born of the Virgin Mary, Suffered under Pontius Pilate, Was crucified, dead, and buried, He descended into hell; The third day he rose again from the dead, He ascended into**

heaven, And sitteth on the right hand of God the Father almighty; From thence he shall come to judge the quick and the dead.

I believe in the Holy Spirit; The holy catholic Church; The Communion of Saints; The Forgiveness of sins; The Resurrection of the body; And the Life everlasting. Amen.

### THE PROMISES

Do you desire to be baptized in this faith?
*Answer:* I do.

Will you keep God's holy will and commandments and walk in them all the days of your life?
*Answer:* By God's grace, I will.

*If the candidates are husband and wife, the minister says to them:*

Will you, in obedience to Christ's teaching, continue together in love, and nurture your children in the Christian faith?

*Husband and wife answer together:*

By God's grace, we will.

*The minister says to all the candidates:*

MAY almighty God grant that the evil spirit of pride, faction, and sinful desire, may never hereafter have dominion over you: for Christ has bought you with his precious blood, and in your baptism delivers you from the power of darkness and accepts you as *children* of light. May your ears be open to hear God's voice, and your mouth to declare the glory of his name, who liveth and reigneth one God, Father, Son, and Holy Spirit, ever world without end. **Amen.**

## THE BAPTISM

*The minister says:*

Let us pray in silence for *those* about to be baptized, that *they* may receive the fullness of God's grace.

*The people may kneel.*

*Silence is kept for a space. Then the minister says:*

The Lord be with you:
**And with thy spirit.**

*The minister prays in his own words.*

---

¶ *Or the following litany is said or sung:*

Blessed art thou, O Lord God, heavenly Father, who hast created all things and given us the element of water:
**Blessed art thou, O Lord.**

Blessed art thou, O Lord Jesus Christ, the only-begotten Son of God, who wast baptized in the Jordan and didst die and rise again:
**Blessed art thou, O Lord.**

Blessed art thou, O Lord, the Holy Spirit, who didst descend upon Jesus Christ and upon the Church:
**Blessed art thou, O Lord.**

Be present, O God, with us who call upon thy threefold name, and bless this water, that it may signify the washing away of sin, and that *those* who are baptized therein may be born again to eternal life:
**Hear us, we beseech thee.**

Grant *them* thy Holy Spirit, that *they* may be baptized into the one body, and ever remain in the number of thy faithful and elect people:
**Hear us, we beseech thee.**

Grant that, being united with Christ in his death and resurrection, *they* may die unto sin and live unto righteousness:
**Hear us, we beseech thee.**

Grant that *they* may put off the old man and become a new creation in Christ Jesus:
**Hear us, we beseech thee.**

From darkness lead *them* to light; from death lead *them* to everlasting life:
**Hear us, we beseech thee.**

---

*All stand; and the minister, having asked the Christian name, dips each candidate in the water, or pours water upon him, saying:*

*N,* I baptize thee in the name of the Father, and of the Son, and of the Holy Spirit.  **Amen.**

*The minister says over each person baptized:*

We have received this person into the congregation of Christ's flock [✠ and do sign *him* with the sign of the cross].[1]

*Then he says for all together:*

May *these persons* never be ashamed to confess the faith of Christ crucified, but continue Christ's faithful servants unto *their lives'* end.  **Amen.**

*Then may be said or sung:*

THE Lord bless you and keep you: the Lord make

[1] *Here the minister may make a cross upon the person's forehead.*

his face to shine upon you, and be gracious to you: the Lord lift up his countenance upon you, and give you peace. **Amen.**  Num. 6:24-26

*A hymn of praise is sung.*

*A procession may be made from the place of baptism into the body of the church.*

---

## *THE PUTTING ON OF A WHITE GARMENT

*The newly baptized may now put on white garments.*
*When they have assembled, the minister says to them:*

We will rejoice greatly in the Lord:
**Our souls shall be joyful in our God.**

For he hath clothed us with the garments of salvation:
**He hath covered us with the robes of righteousness.**

Put off your old nature, and be renewed in the spirit of your minds:
**We will put on the new nature, created after the likeness of God.**

---

## *THE LIGHT

*The newly baptized may be given lighted lamps or tapers.*
*When they have received them, the minister says:*

Let your light so shine before men, that they may see your good works:
**And give glory to our Father who is in heaven.**

Matt. 5:16

¶ *Or some other brief forms of words may be used.*

---

## THE THANKSGIVING

*The minister says:*

Let us pray

**Our Father, who art in heaven, Hallowed be thy name. Thy kingdom come; Thy will be done; In earth as it is in heaven. Give us this day our daily bread; And forgive us our trespasses, As we forgive them that trespass against us; And lead us not into temptation, But deliver us from evil. For thine is the kingdom, The power, and the glory, For ever and ever. Amen.**

*The minister says, or the minister and people say together:*

WE yield thee hearty thanks, most merciful Father, that it has pleased thee to receive *these* thy *servants* for thine own *children* by adoption and to incorporate *them* into thy holy Church. And we humbly beseech thee to grant that *they* may more and more show forth in *their lives* that which *they* now *are* by thy calling; so that as *they are* made *partakers* of the death of thy Son, *they may* also be *partakers* of his resurrection, and finally, with all thy Church, inherit thine everlasting kingdom; through the same Jesus Christ our Lord. **Amen.**

## A CHARGE

*The minister exhorts the congregation and the newly baptized briefly in his own words.*

¶ *Or he may say to the congregation:*

*These* our *brothers and sisters* in Christ *have*, after profession of *their* repentance and faith, been received into the household of God. I charge you, and especially the elders among you, to befriend *them*, and to remind *them* what solemn promises *they have* made before this congregation. Support *them* therefore with your prayers, and encourage *them* to attend diligently to right instruction in God's holy word, and so to prepare *themselves* for Confirmation, that, being established in faith by the Holy Spirit, *they* may come with due preparation to receive the Lord's Supper, and may go forth into the world to serve God faithfully in the fellowship of his Church. Will you endeavour to do all these things?

**We will, God being our helper ; and we receive *them* into our fellowship.**

*And then, speaking to the newly baptized, he says:*

AND you, beloved, have now by baptism put off your old nature and put on Christ. You are accepted as *children* of God and of the light by faith in Jesus Christ, and should walk as becomes *children* of light. Remember always that baptism unites us with Christ in the likeness of his death and resurrection. We who are baptized must reckon ourselves dead unto sin and no longer in bondage to it. We have been raised together with Christ, so that we may overcome all evil desires and walk in newness of life. Let us therefore bear witness to the world that Christ is our life, knowing that when he is manifested, then they that are his shall also be manifested with him in glory.

*A hymn may be sung here, and the thankoffering is taken.*

*If the baptism is administered otherwise than at the Lord's Supper or at Morning or Evening Worship, the minister dismisses those that are gathered together with this blessing:*

MAY God almighty, the Father of our Lord Jesus Christ, grant you to be strengthened with might through his Spirit in the inner man ; that Christ may dwell in your hearts through faith, and that you may be filled with all the fullness of God. **Amen.**

# II

# THE BAPTISM OF INFANTS

## A THANKSGIVING AFTER CHILDBIRTH

*This thanksgiving should be made at a public service of the
Church, and the congregation should join in the saying of the
Psalm and the Lord's Prayer.*

*The Mother and Father, bringing the newly born child, kneel
before the Holy Table, or at some other convenient place,
and the minister facing them says:*

Almighty God has been good to you in giving you the gift
of *a child*.

Let us therefore give thanks to him.

*The minister and parents together with the congregation say the
following Psalm responsively:*

### Psalm 145 : 1–8

I WILL magnify thee, O God, my King : and I will praise
thy name for ever and ever.
Every day will I give thanks unto thee : and praise thy
name for ever and ever.
Great is the Lord, and marvellous worthy to be praised :
there is no end of his greatness.
One generation shall praise thy works unto another : and
declare thy power.
As for me, I will be talking of thy worship : thy glory, thy
praise, and wondrous works;
So that men shall speak of the might of thy marvellous
acts : and I will also tell of thy greatness.
The memorial of thine abundant kindness shall be showed :
and men shall sing of thy righteousness.

The Lord is gracious and merciful : long-suffering, and of great goodness.

Glory be to the Father : and to the Son, and to the Holy Spirit;
As it was in the beginning, is now, and ever shall be : world without end. **Amen.**

*Minister:*

Let us pray

Lord, have mercy upon us:
**Christ, have mercy upon us :**
Lord, have mercy upon us.

**Our Father, who art in heaven, Hallowed be thy name. Thy kingdom come ; Thy will be done ; In earth as it is in heaven. Give us this day our daily bread ; And forgive us our trespasses, As we forgive them that trespass against us ; And lead us not into temptation, But deliver us from evil. For thine is the kingdom, The power, and the glory, For ever and ever. Amen.**

ALMIGHTY God, we give thee hearty thanks for thy love and mercy in giving this woman, thy servant, a safe and happy childbirth. Grant that she, having in remembrance thy care and love for her, may never cease to give thee thanks and serve thee faithfully; through Jesus Christ our Lord. **Amen.**

O GOD, our heavenly Father, by whose creative power and love this woman has been granted the gift of *a child*, give to her and her husband wisdom and guidance, that they may know how to train their *child* in the way that leadeth to eternal life, through Jesus Christ our Lord. **Amen.**

*The parents say:*

O GOD, our Father, we give thanks to thee for the *child* whom thou hast given to us: help us to live together as a family in love, joy and peace; give us wisdom to be good parents, that we may all love and serve thee faithfully; through Jesus Christ our Lord. **Amen.**

---

*If the child has died, Psalm 63:1–8 is said instead of Psalm*

*145: 1–8. Instead of the three prayers appointed above, the minister alone says the following prayer:*

ALMIGHTY God, we humbly praise thee that thou hast saved thy handmaid from all the dangers of her delivery, so that she can again come to thy house today. Beloved Father, comfort her and her husband in their sorrow, and strengthen them that they may continue in faith, do thy will, and at the end of the days of their journey attain the glory of life eternal, through Jesus Christ our Lord. **Amen.**

---

*The minister dismisses them with this blessing:*

THE blessing of God almighty, the Father, the Son, and the Holy Spirit, be upon your going out and your coming in; upon your down-sitting and upon your uprising; upon your talking and upon your silence; upon your prayers and upon your work; upon your home and upon your fellowship therein, this day, henceforth, and forever. **Amen.**

*The parents may make a thankoffering, and, if there is a service of Holy Communion, they may receive the Communion together.*

---

# THE BAPTISM

*The minister ascertains beforehand that the children have not already been baptized.*

## THE DECLARATION OF THE WORD

*When the people are gathered at, or proceeding to, the place of baptism, a hymn may be sung, after which the minister says:*

Our help is in the name of the Lord:
**Who hath made heaven and earth.**

---

*Let us pray

*ALMIGHTY God, thou Shepherd of Israel, who didst deliver thy chosen people from the bondage of

* Passages so marked may be omitted.

Egypt, and didst establish with them a sure covenant: Have mercy, we beseech thee, on thy flock, and grant that *these children* who *are* by baptism to be received into thy heritage, may be delivered from the bondage of sin through thy covenant of grace, and attain the promise of eternal life which thou hast given us in thy Son our Saviour Jesus Christ; who liveth and reigneth with thee and the Holy Spirit, ever one God, world without end. **Amen.**

----

*The people may sit.*

Dearly beloved, we are met together to administer holy baptism to *these children*, that, according to Christ's command, *they* may be sealed as *members* of Christ, *children* of God, and *heirs* of the kingdom of heaven.

Hear therefore the words of our Lord and Saviour Jesus Christ:

Go and make disciples of all nations, baptizing them in the name of the Father, and of the Son, and of the Holy Spirit.                      Matt. 28:19

Truly, truly, I say to you, unless one is born of water and the Spirit, he cannot enter the kingdom of God.                                         John 3:5

Hear also what is written in the Gospel according to St. Mark:

They were bringing children to him, that he might touch them; and the disciples rebuked them. But when Jesus saw it he was indignant, and said to them, 'Let the children come to me, do not hinder them; for to such belongs the kingdom of God.

Truly, I say to you, whoever does not receive the
kingdom of God like a child shall not enter it.'
And he took them in his arms and blessed them,
laying his hands upon them.          Mark 10:13–16

*The minister expounds the teaching of Scripture concerning
baptism in his own words.*

¶ *Or he says:*

You hear in this Gospel the words of our Saviour
Christ, when he commanded the children to be
brought to him. You perceive how he took them
in his arms and blessed them. Jesus Christ is the
same yesterday and today and for ever. He loves
*these children* and is ready to receive *them*, to embrace *them* with the arms of his mercy, and to give
*them* the blessing of eternal life.

*These* little *children belong* with you to God. In
Holy Baptism he establishes *them* in the family and
household of faith, that *they* may grow up as *members* of Christ and *heirs* of the kingdom of heaven.

### THE PROFESSION OF FAITH

*All stand. The minister says to the parents (and godparents):*

It is the duty of those who present *children* for
baptism to make confession of the faith in which
*they are* baptized and to promise to bring *them* up
in the way of Christ.

Do you believe in one God, the Father, the Son,
and the Holy Spirit?

*The parents (and godparents) answer:*

I believe.

Let us therefore profess our faith.

*The Apostles' Creed is said or sung by all:*

I believe in God the Father almighty, Maker of heaven and earth:

And in Jesus Christ his only Son our Lord, Who was conceived by the Holy Spirit, Born of the Virgin Mary, Suffered under Pontius Pilate, Was crucified, dead, and buried, He descended into hell; The third day he rose again from the dead, He ascended into heaven, And sitteth on the right hand of God the Father almighty; From thence he shall come to judge the quick and the dead.

I believe in the Holy Spirit; The holy catholic Church; The Communion of Saints; The Forgiveness of sins; The Resurrection of the body; And the Life everlasting. Amen.

### THE PROMISES

Will you, by God's help, provide a Christian home for this child and bring *him* up in the worship and teaching of the Church, that *he* may come to know Christ *his* saviour?

*Answer:* We will, God being our helper.

Will you so order your own lives that you do not cause this little one to stumble?

*Answer:* We will, God being our helper.

Will you encourage *him* later to be received into the full fellowship of the Church by Confirmation; so that, established in faith by the Holy Spirit, *he* may partake of the Lord's Supper and go forth into the world to serve God faithfully in his Church?

*Answer:* We will, God being our helper.

*The minister says to the congregation:*

Dearly beloved, will you be faithful to your calling as members of the Church of Christ, so that *these* and all other children in your midst may grow up in the knowledge and love of him?

*The congregation answer:*

**We will, God being our helper; and we welcome *them* into our fellowship.**

### THE BAPTISM

*The minister says:*

Let us pray in silence for *the children* about to be baptized, that *they* may receive the fullness of God's grace.

*The people may kneel.*

*Silence is kept for a space. Then the minister says.*

The Lord be with you:
**And with thy spirit.**

*The minister prays in his own words.*

---

¶ *Or the following litany is said or sung:*

Blessed art thou, O Lord God, heavenly Father, who hast created all things and given us the element of water:
**Blessed art thou, O Lord.**

Blessed art thou, O Lord Jesus Christ, the only-begotten Son of God, who wast baptized in the Jordan and didst die and rise again:
**Blessed art thou, O Lord.**

Blessed art thou, O Lord, the Holy Spirit, who didst descend upon Jesus Christ and upon the Church:
**Blessed art thou, O Lord.**

Be present, O God, with us who call upon thy threefold name, and bless this water, that it may signify the washing away of sin, and that *those* baptized therein may be born again to eternal life:
**Hear us, we beseech thee.**

Grant *them* thy Holy Spirit, that *they* may be baptized into the one body, and ever remain in the number of thy faithful and elect people:
**Hear us, we beseech thee.**

Grant that, being united with Christ in his death and resurrection, *they* may die unto sin and live unto righteousness:
**Hear us, we beseech thee.**

Grant that *they* may put off the old man and become a new creation in Christ Jesus:
**Hear us, we beseech thee.**

From darkness lead *them* to light; from death lead *them* to everlasting life:
**Hear us, we beseech thee.**

---

*All stand. The minister, having asked the Christian name, pours water upon each child, saying:*

*N*, I baptize thee in the name of the Father, and of the Son, and of the Holy Spirit. **Amen.**

*The minister says over each child baptized:*

We have received this child into the congregation of Christ's flock [✠ and do sign *him* with the sign of the cross].[1]

[1] *Here the minister may make a cross upon the child's forehead.*

*Then he says for all together:*

MAY *these children* never be ashamed to confess the faith of Christ crucified, but continue his faithful *servants* unto *their* lives' end. **Amen.**

*Then may be said or sung:*

\*THE Lord bless you and keep you: the Lord make his face to shine upon you, and be gracious to you: the Lord lift up his countenance upon you, and give you peace. **Amen.**                    Num. 6:24–26

*A hymn of praise is sung. A procession may be made from the place of baptism into the body of the church.*

---

### \*THE LIGHT

*The parents of the children baptized may be given lighted lamps or tapers. When they have received them, the minister says:*

Let your light so shine before men, that they may see your good works:
   **And give glory to our Father who is in heaven.**
                                   Matt. 5:16

¶ *Or some other brief forms of words may be said.*

---

### THE THANKSGIVING

*The minister says:*

Let us pray

**Our Father, who art in heaven, Hallowed be thy name. Thy kingdom come; Thy will be done; In earth as it is in heaven. Give us this day our daily bread; And forgive us our trespasses, As we forgive them that trespass against us; And lead us not into**

temptation, But deliver us from evil. For thine is the kingdom, The power, and the glory, For ever and ever. Amen.

*The minister says, or the minister and people say together:*

WE yield thee hearty thanks, most merciful Father, that it has pleased thee to receive *these children* for thine own *children* by adoption and to incorporate *them* into thy holy Church. And we humbly beseech thee to grant that *they* may more and more show forth in *their lives* that which *they* now *are* by thy calling; so that, as *they are* made *partakers* of the death of thy Son, *they* may also be *partakers* of his resurrection, and finally, with all thy Church, inherit thine everlasting kingdom; through the same Jesus Christ our Lord. **Amen.**

*The minister says:*

ALMIGHTY God our heavenly Father, whose blessed Son shared at Nazareth the life of an earthly home: Bless, we beseech thee, the *homes* of *these children*, and grant wisdom and understanding to all who have the care of *them*, that *they* may grow up in thy constant fear and love; through the same thy Son Jesus Christ our Lord. **Amen.**

*A hymn may be sung, and the thankoffering is taken.*

*If baptism is administered otherwise than at the Lord's Supper or at Morning or Evening Worship, the minister dismisses those that are gathered together with this blessing:*

MAY God almighty, the Father of our Lord Jesus Christ, grant you to be strengthened with might through his Spirit in the inner man; that Christ may dwell in your hearts through faith, and that you may be filled with all the fullness of God. **Amen.**

# AN ORDER OF SERVICE

## FOR THE RECEPTION OF BAPTIZED PERSONS INTO THE FULL FELLOWSHIP OF THE CHURCH COMMONLY CALLED

# CONFIRMATION

## INTRODUCTION

*A hymn is sung.*

*The minister says:*

Our help is in the name of the Lord:
**Who hath made heaven and earth.**

### Let us pray

*The people kneel, and the minister prays in his own words.*

---

*If there is no celebration of the Lord's Supper, there is a Confession and Declaration of Forgiveness such as the following:*

*The minister says:*

I will arise and go to my father, and I will say to him, 'Father, I have sinned against heaven and before you; I am no longer worthy to be called your son'.                                    Luke 15:18

Let us examine ourselves in silence.

*All are silent for a space. After this, the minister says:*

Let us humbly confess our sins to almighty God.

*All say:*

**O God, our Father, We have sinned against thee in thought, word, and deed: We have not loved thee with all our heart; We have not loved our neighbours as ourselves. Have mercy upon us, we beseech thee; Cleanse us from our sins; And help us to overcome our faults; Through Jesus Christ our Lord. Amen.**

*The minister says:*

MAY the almighty and merciful Lord grant unto us pardon and remission of all our sins, time for amendment of life, and the grace and comfort of the Holy Spirit. **Amen.**

*Or he may say* you *and* your *instead of* us *and* our.

---

*All sit.*

*The presbyter reads the names of the candidates, who stand one by one as they are called.*

*The minister says to them:*

BELOVED in the Lord, in your baptism you were received into the fellowship of Christ and sealed as members of the family and household of God.

Now you come, of your own choice, to ratify the solemn covenant then made, to profess your faith in the Lord Jesus, to consecrate yourselves to him, and to receive the gifts which he is waiting to bestow.

You come that, in accordance with the practice of the apostles, we may lay our hands upon you, praying that the Holy Spirit may strengthen you in every good work.

You come that this congregation may welcome you into the full fellowship of Christ's people, and that together we may worship and serve him all the days of our life.

Hear, therefore, the word of God concerning the gift of the Holy Spirit, in the Book of the Prophet Ezekiel:

A new heart I will give you, and a new spirit I will put within you; and I will take out of your flesh the heart of stone and give you a heart of flesh. And I will put my spirit within you, and cause you to walk in my statutes and be careful to observe my ordinances. You shall dwell in the land which I gave to your fathers; and you shall be my people, and I will be your God.                    Ezek. 36:26–28

In the letter of the Apostle Paul to the Church in Rome:

Brethren, we are debtors, not to the flesh, to live according to the flesh—for if you live according to the flesh you will die, but if by the Spirit you put to death the deeds of the body you will live. For all who are led by the Spirit of God are sons of God. For you did not receive the spirit of slavery to fall back into fear, but you have received the spirit of sonship. When we cry, 'Abba! Father!' it is the Spirit himself bearing witness with our spirit that we are children of God, and if children, then heirs, heirs of God and fellow heirs with Christ, provided we suffer with him in order that we may also be glorified with him.                    Rom. 8:12–17

In the words of our Lord Jesus Christ:

If you love me, you will keep my commandments. And I will pray the Father, and he will give you another Counsellor, to be with you for ever, even the Spirit of truth, whom the world cannot receive, because it neither sees him nor knows him; you know him, for he dwells with you, and will be in you. John 14:15–17

You shall receive power when the Holy Spirit has come upon you; and you shall be my witnesses in Jerusalem, and in all Judea and Samaria, and to the end of the earth. Acts 1:8

¶ *Or the minister may choose other passages.*

*The Sermon is preached.*

## THE VOWS

*The candidates stand, and the minister says:*

I ask you now in the presence of God and of this congregation:

IN the power of Christ, do you renounce the pride and vanity of this world, the sins of the flesh, and all the works of the devil?
*Answer:* I renounce them.

Do you believe in one God, the Father, the Son, and the Holy Spirit?
*Answer:* I believe.

Do you accept the Lord Jesus Christ as your Saviour and the Saviour of the world?
*Answer:* I do.

Let us therefore profess our faith.

**I believe in God the Father almighty, Maker of heaven and earth:**
**And in Jesus Christ his only Son our Lord, Who**

was conceived by the Holy Spirit, Born of the Virgin Mary, Suffered under Pontius Pilate, Was crucified, dead, and buried, He descended into hell; The third day he rose again from the dead, He ascended into heaven, And sitteth on the right hand of God the Father almighty; From thence he shall come to judge the quick and the dead.

I believe in the Holy Spirit; The holy catholic Church; The Communion of Saints; The Forgiveness of sins; The Resurrection of the body; And the Life everlasting. Amen.

Will you keep God's holy will and commandments and walk in them all the days of your life?
*Answer:* I will, God being my helper.

Do you promise to join with your fellow Christians in worship on the Lord's Day, and especially in the Lord's Supper?
*Answer:* I promise.

Do you promise to be faithful in reading or hearing the Bible, and in prayer?
*Answer:* I promise.

Do you promise to give according to your means for God's work?
*Answer:* I promise.

Do you acknowledge yourselves bound to confess the faith of Christ crucified and risen, and to continue his faithful servants unto your lives' end, bearing witness to him both in word and in deed?
*Answer:* I promise.

*The minister says:*

Beloved, you have confessed your faith in God through Christ our only Saviour, and your desire to obey him and live in the fellowship of his people; will you now kneel and pray that the Holy Spirit may enable you truly to perform that which you have promised?

*Silence, all kneeling.*

*Then the candidates, led by the minister, say:*

O GOD, my God, Father of our Lord Jesus Christ, I am not my own, but thine. Relying on thy grace, I give myself to thee, As thy child, To love and to serve thee faithfully, All the days of my life. **Amen.**

## THE CONFIRMATION

*The minister calls the congregation to pray in silence for the candidates.*

*Silence is kept for a space.*

*A hymn or lyric praying for the Holy Spirit may be sung kneeling.*

*The minister says the following prayer alone.*

*Or he may invite the congregation to say it with him.*

ALMIGHTY God, our heavenly Father, who by Holy Baptism hast received these thy children into thy family: Establish them in faith, we beseech thee, by thy Holy Spirit, and daily increase in them thy manifold gifts of grace, the spirit of wisdom and understanding, the spirit of counsel and might, the spirit of knowledge and of the fear of the Lord; and keep them in thy mercy unto life eternal; through Jesus Christ thy Son our Lord. **Amen.**

*The minister lays his hand upon the head of each of the candidates in turn, saying:*

STRENGTHEN, O Lord, this thy child with thy heavenly grace, that *he* may continue thine for ever, and daily increase in thy Holy Spirit, until *he* come unto thine everlasting kingdom.

*The people each time say:*

**Amen.**

*When all have been confirmed, the minister says:*

The Lord be with you:
**And with thy spirit.**

## Let us pray

**Our Father, who art in heaven, Hallowed be thy name. Thy kingdom come; Thy will be done; In earth as it is in heaven. Give us this day our daily bread; And forgive us our trespasses, As we forgive them that trespass against us; And lead us not into temptation, But deliver us from evil. For thine is the kingdom, The power, and the glory, For ever and ever. Amen.**

*The minister prays:*

ALMIGHTY and everliving God, who, according to the promise of thy Son our Saviour Jesus Christ, hast ordained thy Church to be the temple of the Holy Spirit: Mercifully hear our prayers for these thy children, upon whom we have laid our hands. Let thy fatherly hand, we beseech thee, be over them; let thy Holy Spirit ever be with them; and so lead them in the knowledge and obedience of thy word, that they may serve thee all their days and be with thee for ever; through our Lord and Saviour Jesus Christ, who with thee and the Holy Spirit liveth and reigneth, ever one God, world without end. **Amen.**

## THE RECEPTION

*If the Lord's Supper is celebrated together with Confirmation, the Reception takes place after the offertory sentences, and the Peace is given first to the newly confirmed and by them to the rest of the congregation.*

*The newly confirmed persons stand and face the congregation, while the minister and the congregation stand and together say to them:*

**Beloved, we, the members of this congregation, Welcome you with joy As partners in the common life of the Church. We pledge to you our friendship and our prayers, That you may grow in the knowledge and love of God And of his Son Jesus Christ our Lord. God grant that we may all serve him here on earth In the unity of the Spirit, And come to the perfect fellowship of the saints above.**

*The newly confirmed persons turn again to the minister.*

*Each is given a membership card. A Bible, a New Testament, or* The Book of Common Worship *of the Church of South India may also be given.*

*The minister says to them:*

In token of our brotherly love in Christ, we give you the greeting of peace.

*The Peace is given, and a hymn is sung, during which the offerings of the newly confirmed and of the congregation are received.*

*If there is no celebration of the Lord's Supper, the minister says this blessing:*

Go forth into the world in peace; and the blessing of God almighty, the Father, the Son, and the Holy Spirit, be upon you and remain with you for ever. **Amen.**

# THE COVENANT SERVICE

## INTRODUCTION

*The following hymn (to the tune called 'French' or 'Dundee')*
*or some other suitable hymn or lyric is sung:*

> COME, let us use the grace divine,
>     And all, with one accord,
> In a perpetual covenant join
>     Ourselves to Christ the Lord:
>
> Give up ourselves, through Jesu's power,
>     His name to glorify;
> And promise, in this sacred hour,
>     For God to live and die.
>
> The covenant we this moment make
>     Be ever kept in mind;
> We will no more our God forsake,
>     Or cast his words behind.
>
> We never will throw off his fear
>     Who hears our solemn vow;
> And if thou art well pleased to hear,
>     Come down and meet us now.
>
> To each the covenant blood apply,
>     Which takes our sins away;
> And register our names on high,
>     And keep us to that day. Amen.

*The minister says, while the people stand:*

## Let us pray

ALMIGHTY God, unto whom all hearts be open, all desires known, and from whom no secrets are hid: Cleanse the thoughts of our hearts by the inspiration of thy Holy Spirit, that we may perfectly love thee, and worthily magnify thy holy name; through Christ our Lord. **Amen.**

*Then the people sit, and the minister says:*

DEARLY beloved, the Christian life, to which we are called, is a life in Christ, redeemed from sin by him and, through him, consecrated to God. Upon this life we have entered, having been admitted into that New Covenant of which our Lord Jesus Christ is Mediator, and which he sealed with his own blood, that it might stand for ever.

On God's part, the covenant is his reconciling of the world to himself in Jesus Christ and his promise that he will fulfil in and through us all that he declared in him, who is the Author and Perfecter of our faith. That his promise stands we are sure, for we have known his goodness and proved his grace in our lives day by day.

On our part we have received this covenant through faith, and stand pledged to live no more unto ourselves, but unto him who loved us and gave himself for us and has called us to serve him to the praise of his glory.

From time to time we renew our vows of consecration, especially when we gather at the Table of the Lord; and on this day we meet expressly, that we may joyfully and solemnly renew the covenant which binds us to God.

Let us then, remembering the mercies of God, and the hope of his calling, lift up our hearts to him in adoration.

## ADORATION

### Let us pray

*All kneel.*

LET us adore the Father, the God of love;
Who created us;
Who every moment preserves and sustains us;
Who has loved us with an everlasting love, and given us the light of the knowledge of his glory in the face of Jesus Christ.

**We adore thee, O God, we acknowledge thee to be the Lord.**

Let us glory in the grace of our Lord Jesus Christ;
Who, though he was rich, yet for our sakes became poor;
Who was tempted in all points like as we are, yet without sin;
Who went about doing good and preaching the gospel of the kingdom;
Who became obedient unto death, even the death of the cross;
Who was dead and is alive for evermore;
Who has opened the kingdom of heaven to all believers;
Who sitteth at the right hand of God in the glory of the Father;
Who shall come again as Judge and King.

**Thou art the King of glory, O Christ.**

Let us rejoice in the fellowship of the Holy Spirit, the Lord, the Giver of life, by whom we are born into the family of God, and made members of the body of Christ;
Whose witness confirms us;
Whose wisdom teaches us;
Whose power enables us;

Who is ready to do for us exceeding abundantly above all that we ask or think.

**All praise to thee, O Holy Spirit.**

*Here follows a period of silent prayer.*

### THANKSGIVING

Let us give thanks to God for his manifold mercies.

O GOD our Father, the Fountain of all goodness, who hast been gracious to us [not only in the year that is past, but[1]] through all the years of our life: We give thee thanks for thy loving-kindness which has filled our days and brought us to this time and place.

**We praise thy holy name, O Lord.**

Thou hast redeemed us and called us with a high calling in Jesus Christ. Thou hast given us a place in the fellowship of thy Spirit and the witness of thy Church.

**We praise thy holy name, O Lord.**

In darkness thou hast been our light; in adversity and temptation a rock of strength; in our joys the very crown of joy; in our labours the all-sufficient reward. For all thy long-suffering and the abundance of thy grace,

**We praise thy holy name, O Lord.**

### CONFESSION

And now let us examine ourselves, asking God to search our hearts.

---

[1] *The words in brackets are omitted except at an Annual Covenant Service.*

*Silent confession.*

Let us humbly confess our sins to God, lest by self-deceit we shut ourselves out from his presence.

Let us pray

O GOD our Father, who hast set forth the way of life for us in thy beloved Son: We confess with shame our slowness to learn of him, our failure to follow him, our reluctance to bear the cross.
**Have mercy upon us and forgive us, O Lord.**

Forgive us, we beseech thee, the poverty of our worship, our neglect of fellowship and of the means of grace, our hesitating witness for Christ, our evasion of our responsibilities in thy service, our imperfect stewardship of thy gifts.
**Have mercy upon us and forgive us, O Lord.**

Forgive us that so little of thy love has reached others through us, that we have been thoughtless in our judgements, hasty in condemnation, grudging in forgiveness, slow to seek reconciliation, unwilling to help our neighbour as we ought.
**Have mercy upon us and forgive us, O Lord.**

**Have mercy on me, O God, according to thy steadfast love; according to thy abundant mercy blot out my transgressions. Wash me thoroughly from my iniquity, and cleanse me from my sin. Create in me a clean heart, O God, and put a new and right spirit within me.** Ps. 51 1, 2, 10

*The people still kneeling, the minister rises and says:*

This is the message we have heard from him and proclaim to you, that God is light and in him is no darkness at all. If we walk in the light, as he is in the light, we have fellowship with one another, and the blood of Jesus his Son cleanses us from all sin. If we say we have no sin, we deceive ourselves, and the truth is not in us. If we confess our sins, he is faithful and just, and will forgive our sins and cleanse us from all unrighteousness. 1 John 1:5, 7–9

**Amen. Thanks be to God.**

The Lord be with you:
**And with thy spirit.**

Let us pray

O GOD, who hast appointed our Lord Jesus Christ as Mediator of a new covenant, grant us grace, we beseech thee, to draw near with fullness of faith and join ourselves in a perpetual covenant to thee; through the same Jesus Christ our Lord. **Amen.**

*All stand, and the lessons are read:*
   *Old Testament:* Jeremiah 31:31–33
   *Epistle:* Hebrews 12:22–25a
   *Gospel:* Matthew 11:27–30

*A sermon may be preached.*


## THE COVENANT

*All remain standing, and the minister says:*

And now, beloved, let us with all our heart renew our part in the covenant that God has made with his people, and take the yoke of Christ upon us.

This taking of his yoke means that we are heartily content that he should appoint us our place and work, and that he alone should be our reward.

Christ has many services to be done; some are easy, others are difficult; some bring honour, others bring reproach; some are suitable to our natural inclinations and temporal interests, others are contrary to both. In some we may please Christ and please ourselves, in others we cannot please Christ except by denying ourselves. Yet the power to do all these things is assuredly given us in Christ, who strengtheneth us.

Therefore let us make the covenant of God our own. Let us engage our heart to the Lord, and resolve in his strength never to go back.

Being thus prepared, let us now, in sincere dependence on his grace and trusting in his promises, yield ourselves anew to him, meekly kneeling upon our knees.

*All kneel.*

*The minister says in the name of all:*

O LORD God, Holy Father, who hast called us through Christ to be partakers in this gracious covenant, we take upon ourselves with joy the yoke of obedience, and engage ourselves, for love of thee, to seek and do thy perfect will. We are no longer our own, but thine.

*Here all the people join.*

**I am no longer my own, but thine. Put me to what thou wilt, rank me with whom thou wilt; put me to doing, put me to suffering; let me be employed for thee or laid aside for thee, exalted for thee or brought low for thee; let me be full, let me be empty; let me have all things, let me have nothing; I freely and heartily yield all things to thy pleasure and disposal.**

**And now, O glorious and blessed God, Father, Son, and Holy Spirit, thou art mine, and I am thine. So be it. And the covenant which I have made on earth, let it be ratified in heaven. Amen.**

*Silence.*

*If a celebration of the Lord's Supper is to follow, the minister and people rise, and the minister says:*

JESUS said: 'This is my blood of the covenant, which is poured out for many for the forgiveness of sins'.                                           Matt. 26:28

**Praise be to Thee, O Christ.**

Behold, how good and joyful a thing it is, brethren, to dwell together in unity.

*The service of the Lord's Supper continues from this place.*

*If there is no celebration of the Lord's Supper, the service ends as follows:*

*Silence after the Covenant.*

*The Lord's Prayer.*

*Hymn or lyric, during which the offerings are collected.*

*Dedication of offerings.*

*Ascription:*

GLORY be to thee, O God the Father, who hast loved us and made us accepted in thy beloved Son.

**Amen. Glory to thee, our Father.**

Glory be to thee, O God the Son, who hast loved us and loosed us from our sins by thine own blood.

**Amen. Glory to thee, our Saviour.**

Glory be to thee, O God the Holy Spirit, who sheddest the love of God abroad in our hearts and dost free us from the law of sin and death.

**Amen. Glory to thee, our Guide and Strengthener.**

O one true God, Father, Son, and Holy Spirit, to thee be all love and all glory for time and for eternity.

**Amen. Blessing, and glory, and wisdom, and thanksgiving, and honour, and power, and might, be unto our God for ever and ever. Amen.**

# THE MARRIAGE SERVICE

## INTRODUCTION

*A lyric or hymn is sung.*

*The persons to be married present themselves before the minister, the man standing at the right hand of the woman.*

*The minister says:*

DEARLY beloved, we are gathered here in the presence of God to join this man and this woman in marriage. This is a way of life instituted by God, and Holy Scripture commands all men to hold it in honour. Our Lord Jesus Christ blessed it by his presence at Cana of Galilee.

About this way of life, hear what our Lord says:

'From the beginning of creation, "God made them male and female". "For this reason a man shall leave his father and mother and be joined to his wife, and the two shall become one." So they are no longer two but one. What therefore God has joined together, let not man put asunder.'

Mark 10:6–9

Marriage is therefore not by any to be undertaken lightly or ill-advisedly, but seriously and prayerfully, duly considering the purposes for which it is ordained.

It is ordained:

That husband and wife may give to each other life-long companionship, help, and comfort, both in prosperity and in adversity;

That God may hallow and direct the natural instincts and affections created by himself, and redeemed in Christ;

That children may be born and brought up in families in the knowledge of our Lord Jesus Christ to the glory of God;

That, marriage being thus held in honour, human society may stand upon firm foundations.

## THE MARRIAGE

*The minister says:*

These two persons have come here to be made one in this holy estate. But if anyone here knows any just cause why they may not be married according to the discipline of the Church and the law of this land, let him now make it known, or else for ever hold his peace.

*If no impediment is alleged, he says to the persons who are to be married:*

I charge you both in the presence of God, that if either of you knows any reason why you may not be joined together in marriage, you do now confess it.

*If no impediment is alleged, the man and woman may now garland each other; and the minister says:*

ALMIGHTY and most merciful Father, without whose help we cannot do anything as we ought, we pray that, as thou hast brought these persons together by thy providence, thou wilt enrich them with thy grace, that they may enter into the marriage covenant as in thy sight, and truly keep the vows they are about to make; through Jesus Christ our Lord. **Amen.**

*Then the minister says to the man:*

N, will you have this woman, M, to be your wife, and cleave to her alone?

*And the man answers:*

I will.

*The minister says to the woman:*

M, will you have this man, N, to be your husband, and cleave to him alone?

*And the woman answers:*

I will.

*If the woman is given in marriage by her parent or guardian, the minister says:*

Who gives this woman to be married to this man?

*And the parent or guardian puts the woman's right hand into the right hand of the man.*

*If the parent or guardian is not present, the minister says:*

N and M, give each other the right hand.

*And the man says after the minister:*

I, N, Take you, M, to be my wife, To have and to hold from this day forward; For better, for worse; For richer, for poorer; In sickness and in health; To love, cherish, and protect, till death us do part, According to God's holy law; And to this I give you my pledge.

*They still hold hands, and the woman says after the minister:*

I, M, Take you, N, to be my husband, To have and to hold from this day forward; For better, for worse; For richer, for poorer; In sickness and in health; To love, cherish, and obey, till death us do part, According to God's holy law; And to this I give you my pledge.

*The minister says:*

God has heard your vows, and we are witnesses.

*The minister may bless the mangalasutra, ring, or rings, saying:*

BLESS this mangalasutra [ring], O merciful Lord, that *he who gives it and she who wears it* may ever be faithful one to the other, and continue together in love so long as they both shall live; through Jesus Christ our Lord. **Amen.**

*The minister delivers the mangalasutra to the man, who puts it on the woman in the customary manner, and holds it. Or else the minister delivers the ring to the man, who puts it on the woman's finger, and holds it. The man then says after the minister:*

This mangalasutra [ring] I give you in token of constant faith and abiding love. I honour you with my body, and all my worldly goods with you I share.

*\* If the woman gives a ring to the man, she puts it on his finger, and holds it, saying after the minister:*

This ring I give you in token of constant faith and abiding love. I honour you with my body, and all my worldly goods with you I share.

*The minister declares:*

As *N* and *M* have made their pledge to each other before God and before this congregation, I declare that they are now husband and wife, according to the law of this land and the ordinance of God; in the name of the Father, and of the Son, and of the Holy Spirit. **Amen.**

Whom therefore God has joined together, let not man put asunder.

*\* Passages thus marked may be omitted at the discretion of the minister.*

*The man and the woman kneel, while the congregation remains standing, and the minister says:*

MOST merciful and gracious God, our Father, of whom the whole family in heaven and earth is named: Send thy blessing upon *N* and *M*, whom we bless in thy name; that, living faithfully together, they may surely perform and keep the vow and covenant between them made, and may ever remain in perfect love and peace together, and live according to thy law; through Jesus Christ our Lord. **Amen.**

GOD the Father, God the Son, God the Holy Spirit, bless, preserve, and keep you; the Lord mercifully look upon you with favour, and fill you with all spiritual benediction and grace: that you may so live together in this life that in the world to come you may have life everlasting. **Amen.**

## THE PRAYERS

*A lyric or hymn is sung; or one or both of the following psalms may be said or sung.*[1] *The man and woman go to the Lord's Table. If the ceremony of the Saptapadi (Seven Steps) is observed, the people say or sing Psalm 67, pausing after each verse while the man and woman take one step forward.*

### *Psalm 67

May God be gracious to us and bless us,
    and make his face to shine upon us,
that thy way may be known upon earth,
    thy saving power among all nations.
Let the peoples praise thee, O God;
    let all the peoples praise thee!

[1] *Any other recognised version of the psalms may be used.*

Let the nations be glad and sing for joy,
>for thou dost judge the peoples with equity
>and guide the nations upon earth.
Let the peoples praise thee, O God;
>let all the peoples praise thee!

The earth has yielded its increase;
>God, our God, has blessed us.
God has blessed us;
>Let all the ends of the earth fear him!

### *Psalm 128

Blessed is everyone who fears the Lord,
>who walks in his ways!
You shall eat the fruit of the labour of your hands;
>you shall be happy, and it shall be well with
>you.

Your wife will be like a fruitful vine
>within your house;
your children will be like olive shoots
>around your table.
Lo, thus shall the man be blessed
>who fears the Lord.

The Lord bless you from Zion!
>May you see the prosperity of Jerusalem
>all the days of your life!
May you see your children's children!
>Peace be upon Israel!

*After each psalm all say or sing:*

Glory be to the Father: and to the Son, and to
the Holy Spirit;

As it was in the beginning, is now, and ever shall be : world without end. Amen.

*A Bible or New Testament may then be placed in the hands of the newly married couple by the minister, with the words:*

May the Word of God be a lamp to your feet and a light to your path.

*The following passage of Scripture is read:*

1 Corinthians 13:4–13.

*A sermon may be preached.*

*Then the minister says:*

Let us pray

Lord, have mercy upon us.
**Christ, have mercy upon us.**
Lord, have mercy upon us.

**Our Father, who art in heaven, Hallowed be thy name. Thy kingdom come; Thy will be done; In earth as it is in heaven. Give us this day our daily bread; And forgive us our trespasses, As we forgive them that trespass against us; And lead us not into temptation, But deliver us from evil. For thine is the kingdom, The power and the glory, For ever and ever. Amen.**

Lord, save thy servant and thy handmaid:
**And let them put their trust in thee.**

O Lord, send help from thy holy place:
**And evermore defend them.**

Be unto them a tower of strength:
**From the face of their enemy.**

O Lord, hear our prayer:
**And let our cry come unto thee.**

ALMIGHTY and everlasting Father, who hast given to mankind the ordinance of marriage, and dost hallow it with thy blessing: Bless, we beseech thee, thy servants *N* and *M*, now joined together as husband and wife; and grant that, bearing one another's burdens, sharing one another's joys, and together fulfilling the duties of their home, they may ever be faithful to each other in love and obedience to thy word; through Jesus Christ our Lord. **Amen.**

O LORD and Saviour Jesus Christ, who didst share at Nazareth the life of an earthly home: Reign, we beseech thee, in the home of these thy servants as Lord and King; give them grace that they may minister to others as thou didst minister to men, and grant that by deed and word they may be witnesses of thy saving love to those amongst whom they live; for thy holy name's sake, who livest and reignest with the Father and the Holy Spirit, one God, world without end. **Amen.**

*The following prayer may be omitted if the woman is past child-bearing.*

O MERCIFUL Lord and heavenly Father, by whose gracious gift mankind is increased: Bestow, we beseech thee, upon these thy servants the heritage and gift of children, and grant that they may live together so long in godly love and honour, that they may see their children brought up in Christian faith and virtue, to thy praise and glory; through Jesus Christ our Lord. **Amen.**

O ALMIGHTY Lord, and everlasting God, vouchsafe, we beseech thee, to direct, sanctify, and govern, both our hearts and bodies in the ways of thy laws, and in the works of thy commandments; that through thy most mighty protection, both here and ever, we may be preserved in body and soul; through our Lord and Saviour Jesus Christ. **Amen.**

*If the Lord's Supper follows, the service begins at the Breaking of the Bread. Otherwise, the minister says:*

THE grace of our Lord Jesus Christ, and the love of God, and the fellowship of the Holy Spirit, be with you all. **Amen.**

*A lyric or hymn may be sung while the register is being signed.*

# THE BURIAL SERVICE

## THE SERVICE
## IN THE HOUSE OR CHURCH

*A lyric or hymn is sung. If the service is held in the house, the minister and people gather in the place where the body lies, and the minister reads some or all of the following sentences. If the service is held in the church, the sentences may be read while the body is carried into the church.*

BLESSED be the God and Father of our Lord Jesus Christ, the Father of mercies and God of all comfort, who comforts us in all our affliction, so that we may be able to comfort those who are in any affliction, with the comfort with which we ourselves are comforted by God. 2 Cor. 1:3, 4

Thou dost show me the path of life; in thy presence there is fullness of joy, in thy right hand are pleasures for evermore. Ps. 16:11

His favour is for a lifetime. Weeping may tarry for the night, but joy comes with the morning.
Ps. 30:5

Jesus said: 'I am the resurrection and the life; he who believes in me, though he die, yet shall he live, and whoever lives and believes in me shall never die'. John 11:25, 26

Because I live, you will live also. John 14:19

Truly, truly, I say to you, the hour is coming, and now is, when the dead will hear the voice of the Son of God, and those who hear will live. John 5:25

*At the burial of a child, the following may be used:*

HE will feed his flock like a shepherd, he will gather the lambs in his arms, he will carry them in his bosom, and gently lead those that are with young.

Isa. 40:11

Jesus said: 'It is not the will of my Father who is in heaven that one of these little ones should perish. For I tell you that in heaven their angels always behold the face of my Father who is in heaven.'                    Matt. 18:14, 10

*One or more of the following psalms¹ are said or sung:*

### Psalm 90

LORD, thou hast been our dwelling place
    in all generations.
Before the mountains were brought forth,
    or ever thou hadst formed the earth and the
        world,
        from everlasting to everlasting thou art
        God.

Thou turnest man back to the dust,
    and sayest, 'Turn back, O children of men!'
For a thousand years in thy sight
    are but as yesterday when it is past,
    or as a watch in the night.

Thou dost sweep men away; they are like a
        dream,
    like grass which is renewed in the morning:
in the morning it flourishes and is renewed;
    in the evening it fades and withers.

¹ *Any other recognised version may be used.*

For we are consumed by thy anger;
    by thy wrath we are overwhelmed.
Thou hast set our iniquities before thee,
    our secret sins in the light of thy countenance.

For all our days pass away under thy wrath,
    our years come to an end like a sigh.
The years of our life are threescore and ten,
    or even by reason of strength fourscore;
Yet their span is but toil and trouble;
    they are soon gone, and we fly away.

Who considers the power of thy anger,
    and thy wrath according to the fear of thee?
So teach us to number our days
    that we may get a heart of wisdom.

Return, O Lord!  How long?
    Have pity on thy servants!
Satisfy us in the morning with thy steadfast love,
    that we may rejoice and be glad all our days.

Make us glad as many days as thou hast afflicted
        us,
    and as many years as we have seen evil.
Let thy work be manifest to thy servants,
    and thy glorious power to their children.
Let the favour of the Lord our God be upon us,
    and establish thou the work of our hands
        upon us,
        yea, the work of our hands establish thou it.


*Psalm 130*

OUT of the depths I cry to thee, O Lord!
    Lord, hear my voice!
Let thy ears be attentive
    to the voice of my supplications!

If thou, O Lord, shouldst mark iniquities,
    Lord, who could stand?
But there is forgiveness with thee,
    that thou mayest be feared.

I wait for the Lord, my soul waits,
    and in his word I hope;
my soul waits for the Lord
    more than watchmen for the morning,
    more than watchmen for the morning.

O Israel, hope in the Lord!
    For with the Lord there is steadfast love,
    and with him is plenteous redemption.
And he will redeem Israel
    from all his iniquities.

### *Psalm 23*

THE Lord is my shepherd, I shall not want;
    he makes me lie down in green pastures.
He leads me beside still waters;
    he restores my soul.
He leads me in paths of righteousness
    for his name's sake.

Even though I walk through the valley of the
    shadow of death,
    I fear no evil;
for thou art with me;
    thy rod and thy staff,
    they comfort me.

Thou preparest a table before me
    in the presence of my enemies;
thou anointest my head with oil,
    my cup overflows.

Surely goodness and mercy shall follow me
all the days of my life;
And I shall dwell in the house of the Lord
for ever.

*After each psalm, all say or sing:*

Glory be to the Father : and to the Son, and to
the Holy Spirit;
As it was in the beginning, is now, and ever shall
be : world without end. Amen.

*One or more of the following passages of Scripture are read:*
1 Corinthians 15:20–28 and 35–58.
Revelation 7:9–17 and 21:1–7.

*A short address may be given here, and after it the minister says:*

The Lord be with you:
**And with thy spirit.**

Let us pray

Lord, have mercy upon us.
**Christ, have mercy upon us.**
Lord, have mercy upon us.

**Our Father, who art in heaven, Hallowed be thy
name. Thy kingdom come ; Thy will be done ; In
earth as it is in heaven. Give us this day our daily
bread ; And forgive us our trespasses, As we forgive
them that trespass against us; And lead us not into
temptation, But deliver us from evil. For thine is the
kingdom, The power and the glory, For ever and ever.
Amen.**

*Minister:* Let us commend our *brother* departed
to God.

The souls of the righteous are in the hand of God:
**And no torment will ever touch them.**

Wisdom 3:1

Let us pray

ALMIGHTY God, with whom do live the spirits of them that depart hence in the Lord, and with whom the souls of the faithful are in joy and felicity: We commend into thy hands the soul of this our *brother*; trusting that thou wilt bring *him* into sure consolation and rest. Grant, we beseech thee, that at the day of Judgement *he* and all thy people, departed out of this life, may with us, and we with them, fully receive thy promises, and be made perfect; through the glorious resurrection of thy Son Jesus Christ our Lord. **Amen.**

Let us pray for those who mourn.

Blessed are those who mourn:
**For they shall be comforted.**                    Matt. 5:4

Let us pray

FATHER of mercies, and God of all comfort: Look in thy tender love and pity, we beseech thee, on thy sorrowing servants. Be thou to them their refuge and strength, a very present help in trouble; make them to know the love of Christ, which passeth knowledge; who by death hath conquered death, and by rising again hath opened the gates of everlasting life; even Jesus Christ our Lord. **Amen.**

Let us pray for faith and hope.

I believe that I shall see the goodness of the Lord:
**In the land of the living.**                    Ps. 27:13

Let us pray

O HEAVENLY Father, who in thy Son Jesus Christ hast given us a true faith, and a sure hope: Help us, we pray thee, to live as those who believe and trust in the communion of saints, the forgiveness of sins, and the resurrection to life everlasting; and strengthen this faith and hope in us all the days of our life; through thy Son Jesus Christ. **Amen.**

And now, in sure and steadfast hope, let us declare our faith:

**I believe in God the Father almighty, Maker of heaven and earth :**

**And in Jesus Christ his only Son our Lord, Who was conceived by the Holy Spirit, Born of the Virgin Mary, Suffered under Pontius Pilate, Was crucified, dead, and buried, He descended into hell; The third day he rose again from the dead, He ascended into heaven, And sitteth on the right hand of God the Father almighty; From thence he shall come to judge the quick and the dead.**

**I believe in the Holy Spirit; The holy catholic Church; The Communion of Saints; The Forgiveness of sins; The Resurrection of the body; And the Life everlasting. Amen.**

*The people may sing a lyric or hymn.*

*The minister and people say together:*

**The grace of our Lord Jesus Christ, and the love of God, and the fellowship of the Holy Spirit, be with us all. Amen.**

*As the body is taken from the church or house, the people sing.*

---

## THE BURIAL

*The minister meets the procession at the gate of the cemetery, and says:*

Blessed be the God and Father of our Lord Jesus Christ! By his great mercy we have been born

anew to a living hope through the resurrection of
Jesus Christ from the dead. 1 Pet. 1:3

*As the body is taken to the grave, the minister says sentences
from the Bible, such as the following:*

Christ has been raised from the dead, the firstfruits of those who have fallen asleep. For as by
a man came death, by a man has come also the
resurrection of the dead. For as in Adam all die,
so also in Christ shall all be made alive.

1 Cor. 15:20–22

Fear not, says the Lord; I am the first and the
last, and the living one; I died, and behold I am
alive for evermore. Rev. 1:17, 18

Even though I walk through the valley of the
shadow of death, I fear no evil; for thou art with
me; thy rod and thy staff, they comfort me. Ps. 23:4

*At the graveside the minister says:*

## Let us pray

O LORD Jesus Christ, who didst rest in a sepulchre,
and didst thereby sanctify the grave to be a bed of
hope to thy people: Grant, we pray thee, that this
grave may be a resting place for the body of thy
servant, who we believe is at rest in thee; who art
the resurrection and the life. **Amen.**

Eternal rest grant unto him, O Lord:
**And let light perpetual shine upon him.**

### THE COMMITTAL

*While the body is being lowered into the grave, a short lyric or
hymn may be sung.*

*Some earth is cast upon the coffin, and the minister says:*

We commend into thy hands, most merciful Father,

the soul of this our *brother* departed, and we commit *his* body to the ground, earth to earth, ashes to ashes, dust to dust; in sure and certain hope of the resurrection in the last day, and the life of the world to come; through our Lord Jesus Christ, who shall fashion anew the body of our low estate that it may be like unto his glorious body, according to the mighty working, whereby he is able to subdue all things unto himself.

---

*When the body is cremated, the minister says:*

WE commend into thy hands, most merciful Father, the soul of this our *brother* departed, and we commit *his* body to the fire; in sure and certain hope....

*At the burial of the ashes after cremation, he says:*

WE commend into thy hands, most merciful Father, the soul of this our *brother* departed, and we commit *his* ashes to the ground; in sure and certain hope....

---

*The Lord's Prayer may be said by all. Then is said:*

Thou art the King of glory, O Christ:
**Thou art the everlasting Son of the Father.**

We therefore pray thee, help thy servants, whom thou hast redeemed with thy precious blood:
**Make them to be numbered with thy saints, in glory everlasting.**

Lord, now lettest thou thy servant depart in peace, according to thy word:
**For mine eyes have seen thy salvation.**

Luke 2:29, 30

I heard a voice from heaven saying, 'Write this: Blessed are the dead who die in the Lord henceforth'. 'Blessed indeed,' says the Spirit, 'that they may rest from their labours, for their deeds follow them!'                    Rev. 14:13

*The minister says this blessing:*

Now may the God of peace who brought again from the dead our Lord Jesus, the great Shepherd of the sheep, by the blood of the eternal covenant, equip you with everything good that you may do his will, working in you that which is pleasing in his sight, through Jesus Christ; to whom be glory for ever and ever. **Amen.**                    Heb. 13:20, 21

# THE ORDINAL

# ORDERS FOR
## THE ORDINATION OF DEACONS
## THE ORDINATION OF PRESBYTERS
## THE CONSECRATION OF BISHOPS

### PREFACE

'The Church of South India believes that the ministry is a gift of God through Christ to His Church, which He has given for the perfecting of the life and service of all its members' (Constitution II. 7). The Church as a whole is a priestly body, since it is the body of Christ the great High Priest. All its members, according to the measure of the gift of Christ, share in its priestly nature. Yet from the beginning God has entrusted particular ministries to particular persons within it, and these have, through the Church, received the commission of Christ. The ordained ministry of the Church of South India consists of Bishops, Presbyters, and Deacons. In accepting this ministry the Church of South India desires to maintain continuity with the historic ministry of the Church as it has come down to us from early times through the uniting Churches.

An ordination service is the rite by which one of these ministries is conferred. It is an act of God in his Church. 'The Church of South India believes that in all ordinations and consecrations the true Ordainer and Consecrator is God, who, in response to the prayers of His Church, and through the words and acts of its representatives, commissions and empowers for the office and work to which they are called the persons whom it has selected' (Constitution II. 11; see also II. 7).

In the earliest ordination of which we have record, that described in Acts 6:1–6, the following parts appear: election by the people, prayer, and the laying on of apostolic hands. In accordance with this pattern, which is the scriptural authority for what is said in the Constitution (IV. 25 and V. 5) of the essential elements in ordination services, the same three parts form the basis of the services in this book:

(1) the presentation of the candidates to the presiding Bishop, this being the last step in the process of choice of them by the Church;

(2) prayer for those about to be ordained or consecrated, that they may receive the gift of the Holy Spirit for their ministry; and

(3) the laying on of hands of at least three Bishops (in an episcopal consecration), of the Bishop and Presbyters (in an ordination of Presbyters), or of the Bishop (in an ordination of Deacons).

To these have been added an examination of the candidates concerning their beliefs and duties, the delivery to them of the instruments of their office (Bible, pastoral staff), and the giving of the right hand of fellowship. These ceremonies, however valuable for their symbolism, are not essential elements in the rites of ordination.

---

# THE ORDINATION OF DEACONS

*The service begins with the first part of* The Order for the Lord's Supper, *called* THE PREPARATION.

## THE PRESENTATION OF THE CANDIDATES

*The people sit. A person duly appointed presents the candidates and says to the Bishop seated in his chair:*

REVEREND Father in God, we present unto you these persons to be ordained Deacons.

*Bishop:* Let the authority for their ordination be read.

*The authorisation of the Diocese for the ordaining of the candidates is read. This shall include a statement of the work to which each candidate has been called.*

*The Bishop to the people:*

BELOVED, these are they whom we intend, God willing, to ordain Deacons. You have heard that those appointed to inquire about them and examine them believe them to be men of sound learning and godly life, and find them to be duly called to serve

God in this ministry. We therefore ask you to declare your assent.

*The people stand, and the Bishop says:*

We are not sufficient of ourselves; our sufficiency is from God.

Do you trust that these persons are, by God's grace, worthy to be ordained?

*People:* **We trust that they are worthy. To God be the glory.**

## THE MINISTRY OF THE WORD OF GOD[1]

The Lord be with you:
**And with thy spirit.**

### Let us pray

*The people kneel.*

ALMIGHTY God, Giver of all good things, who by thy one Spirit hast appointed a diversity of ministrations in thy Church: Mercifully behold these thy servants now called to the office of Deacon; and so replenish them with the truth of thy gospel, adorn them with innocency of life, and fill them with the power of thy Holy Spirit, that both by word and good example, they may faithfully and joyfully serve thee, to the glory of thy name and the building up of thy Church; through the merits of our Saviour Jesus Christ, who liveth and reigneth with thee and the Holy Spirit, world without end. **Amen.**

*The lesson from the Old Testament:* Isaiah 42:1-9

*Psalm 84 or a hymn*

*The Epistle:* 1 Timothy 3:8-13

*The Gospel:* Luke 12:35-38

*The Sermon*

[1] *For rubrics see* The Lord's Supper, *p. 9.*

*The Nicene Creed*
*Hymn*

## THE EXAMINATION

*The candidates stand. The people sit. The Bishop is seated in his chair and says:*

IT belongs to the office of a Deacon, in the church where he shall be appointed to serve, to preach the word, to assist the Presbyter in the ministration of the Lord's Supper and in other services of the Church to administer baptism, to minister in the temporalities of the Church, to give succour to the poor, the needy, and the sick, to instruct children and catechumens in the faith, and generally to give assistance in pastoral and evangelistic work.

Brothers, these are the duties of a Deacon. Do you trust that you are truly called by God to this ministry in his Church?

*Answer:* I do so trust.

Are zeal for the glory of God, love for our Lord Jesus Christ, and a desire for the salvation of men, so far as you know your own heart, your chief motives for entering into this ministry?

*Answer:* So far as I know my own heart, they are.

Do you accept the Holy Scriptures as containing all things necessary for salvation, and as the supreme and decisive standard of faith?

*Answer:* I do.

Do you accept the Apostles' and Nicene Creeds as witnessing to and safeguarding the faith that is set forth in Scripture?

*Answer:* I do.

Will you be diligent in the reading of the Holy

Scriptures and in such studies as help to the knowledge of the same?

*Answer:* I will, the Lord being my helper.

Will you continually stir up the gift of God that
is in you to preach the gospel to all men?

*Answer:* I will, the Lord being my helper.

Will you endeavour to lead a prayerful and
disciplined life, and so to guide your households
that both you and they may be wholesome examples
to the flock of Christ?

*Answer:* I will, the Lord being my helper.

Seeing you believe you are called to exercise this
ministry within the Church of South India, will you
accept its discipline and submit yourselves as sons
in the gospel to those whom this Church shall appoint over you?

*Answer:* I will, by the help of God.

*All kneel, the ordinands kneeling before the Bishop, who
stands and says:*

ALMIGHTY God, our heavenly Father, who has
given you the will to do all these things, grant you
also grace to perform them. Faithful is he that
calleth you, who also will do it. **Amen.**

## THE ORDINATION

*The Bishop calls the people to silent prayer.*
*The hymn 'Come, Holy Ghost' is sung kneeling.*
*The Bishop stands and says:*

WE glorify thee, O God, most merciful Father, that
thou of thy great goodness didst send thy Son Jesus
Christ to take the form of a servant and to humble
himself, becoming obedient, even to the death of
the cross. We praise thee that thou hast exalted

him and given him the name which is above every name, and through him hast taught us that he who would be great should be the servant of all. We thank thee that thou hast graciously called these thy servants to be Deacons in thy Church; and, we humbly beseech thee,

*Here the Bishop remains standing, lays his hand upon the head of each ordinand in turn, and repeats the following words:*

SEND DOWN THY HOLY SPIRIT UPON THY SERVANT . . ., WHOM WE, IN THY NAME, AND IN OBEDIENCE TO THY MOST BLESSED WILL, DO NOW ORDAIN DEACON IN THY CHURCH.

*The people each time repeat:* **Amen.**

*And the Bishop continues, praying for all those ordained:*

Give them grace, we beseech thee, to be faithful to their promises, constant in their service, and bold to proclaim thy gospel; that, having always the full assurance of faith, they may abound in hope, and continue rooted and grounded in the love of thy Son Jesus Christ our Lord, to whom, with thee and the Holy Spirit, be honour and glory, world without end. **Amen.**

*The Bishop delivers to each one, still kneeling, a Bible, saying:*

Take this, a token of the authority which you have received to preach the word of God and to serve his people.

*The Bishop then gives him the right hand of fellowship and says:*

We give you the right hand of fellowship, and receive you to take part with us in this ministry.

*All stand. The Bishop says:*

We declare that . . . are Deacons in the Church of

God, in the name of the Father, and of the Son, and of the Holy Spirit.

**Amen. Thanks be to God.**

*A doxology is sung.*

The Order for the Lord's Supper *continues at the Intercession. The second litany may be used, with the addition of the following petitions after that for* our bishops and all other ministers:

For the servants of God now ordained Deacons, that they may faithfully minister to the glory of his name, let us pray to the Lord.

For the wives and homes of our ministers, especially of those now ordained, that they may show forth the love of Christ, let us pray to the Lord.

*Proper Preface (after* It is verily meet . . . everlasting God):

Through Jesus Christ our Lord, who came not to be ministered unto, but to minister, and to give his life a ransom for many.

**Therefore with angels . . .**

---

# THE ORDINATION OF PRESBYTERS

*The service begins with the first part of* The Order for the Lord's Supper, *called* THE PREPARATION.

## THE PRESENTATION OF THE CANDIDATES

*The people sit. A person duly appointed presents the candidates and says to the Bishop, seated in his chair:*

REVEREND Father in God, we present unto you these persons to be ordained Presbyters.

*Bishop:* Let the authority for their ordination be read.

*The authorisation of the Diocese for the ordaining of the candidates is read. This shall include a statement of the work to which each candidate has been called.*

*The Bishop says to the people:*

Beloved, these are they whom we intend, God willing, to ordain Presbyters. You have heard that those appointed to inquire about them and examine them believe them to be men of sound learning and godly life, and find them to be duly called to serve God in this ministry. We therefore ask you to declare your assent.

*The people stand, and the Bishop says:*

We are not sufficient of ourselves; our sufficiency is from God.

Do you trust that these persons are, by God's grace, worthy to be ordained?

*People:* **We trust that they are worthy. To God be the glory.**

THE MINISTRY OF THE WORD OF GOD[1]

The Lord be with you:
**And with thy spirit.**

Let us pray

*The people kneel.*

ALMIGHTY God, Giver of all good things, who by thy one Spirit hast appointed a diversity of ministrations in thy Church: Mercifully behold these thy servants now called to the office of Presbyter; and so replenish them with the truth of thy gospel, adorn them with innocency of life, and fill them with the power of thy Holy Spirit, that both by word and good example, they may faithfully and joyfully serve thee, to the glory of thy name and the building

---

[1] *For rubrics see* The Lord's Supper, *p. 9.*

up of thy Church; through the merits of our Saviour Jesus Christ, who liveth and reigneth with thee and the Holy Spirit, world without end. **Amen.**

*The Lesson from the Old Testament:* Ezekiel 33:1–9
*Psalm 99 or a hymn*
*The Epistle:* 1 Peter 5:1–11
*The Gospel:* John 10:1–16
*The Sermon*
*The Nicene Creed*
*Hymn*

## THE EXAMINATION

*The candidates stand. The people sit. The Bishop is seated in his chair and says:*

In the name of the Lord Jesus Christ, the King and Head of the Church, who, being ascended on high, has given gifts unto men for the building up of his Body, we are met here to ordain you Presbyters by prayer and the laying on of hands.

In this act of ordination we believe that it is God who gives you grace and authority for the office and work to which you are called, and that he does so in answer to the prayers of his Church and through the actions and words of his appointed ministers. We act and speak as part of the One, Holy, Catholic, and Apostolic Church, and in the faith which we have now with united voice declared in the words of the Creed.

Wherefore, that we may know that you truly profess this faith, and desire by God's grace to fulfil this ministry, we require you to answer these questions:

Do you trust that you are truly called by God to this ministry in his Church?
*Answer:* I do so trust.

Are zeal for the glory of God, love for our Lord
Jesus Christ, and a desire for the salvation of men,
so far as you know your own heart, your chief
motives for entering into this ministry?

*Answer:* So far as I know my own heart, they are.

Do you accept the Holy Scriptures as containing all things necessary for salvation, and as the
supreme and decisive standard of faith?

*Answer:* I do.

Do you accept the Apostles' and Nicene Creeds
as witnessing to and safeguarding the faith that is
set forth in Scripture?

*Answer:* I do.

Will you be diligent in the reading of the Holy
Scriptures and in such studies as help to the knowledge of the same?

*Answer:* I will, the Lord being my helper.

Seeing you are called to be ambassadors for
Christ, will you, by the help of the Holy Spirit,
continually stir up the gift of God that is in you to
testify to all men the gospel of the grace of God?

*Answer:* I will, the Lord being my helper.

Will you faithfully teach and preach the word of
God to the people committed to your charge, and
minister the sacraments as commanded by our Lord
Jesus Christ?

*Answer:* I will, the Lord being my helper.

Will you be faithful watchmen and shepherds of
the flock? Will you endeavour to maintain peace
and love among them, to bring sinners to repentance, and to declare to them God's forgiveness?

*Answer:* I will, the Lord being my helper.

Will you, for Christ's sake, be faithful in visiting the sick, in caring for the poor and needy, and in helping the oppressed?

*Answer:* I will, the Lord being my helper.

Will you help your people to be good stewards of the manifold gifts of God, that every member may be equipped for the work of ministering, and the whole Body built up in love?

*Answer:* I will, the Lord being my helper.

Will you endeavour to lead a prayerful and disciplined life, and so to guide your households that both you and they may be wholesome examples to the flock of Christ?

*Answer:* I will, the Lord being my helper.

Seeing you believe you are called to exercise this ministry within the Church of South India, will you accept its discipline and submit yourselves as sons in the gospel to those whom this Church shall appoint to have the rule over you?

*Answer:* I will, by the help of God.

*All kneel, the ordinands kneeling before the Bishop, who stands and says:*

ALMIGHTY God, our heavenly Father, who has given you the will to do all these things, grant you also grace to perform them. Faithful is he that calleth you, who also will do it. **Amen.**

### THE ORDINATION

*The Bishop calls the people to silent prayer.*

*The hymn 'Come, Holy Ghost' is sung kneeling.*

*The Bishop, standing together with the Presbyters, says:*

WE glorify thee, O God, most merciful Father, that of thine infinite love and goodness towards us thou didst choose a people for thine own possession to be a royal priesthood and a holy nation, and hast given thine only Son Jesus Christ to be our great High Priest and the Author of eternal salvation. We thank thee that by his death he has overcome death and, having ascended into heaven, has poured forth his gifts abundantly upon thy people, making some apostles, some prophets, some evangelists, some pastors and teachers, for the building up of his Body the Church, until his coming again in glory; and, we humbly beseech thee,

*The Bishop lays his hand upon the head of each person to be ordained in turn, the Presbyters also laying on their right hands; and the Bishop repeats the following words:*

SEND DOWN THY HOLY SPIRIT UPON THY SERVANT..., WHOM WE, IN THY NAME, AND IN OBEDIENCE TO THY MOST BLESSED WILL, DO NOW ORDAIN PRESBYTER IN THY CHURCH, COMMITTING UNTO HIM AUTHORITY TO MINISTER THY WORD AND SACRAMENTS, TO DECLARE THY FORGIVENESS TO PENITENT SINNERS, AND TO SHEPHERD THY FLOCK.

*The people each time repeat:* **Amen.**

*And the Bishop continues, praying for all those ordained:*

GIVE them grace, we beseech thee, O Lord, to offer with all thy people spiritual sacrifices acceptable to thee. Enrich them in all utterance and all knowledge, that they may proclaim the gospel of thy salvation. Make them watchful and loving guardians over thy flock, as followers of the Good Shepherd who gave his life for the sheep. Enable them in all things to fulfil their ministry without reproach in thy sight; so that, abiding steadfast to the end, with all thy faithful servants they may be received into thine eternal joy; through Jesus Christ our Lord, who liveth and reigneth and is worshipped and glorified with thee, O Father, and the Holy Spirit, one God, world without end. **Amen.**

*The Bishop delivers to each one, still kneeling, a Bible, saying:*

Take this, a token of the authority which you have received to preach the word of God and to minister the sacraments in the congregations to which you shall be appointed.

*The Bishop gives him the right hand of fellowship and says:*

We give you the right hand of fellowship, and receive you to take part with us in this ministry.

*All stand. The Bishop says:*

We declare that . . . are Presbyters in the Church of God, in the name of the Father, and of the Son, and of the Holy Spirit.

**Amen. Thanks be to God.**

*A doxology is sung.*

The Order for the Lord's Supper *continues at the Intercession. The second litany may be used, with the addition of the following petitions after that for* our bishops and all other ministers:

For the servants of God now ordained Presbyters, that they may faithfully minister to the glory of his name, let us pray to the Lord.

For the wives and homes of our ministers, especially of those now ordained, that they may show forth the love of Christ, let us pray to the Lord.

*Proper Preface (after* It is verily meet . . . everlasting God)*:*

Through Jesus Christ our Lord, who gave authority to his disciples, saying, 'As the Father hath sent me, even so send I you'.

**Therefore with angels . . .**

# THE CONSECRATION OF BISHOPS

*The service begins with the first part of* The Order for the Lord's Supper, *called* THE PREPARATION.

## THE PRESENTATION OF THE BISHOP-ELECT

*The Bishop-elect is presented to the Moderator or his deputy by three presbyters of the Diocese to which he is appointed, and one of the presbyters says:*

REVEREND Father in God, we present unto you this godly and well-learned man to be consecrated Bishop.

*The Moderator says:*

Let the instrument of his election and appointment be read.

*The Secretary of the Synod, or some other duly appointed person, reads the instrument.*

*The Moderator says to the people:*

Beloved, this is he whom we intend, God willing, this day to consecrate Bishop. You have heard that he has been duly elected and appointed, and that the appointment has been confirmed by those who have authority to do so. We therefore ask you to declare your assent.

*The people stand, and the Moderator says:*

We are not sufficient of ourselves; our sufficiency is from God.

Do you trust that he is, by God's grace, worthy to be consecrated?

*The people say:* **We trust that he is worthy. To God be the glory.**

# THE MINISTRY OF THE WORD OF GOD[1]

*The Moderator says:*

The Lord be with you:
**And with thy spirit.**

Let us pray

*The people kneel.*

ALMIGHTY God, Giver of all good things, who by thy one Spirit hast appointed a diversity of ministrations in thy Church: Mercifully behold this thy servant now called to the office of Bishop; and so replenish him with the truth of thy gospel, adorn him with innocency of life, and fill him with the power of thy Holy Spirit, that, both by word and good example, he may faithfully and joyfully serve thee to the glory of thy name and the building up of thy Church; through the merits of our Saviour Jesus Christ, who liveth and reigneth with thee and the Holy Spirit, one God, world without end. **Amen.**

*The lesson from the Old Testament:* Ezekiel 34:11–16
*Psalm 119:105–112 or a hymn*
*The Epistle:* Acts 20:28–35
*The Gospel:* John 20:19–23
*The Sermon*
*The Nicene Creed*
*Hymn*

# THE EXAMINATION OF THE BISHOP-ELECT

*The Bishop-elect stands before the Moderator, who sits. The Moderator says:*

IN the name of the Lord Jesus Christ, the King and Head of the Church, who being ascended on high, has given gifts unto men for the building up of his

---

[1] *For rubrics see* The Lord's Supper, *p. 9.*

Body, we are met here to consecrate you Bishop in the One, Holy, Catholic, and Apostolic Church, by prayer and the laying on of hands.

In this act of consecration we believe that it is God who gives you grace and authority for the office and work to which you are called, and that he does so in answer to the prayers of his Church and through the actions and words of his appointed ministers. We act and speak as part of the universal Church, and in the faith which we have now with united voice declared in the words of the Creed.

Wherefore, that we may know that you indeed profess this faith, and desire by God's grace to fulfil this ministry, we require you to answer these questions:

Do you trust that you are called to the office of Bishop in the Church of God?
*Answer:* I do.

Are zeal for the glory of God, love for our Lord Jesus Christ, and a desire for the salvation of men, so far as you know your own heart, your chief motives for accepting this office?
*Answer:* So far as I know my own heart, they are.

Do you accept the Holy Scriptures as containing all things necessary for salvation, and as the supreme and decisive standard of faith?
*Answer:* I do.

Do you accept the Apostles' and Nicene Creeds as witnessing to and safeguarding the faith which is set forth in Scripture?
*Answer:* I do.

Will you be diligent in the study of the Holy Scriptures, praying for a true understanding of them, that you may be able to feed your people with the Bread of life, to lead them in accordance with God's will, and to withstand and convince false teachers?

*Answer:* I will, God being my helper.

Will you faithfully administer discipline in accordance with God's word and the order of this Church?

*Answer:* I will, God being my helper.

Will you be a faithful witness of Christ to those among whom you live, and lead your people to obey our Saviour's command to make disciples of all nations?

*Answer:* I will, God being my helper.

Will you do all in your power to ensure that the worship offered by the ministers and people committed to your charge shall be worthy of God's majesty and love?

*Answer:* I will, God being my helper.

Will you seek always the unity and peace of this Church and of the whole Church of God?

*Answer:* I will, God being my helper.

Will you order your own life, and that of your household, in accordance with God's holy laws, that you may be an example to your people?

*Answer:* I will, God being my helper.

Will you for Christ's sake be gentle and merciful to the poor and needy?

*Answer:* I will, God being my helper.

Will you see that Baptism and Confirmation are duly and regularly administered in your diocese, and will you be faithful and discreet in ordaining men to the sacred ministry?

*Answer:* I will, God being my helper.

Seeing you believe you are called to exercise this ministry within the Church of South India, do you promise to fulfil the duties of your office in accordance with the constitution of this Church and of the diocese to which you are appointed?

*Answer:* I do, by the help of God.

*All kneel, and the Moderator says:*

ALMIGHTY God, our heavenly Father, who has given you the will to do all these things, grant you also grace to perform them. Faithful is he that calleth you, who also will do it. **Amen.**

## THE CONSECRATION

*The Moderator calls the people to silent prayer.*

*The hymn 'Come, Holy Ghost' is sung kneeling.*

*The Moderator, standing together with the Bishops (and Presbyters), says:*

WE glorify thee, O God, most merciful Father, that of thine infinite love and goodness towards us thou didst choose a people for thine own possession to be a royal priesthood and a holy nation, and hast given thine only Son Jesus Christ to be our great High Priest and the Author of eternal salvation. We thank thee that by his death he has overcome death and, having ascended into heaven, has poured forth his gifts abundantly upon thy people, making some apostles, some prophets, some evangelists, some pastors and teachers, for the building up of his Body the Church, until his coming again in glory; and, we humbly beseech thee,

*Here the Moderator and the Bishops (and Presbyters) lay their hands upon the head of the Bishop-elect; and the Moderator repeats the following words:*

SEND DOWN THY HOLY SPIRIT UPON THY SERVANT . . ., WHOM WE, IN THY NAME, AND IN OBEDIENCE TO THY MOST BLESSED WILL, DO NOW ORDAIN AND CONSECRATE BISHOP IN THY CHURCH.

*The people say:* **Amen.**

*And the Moderator continues:*

Give him grace, we beseech thee, to be a faithful ambassador of Christ to the world, to offer with all thy people spiritual sacrifices acceptable to thee, to feed and govern thy flock as a true shepherd, and to promote love and unity among all thy people. Deliver him from all assaults of the devil, and grant that in all things he may fulfil his ministry without reproach in thy sight, and, abiding steadfast to the end, may be received with all thy faithful servants into thine eternal glory; through Jesus Christ our Lord, who liveth and reigneth, and is worshipped and glorified, with thee, O Father, and the Holy Spirit, one God, world without end. **Amen.**

## THE PRESENTATION OF THE BIBLE AND PASTORAL STAFF

*The Moderator delivers to him a copy of the Bible, saying:*

Take this, a token of the authority which you have received to be a Bishop in the Church of God. Give heed unto reading, exhortation, and teaching. Think upon the things contained in this book. Give yourself wholly to them, that the increase coming thereby may be manifest unto all men; for by so doing you shall save both yourself and those who hear you.

*The Moderator gives him the right hand of fellowship and says:*

We give you the right hand of fellowship, and receive you to take part with us in this ministry.

*The Moderator delivers to him the Pastoral Staff, saying:*

Be to the flock of Christ a good shepherd. Feed the flock; hold up the weak, heal the sick, bind up the broken, bring again the outcast, seek the lost. So be merciful that you be not remiss; so minister discipline, that you forget not mercy: that when the Chief Shepherd shall appear you may receive the never-fading crown of glory.

*The Moderator says to the people:*

We declare that . . . is a Bishop in the Church of God, in the name of the Father, and of the Son, and of the Holy Spirit.

**Amen. Thanks be to God.**

*A doxology is sung.*

The Order for the Lord's Supper *continues at the Intercession. The second litany may be used, with the addition of the following petitions after that for* our bishops and all other ministers:

For the servant of God now consecrated Bishop, that he may faithfully minister to the glory of his name, let us pray to the Lord.

For the [wife and] home of him who has been consecrated, that *they* may show forth the love of Christ, let us pray to the Lord.

*Proper Preface (after* It is verily meet . . . everlasting God):

Through Jesus Christ our Lord, who gave authority to his disciples, saying, 'As the Father hath sent me, even so send I you'.

**Therefore with angels . . .**

# A SHORT ORDER FOR
# THE LORD'S SUPPER

## THE PREPARATION

*A hymn or psalm may be sung or said.*

*As the ministers come to the Lord's Table, the people stand. The presbyter, or one of those with him, carries in both hands the Bible from which the lessons are to be read, and places it on the Table or on a lectern. The presbyter may stand behind the Table, facing the people.*

*The presbyter says, the people standing:*

## Let us pray

ALMIGHTY God, unto whom all hearts be open, all desires known, and from whom no secrets are hid: Cleanse the thoughts of our hearts by the inspiration of thy Holy Spirit, that we may perfectly love thee, and worthily magnify thy holy name; through Christ our Lord. **Amen.**

*The presbyter says:*

Brethren, we have come together to hear God's most holy word, and to receive the body and blood of the Lord. Let us therefore kneel and examine ourselves in silence, seeking God's grace that we may draw near to him with repentance and faith.

*All kneel. After a short silence, the presbyter says:*

Let us humbly confess our sins to almighty God.

*The deacon leading, all say together:*

**Heavenly Father, we confess that we have sinned against thee and our neighbour. We have walked in**

**darkness rather than in light; we have named the name of Christ, but have not departed from iniquity. Have mercy upon us, we beseech thee; for the sake of Jesus Christ forgive us all our sins; cleanse us by thy Holy Spirit; quicken our consciences; and enable us to forgive others, that we may henceforth serve thee in newness of life, to the glory of thy holy name. Amen.**

*The presbyter stands and says:*

Hear the gracious word of God to all who truly turn to him through Jesus Christ.

God so loved the world, that he gave his only-begotten Son, that whosoever believeth on him should not perish, but have eternal life.     John 3:16

Faithful is the saying, and worthy of all acceptation, that Christ Jesus came into the world to save sinners.                                       1 Tim. 1:15

*After a short silence, the presbyter says:*

ALMIGHTY God, our heavenly Father, who of his great mercy has promised forgiveness of sins to all who forgive their brethren and with hearty repentance and true faith turn unto him: Have mercy upon you; pardon and deliver you from all your sins; confirm and strengthen you in all goodness; and bring you to eternal life; through Jesus Christ our Lord.

**Amen. Thanks be to God.**

*The presbyter may say* us *and* our *for* you *and* your; *if so, the prayer precedes the reading of the Gracious Word of God.*

## THE MINISTRY OF THE WORD OF GOD

The Lord be with you:
**And with thy spirit.**

Let us pray

*The Collect of the Day, or another short prayer, is said.*

*The First Lesson, from the Old Testament or from the Epistles, is read, and after it the people say:*

**Thanks be to thee, O God.**

*The Gospel is read, and the people say:*

**Praise be to thee, O Christ.**

*The Sermon is preached, the people sitting.*

*Then the Apostles' Creed is said or sung by all, standing:*

**I believe in God the Father almighty, Maker of heaven and earth:**

**And in Jesus Christ his only Son our Lord, Who was conceived by the Holy Spirit, Born of the Virgin Mary, Suffered under Pontius Pilate, Was crucified, dead, and buried, He descended into hell; The third day he rose again from the dead, He ascended into heaven, And sitteth on the right hand of God the Father almighty; From thence he shall come to judge the quick and the dead.**

**I believe in the Holy Spirit; The holy catholic Church; The Communion of Saints; The Forgiveness of sins; The Resurrection of the body; And the life everlasting. Amen.**

*Announcements may be made here, and the collection may be taken. A hymn may also be sung.*

*Biddings for prayer may be made, and then, all kneeling, this litany may be said or sung, the deacon leading; or the presbyter may offer intercession in his own words for the Church and the world.*

Let us pray

FOR the peace that is from above, and for the salvation of our souls, let us pray to the Lord.

**Lord, have mercy** (*and so after each bidding*).

For the peace of the whole world, for the welfare of God's holy Churches, and for the union of all, let us pray to the Lord.

For our bishops and all other ministers, espeally . . . . . . . ., our Moderator, and . . . . . . . ., our Bishop, that with a good heart and a pure conscience they may accomplish their ministry, let us pray to the Lord.

For the rulers of our country and all in authority, let us pray to the Lord.

For the sick, the suffering, the sorrowful, and the dying, let us pray to the Lord.

For the poor, the hungry, orphans and widows, and them that suffer persecution, let us pray to the Lord.

For ourselves and all who confess the name of Christ, that we may show forth the excellencies of him who called us out of darkness into his marvellous light, let us pray to the Lord.

That, with all his servants who have served him here and are now at rest, we may enter into the fullness of his unending joy, let us pray to the Lord.

*The presbyter gives the First Benediction:*

THE grace of the Lord Jesus Christ, and the love of God, and the fellowship of the Holy Spirit, be with you all. **Amen.**

*He may say* us *instead of* you.
*Those who leave shall leave now.*

## THE BREAKING OF THE BREAD

*The full Order is followed, the first Thanksgiving Collect being said.*

For the grace of the whole world, for the welfare
of God's holy churches, and for the union of all,
let us render thanks to the Lord.

For our bishops, and all other ministers, and
all ... the Christian people, and ...
on us, that with a quiet heart and pure ...
acknowledge thy commandments, let us ...
praise the Lord.

For the faithful of our country, and of all man ...
let us pray to the Lord.

For those that are sick, that are in suffering, that
desire to pass to the Lord.

For the poor, the hungry, captives and widows,
and the orphan, supplication let us make to the
Lord.

For himself, and for all who ask the help of the
Christian, that they may live in peace all their days,
him who called us out of darkness into his marve-
lous light, let us render to the Lord.

That, with all his servants who have served him
here in the work of God, among whom our forefall
asleep, his enduring love beginning ...

... a better resurrection.

For grace of the Lord Jesus Christ, and the love of
God, and the fellowship of the Holy Spirit, descend
on all. Amen.

*Let them be seated a while.*

*Then we make our prayer.*

*Now when the Bishop, or the Presbyter, has taken the
bread ...*

# DAILY BIBLE
READINGS

*A table to show how the Extra Weeks come*

| Year | 4th before Christmas | 4th after Christmas | Extra | 9th before Easter | 24th after Pentecost | Extra |
|------|------|------|------|------|------|------|
| 1962–3 | Dec. 2 | Jan. 20 | 1, 2 | Feb. 10 | Nov. 17 | 3 |
| 1963–4 | 1 | 19 | — | Jan. 26 | 21 | 1, 2, 3 |
| 1964–5 | Nov. 29 | 17 | 1, 2, 3 | Feb. 14 | 1§ | — |
| 1965–6 | 28 | 16 | 1, 2 | 6 | 13 | 3 |
| 1966–7 | 27 | 15† | — | Jan. 22 | Oct. 29 | 1, 2, 3, 4 |
| 1967–8 | Dec. 3 | 21 | 1, 2 | Feb. 11 | Nov. 17§ | 3 |
| 1968–9 | 1 | 19 | 1 | 2 | 9 | 2, 3 |
| 1969–70 | Nov. 30 | 18 | — | Jan. 25 | 1 | 1, 2, 3 |
| 1970–1 | 29 | 17 | 1, 2 | Feb. 7 | 14 | 3 |
| 1971–2 | 28 | 16 | 1 | Jan. 30 | 5§ | 2, 3, 4 |
| 1972–3 | Dec. 3 | 21 | 1, 2, 3 | Feb. 18 | 25 | — |
| 1973–4 | 2 | 20 | 1, 2 | 10 | 17 | 3 |
| 1974–5 | 1 | 19 | — | Jan. 26 | 2 | 1, 2, 3 |

† Christmas Day is a Sunday in 1966: in 1967 January 15 is the Third Sunday after Christmas. § 1964, 1968, and 1972 are leap-years.

*Note.* Passages marked with asterisks (*) may be omitted, the rest being redistributed evenly among the days of the week.

# FOURTH SUNDAY BEFORE CHRISTMAS
## BEGINNING OF ADVENT

| *THE BEGINNING* | | | *THE END* |
|------|------|------|------|
| | **MONDAY** | | |
| In the Beginning | Gen. 1:1–23 | Mark 13:1–13 | Signs of the End |
| The End of Creation | Gen. 1:24—2:3 | Mark 13:14–20 | Tribulation |
| | **TUESDAY** | | |
| The Garden of Eden | Gen. 2:4–17 | Mark 13:21–27 | The Coming |
| A Help meet for Man | Gen. 2:18–25 | Mark 13:28–37 | 'Therefore watch' |
| | **WEDNESDAY** | | |
| Disobedience | Gen. 3:1–13 | Luke 12:22–34* | Seeking the Kingdom |
| Punishment | Gen. 3:14–24 | Luke 12:35–48* | Faithful Servants |
| | **THURSDAY** | | |
| Cain and Abel | Gen. 4:1–16* | Luke 12:49–59* | The coming Crisis |
| God's Word to Noah | Gen. 6:9–22* | Luke 17:20–37* | The Time |
| | **FRIDAY** | | |
| The Flood | Gen. 7:7–24* | Matt. 13:24–30* | Weeds |
| The End of the Flood | Gen. 8* | Matt. 25:1–13 | The Bridesmaids |
| | **SATURDAY** | | |
| A Covenant | Gen. 9:8–17* | Matt. 25:14–30* | The Talents |
| Babel | Gen. 11:1–9* | Matt. 25:31–46 | Sheep and Goats |

# THIRD BEFORE CHRISTMAS
# SECOND IN ADVENT

*VISIONS OF THE END*                    *REVELATION 1–11*

### MONDAY

| | | | |
|---|---|---|---|
| *The Day of the Lord* | Isa. 13:1–12* | Rev. 1 | *A Voice and a Vision* |
| *The Fall of Babylon* | Isa. 13:13–22 | Rev. 2:1–17 | *Three Churches* |

### TUESDAY

| | | | |
|---|---|---|---|
| *The End of its King* | Isa. 14:3–15* | Rev. 2:18—3:6* | *Thyatira, Sardis* |
| *Moab a Suppliant* | Isa. 15:1—16:5* | Rev. 3:7–22 | *Philadelphia, Laodicea* |

### WEDNESDAY

| | | | |
|---|---|---|---|
| *Doom on Egypt* | Isa. 19:1–10* | Rev. 4 | *The Throne in Heaven* |
| *God smites to heal* | Isa. 19:19–25 | Rev. 5 | *Lamb and Scroll* |

### THURSDAY

| | | | |
|---|---|---|---|
| *The City desolate* | Isa. 24:1–13* | Rev. 6* | *Six Seals opened* |
| *The Lord shall reign* | Isa. 24:17–23 | Rev. 7 | *God's Servants sealed* |

### FRIDAY

| | | | |
|---|---|---|---|
| *Death swallowed up* | Isa. 25:1–8 | Rev. 8* | *A Seal and Trumpets* |
| *The strong City* | Isa. 26:1–6 | Rev. 9* | *More Trumpets* |

### SATURDAY

| | | | |
|---|---|---|---|
| *'Thy dead shall live'* | Isa. 26:13–19 | Rev. 10* | *An Angel's Message* |
| *The Lord's Coming* | Isa. 27:1–6, 12f* | Rev. 11* | *A Trumpet and a Triumph* |

# SECOND BEFORE CHRISTMAS
# THIRD IN ADVENT

*VISIONS OF THE END*                    *REVELATION 12–22*

### MONDAY

| | | | |
|---|---|---|---|
| *Doom on Edom* | Isa. 34:6–17* | Rev. 12* | *A Woman and a Dragon* |
| *The Way of Holiness* | Isa. 35 | Rev. 13* | *The Two Beasts* |

### TUESDAY

| | | | |
|---|---|---|---|
| *A Dream* | Dan. 7:1–14 | Rev. 14* | *The Lamb's People* |
| *Its Interpretation* | Dan. 7:13–27 | Rev. 15 | *The Conquerors' Song* |

### WEDNESDAY

| | | | |
|---|---|---|---|
| *The Resurrection* | Dan. 12:1–10 | Rev. 16* | *Armageddon* |
| *A Remnant; its Glory* | Zeph. 3:11–20* | Rev. 17* | *Babylon and Beast* |

### THURSDAY

| | | | |
|---|---|---|---|
| *'Thy King cometh'* | Zech. 9:9–12 | Rev. 18 | *Epitaph on Babylon* |
| *Israel gathered* | Zech. 10:3–12* | Rev. 19:1—20:3 | *Lamb and Dragon* |

### FRIDAY

| | | | |
|---|---|---|---|
| *The Spirit of Grace* | Zech. 12:1–10* | Rev. 20:4–15* | *The Thousand Years* |
| *A Purging* | Zech. 13:7–9* | Rev. 21:1–14 | *New Heaven and Earth* |

### SATURDAY

| | | | |
|---|---|---|---|
| *Light at Evening* | Zech. 14:1–7 | Rev. 21:15—22:5 | *The Holy City* |
| *Holy Jerusalem* | Zech. 14:16–21* | Rev. 22:6–21 | *His Coming* |

# NEXT BEFORE CHRISTMAS
# FOURTH IN ADVENT

Each year, only the readings for the six days following the Sunday next before Christmas are used.

### DECEMBER 19

| | | | |
|---|---|---|---|
| *'My servant'* | Isa. 41:8–14 | Heb. 11:8–16 | *Faith* |
| *The Servant's Work* | Isa. 61:1–6 | Heb. 11:32—12:2 | *Cloud of Witnesses* |

### DECEMBER 20

| | | | |
|---|---|---|---|
| *God's Salvation* | Isa. 52:7–12 | Mark 12:1–11 | *Vineyard-farmers* |
| *Calling Nations* | Isa. 55:1–5 | Luke 12:22–34 | *The Father's Pleasure* |

### DECEMBER 21

| | | | |
|---|---|---|---|
| *'Arise, shine'* | Isa. 60:1–7 | Luke 12:35–48 | *Faithful Servants* |
| *'God thy glory'* | Isa. 60:13–19 | Luke 21:25–36 | *'Your redemption'* |

### DECEMBER 22

| | | | |
|---|---|---|---|
| *The Fore-runner* | Mal. 4 | Luke 1:5–25 | *Promise to Zechariah* |
| *Manoah's Wife* | Judg. 13:2–20 | Luke 1:26–38 | *The Promise to Mary* |

### DECEMBER 23

| | | | |
|---|---|---|---|
| *Hannah's Son* | 1 Sam. 1:1–20 | Luke 1:39–56 | *Mary and Elizabeth* |
| *Hannah's Thanks* | 1 Sam. 1:21—2:8 | Luke 1:57–66 | *The Birth of John* |

### DECEMBER 24

| | | | |
|---|---|---|---|
| *Comfort for Zion* | Isa. 40:1–11 | Luke 1:67–80 | *Zechariah's Thanks* |
| *Little Bethlehem* | Mic. 5:2–4 | Luke 2:1–20 | *The Birth of Jesus* |

### DECEMBER 25

| | | | |
|---|---|---|---|
| *A great Light* | Isa. 9:2–7 | Heb. 1:1–12 | *These last Days* |
| *'Let me hear'* | Psa. 85:8–13 | John 1:1–14 | *The Word made Flesh* |
| *Immanuel* | Isa. 7:10–14 | Matt. 1:18–25 | *The Spirit* |

### DECEMBER 26

| | | | |
|---|---|---|---|
| *Light to all* | Isa. 42:1–9 | Luke 2:21–40 | *Simeon and Anna* |
| *God the Redeemer* | Isa. 43:1–7 | Matt. 2:13–23 | *The Infant Jesus* |

### DECEMBER 27

| | | | |
|---|---|---|---|
| *God's Witnesses* | Isa. 43:8–13 | Gal. 4:1–7 | *The Fullness of Time* |
| *A new Thing* | Isa. 43:14–21 | 1 Cor. 1:26–31 | *No Flesh to Glory* |

### DECEMBER 28

| | | | |
|---|---|---|---|
| *The End of the Earth* | Isa. 49:1–6 | Eph. 1:3–14 | *God's Purpose* |
| *Restoration* | Jer. 31:10–14 | Eph. 3:14–21 | *The Love of Christ* |

### DECEMBER 29

| | | | |
|---|---|---|---|
| *A holy Nation* | Exod. 19:1–9 | Phil. 2:1–11 | *The Mind of Christ* |
| *'Be holy'* | Lev. 19:1, 9–18 | Col. 1:3–20 | *Christ in Creation* |

### DECEMBER 30

| | | | |
|---|---|---|---|
| *A chosen People* | Deut. 7:6–11 | 1 Tim. 3:16 | *The Mystery of Christ* |
| *Firstfruits* | Deut. 26:1–11 | 1 John 1:1—2:6 | *The Word of Life* |

# NEXT AFTER CHRISTMAS
## (OR CHRISTMAS DAY)†

*AMOS*                                                      *JOHN 1–5*

### MONDAY

| | | |
|---|---|---|
| *Damascus* | Amos 1:1–5* | John 1:1–18 | *The Word* |
| *Moab and Judah* | Amos 2:1–5* | John 1:19–34 | *The Lamb of God* |

### TUESDAY

| | | |
|---|---|---|
| *Northern Israel* | Amos 2:6–16 | John 1:35–51* | *The Son of God* |
| *'God hath spoken'* | Amos 3:1–8, 12 | John 2:1–12 | *The Wedding at Cana* |

### WEDNESDAY

| | | |
|---|---|---|
| *Unteachableness* | Amos 4:4–13 | John 2:13–25* | *Passover, Jerusalem* |
| *'Seek the Lord'* | Amos 5:1–15 | John 3:1–21 | *Nicodemus* |

### THURSDAY

| | | |
|---|---|---|
| *The Day of the Lord* | Amos 5:18–24 | John 3:22–36* | *John and Jesus* |
| *At Ease in Zion* | Amos 6:1–8 | John 4:1–26 | *The Woman of Sychar* |

### FRIDAY

| | | |
|---|---|---|
| *Visions of Judgement* | Amos 7:1–9* | John 4:27–38* | *The Food of Jesus* |
| *Amaziah* | Amos 7:10–17* | John 4:39–54* | *Saviour of the World* |

### SATURDAY

| | | |
|---|---|---|
| *Social Justice* | Amos 8:4–12* | John 5:1–24 | *The Life-giver* |
| *Destruction* | Amos 9:1–10* | John 5:25–47* | *Witnesses to Jesus* |

# SECOND (OR NEXT) AFTER CHRISTMAS

*HOSEA, MICAH*                                             *JOHN 6–9*

### MONDAY

| | | |
|---|---|---|
| *'Not my people'* | Hos. 1:2—2:1* | John 6:1–15* | *A miraculous Meal* |
| *The Lord pleads* | Hos. 2:2–15 | John 6:16–34* | *Manna and Bread* |

### TUESDAY

| | | |
|---|---|---|
| *Redemption* | Hos. 2:18—3:5 | John 6:35–51 | *The Bread of Life* |
| *Unreal Repentance* | Hos. 6:1–6 | John 6:52–71 | *The Disciples sifted* |

### WEDNESDAY

| | | |
|---|---|---|
| *The Lord and Israel* | Hos. 11:1–9* | John 7:1–13* | *Jesus' Time* |
| *An Appeal* | Hos. 14* | John 7:14–31* | *'Is this the Christ?'* |

### THURSDAY

| | | |
|---|---|---|
| *Samaria, Jerusalem* | Mic. 1:1–9* | John 7:32–52* | *A Division* |
| *Social Justice* | Mic. 2:1–4, 12f* | John 7:53—8:11 | *A Woman accused* |

### FRIDAY

| | | |
|---|---|---|
| *Rulers and Prophets* | Mic. 3 | John 8:12–30 | *Light of the World* |
| *The Lord's House* | Mic. 4:1–5 | John 8:31–59* | *Children of Abraham* |

### SATURDAY

| | | |
|---|---|---|
| *Promise to Bethlehem* | Mic. 4:8—5:2* | John 9:1–23 | *A Man born blind* |
| *True Sacrifice* | Mic. 6:1–8 | John 9:24–41 | *Blind Men* |

† When Christmas Day is a Sunday (the fifth Sunday in Advent), we begin
Amos and John on Dec. 26; and in the weeks beginning on the Next, Second, and
Third Sundays after Christmas, we read the passages usually ascribed to the weeks
of the Second, Third, and Fourth Sundays after Christmas.

# THIRD (OR SECOND) AFTER CHRISTMAS

*ISAIAH 1–6*                                                      *JOHN 10–14*

### MONDAY

| Ruin and a Remnant | Isa. 1:1–9 | John 10:1–18 | The Good Shepherd |
| Vain Offerings | Isa. 1:10–20 | John 10:19–39* | 'I and the Father' |

### TUESDAY

| A Purge | Isa. 1:21–31 | John 10:40—11:16 | Death of Lazarus |
| Against Idols | Isa. 2:5–11 | John 11:17–37* | Martha and Mary |

### WEDNESDAY

| The Day of the Lord | Isa. 2:12–22* | John 11:38–53 | Raising of Lazarus |
| Against the Rulers | Isa. 3:1–8, 12f* | John 11:54—12:11* | The Anointing |

### THURSDAY

| Daughters of Zion | Isa. 3:16—4:1* | John 12:12–36* | The Triumphal Entry |
| A holy Remnant | Isa. 4:2–6* | John 12:37–50* | Belief and Unbelief |

### FRIDAY

| The Lord's Vineyard | Isa. 5:1–7 | John 13:1–20 | The Foot-washing |
| Wickedness | Isa. 5:8–23* | John 13:21–38* | Judas and Peter |

### SATURDAY

| Punishment | Isa. 5:24–30* | John 14:1–14 | 'I go to the Father' |
| Isaiah's Call | Isa. 6:1–11 | John 14:15–31 | 'I will come again' |

# FOURTH (OR THIRD) AFTER CHRISTMAS

*ISAIAH 7–12*                                                     *JOHN 15–21*

### MONDAY

| Jerusalem attacked | Isa. 7:1–9 | John 15:1–17 | The true Vine |
| God with us | Isa. 7:10–17* | John 15:18–27* | His Witnesses |

### TUESDAY

| Whom to fear | Isa. 8:1–15* | John 16:1–15* | Sending the Paraclete |
| Isaiah's Disciples | Isa. 8:16–22 | John 16:16–33* | The World overcome |

### WEDNESDAY

| The Prince of Peace | Isa. 9:1–7 | John 17 | Jesus' Prayer |
| Unteachableness | Isa. 9:8–17* | John 18:1–27* | Annas, Caiaphas |

### THURSDAY

| Oppression | Isa. 9:18—10:4* | John 18:28–40 | Before Pilate |
| God and Assyria | Isa. 10:5–15 | John 19:1–27 | Crucifixion |

### FRIDAY

| A Remnant to return | Isa. 10:16–27* | John 19:28–42* | Death and Burial |
| A righteous King | Isa. 11:1–9 | John 20:1–18 | Sunday Morning |

### SATURDAY

| Israel restored | Isa. 11:10–16* | John 20:19–31* | Jesus and Thomas |
| Israel's Thanks | Isa. 11:12 | John 21 | Beside the Lake |

For any weeks between the week of the fourth Sunday after Christmas and the ninth Sunday before Easter, the readings provided for Extra Weeks are used in order (see the table on page 186).

# NINTH BEFORE EASTER

*ISAIAH 28–33*　　　　　　　　　　　　　　　　　　　*HEBREWS 1–7*

### MONDAY

| | | | |
|---|---|---|---|
| *Ephraim and Judah* | Isa. 28:1–13* | Heb. 1 | *The Son of God* |
| *Rulers who scorn God* | Isa. 28:14–22 | Heb. 2:1–4* | *A great Salvation* |

### TUESDAY

| | | | |
|---|---|---|---|
| *Skill in ploughing* | Isa. 28:23–29* | Heb. 2:5–9* | *Suffering, crowned* |
| *'Awake, Jerusalem!'* | Isa. 29:1–14 | Heb. 2:10–18 | *Perfect by suffering* |

### WEDNESDAY

| | | | |
|---|---|---|---|
| *Saved by a Remnant* | Isa. 29:15–24 | Heb. 3:1–11 | *Importance of today* |
| *Returning and Rest* | Isa. 30:1f, 8–18 | Heb. 3:12–19* | *A new Exodus* |

### THURSDAY

| | | | |
|---|---|---|---|
| *God's Redemption* | Isa. 30:19–26 | Heb. 4:1–13* | *The Word a Sword* |
| *'God also is wise'* | Isa. 31 | Heb. 4:14—5:10* | *A High Priest* |

### FRIDAY

| | | | |
|---|---|---|---|
| *A righteous King* | Isa. 32:1–8* | Heb. 5:11—6:8 | *'Do not fall away!'* |
| *A Rebuke to Women* | Isa. 32:9–20* | Heb. 6:9–20 | *Hope the Anchor* |

### SATURDAY

| | | | |
|---|---|---|---|
| *God will arise* | Isa. 33:1–10* | Heb. 7:1–14* | *Melchizedek* |
| *The King's Beauty* | Isa. 33:13–22* | Heb. 7:15–28 | *The eternal Priest* |

# EIGHTH BEFORE EASTER

*JEREMIAH 1–7*　　　　　　　　　　　　　　　　　　　*HEBREWS 8–13*

### MONDAY

| | | | |
|---|---|---|---|
| *Jeremiah's Call* | Jer. 1:4–10 | Heb. 8* | *A better Covenant* |
| *Evil from the North* | Jer. 1:11–19 | Heb. 9:1–14 | *The true Atonement* |

### TUESDAY

| | | | |
|---|---|---|---|
| *Israel's Folly* | Jer. 2:4–13, 32* | Heb. 9:15–28* | *Pattern and Copy* |
| *Judah and Ephraim* | Jer. 3:6–18* | Heb. 10:1–18* | *The true Sacrifice* |

### WEDNESDAY

| | | | |
|---|---|---|---|
| *Evil from the North* | Jer. 4:5–14* | Heb. 10:19–39* | *'Therefore enter in'* |
| *Desolation: A Vision* | Jer. 4:19–31 | Heb. 11:1–16 | *The Nature of Faith* |

### THURSDAY

| | | | |
|---|---|---|---|
| *Seeking Honesty* | Jer. 5:1–9* | Heb. 11:17–31 | *Christ's Reproach* |
| *The Exile foretold* | Jer. 5:20–31* | Heb. 11:32–40 | *Promises unfulfilled* |

### FRIDAY

| | | | |
|---|---|---|---|
| *Saying 'Peace, peace'* | Jer. 6:9–15 | Heb. 12:1–17 | *'Therefore let us run'* |
| *A Foe from the North* | Jer. 6:22–30 | Heb. 12:18–29* | *Sinai and Zion* |

### SATURDAY

| | | | |
|---|---|---|---|
| *Doom on the Temple* | Jer. 7:1–15 | Heb. 13:1–14 | *The Christian Life* |
| *The Prophets ignored* | Jer. 7:21–28* | Heb. 13:15–25* | *Last Words* |

## SEVENTH BEFORE EASTER

*JEREMIAH 8–20*                                           *1, 2, & 3 JOHN*

### MONDAY

| | | | |
|---|---|---|---|
| *His Sorrow* | Jer. 8:18—9:3 | 1 John 1:1—2:6 | *God is Light* |
| *Wherein to glory* | Jer. 9:17–24 | 1 John 2:7–17 | *The new Commandment* |

### TUESDAY

| | | | |
|---|---|---|---|
| *Treachery at Home* | Jer. 12:1–6* | 1 John 2:18–29 | *God is Life* |
| *The Leopard's Spots* | Jer. 13:20–27* | 1 John 3:1–10* | *Hope and Purity* |

### ASH WEDNESDAY

| | | | |
|---|---|---|---|
| *True Fasting* | Isa. 58:1–8 | 2 Cor. 7:2–10 | *Godly Sorrow* |
| *'Behold, thou desirest'* | Psa. 51:6–12 | Matt. 6:16–21 | *Hypocrisy* |
| *'Rend your hearts'* | Joel 2:12–17 | 1 Cor. 9:19–27 | *Paul the Athlete* |

### THURSDAY

| | | | |
|---|---|---|---|
| *Dialogue with God* | Jer. 15:10, 15–21 | 1 John 3:11–24 | *Love and Life* |
| *Dialogue with God* | Jer. 17:9f, 14–18* | 1 John 4 | *God is Love* |

### FRIDAY

| | | | |
|---|---|---|---|
| *A Sign: the Potter* | Jer. 18:1–12* | 1 John 5:1–12* | *Christ's Victory* |
| *Jeremiah's Enemies* | Jer. 18:13–23* | 1 John 5:13–21* | *Praying for Sinners* |

### SATURDAY

| | | | |
|---|---|---|---|
| *A Sign: the Bottle* | Jer. 19:1–13 | 2 John* | *Address to a Church* |
| *Jeremiah and Pashhur* | Jer. 19:14—20:6 | 3 John* | *Messages to Gaius* |

## SIXTH BEFORE EASTER: FIRST IN LENT

*JEREMIAH 20–30*                                            *1 & 2 PETER*

### MONDAY

| | | | |
|---|---|---|---|
| *Jeremiah's Complaints* | Jer. 20:7–18 | 1 Pet. 1:1–12 | *Born anew* |
| *Zedekiah* | Jer. 21:1–10* | 1 Pet. 1:13–25 | *'Therefore be holy'* |

### TUESDAY

| | | | |
|---|---|---|---|
| *Jehoiakim* | Jer. 22:13–19* | 1 Pet. 2:1–10 | *God's own People* |
| *Jehoiachin* | Jer. 22:20–30* | 1 Pet. 2:11–25 | *The Example of Jesus* |

### WEDNESDAY

| | | | |
|---|---|---|---|
| *A Branch of David* | Jer. 23:1–8 | 1 Pet. 3:1–12 | *Love of the Brethren* |
| *False Prophets* | Jer. 23:16–30 | 1 Pet. 3:13—4:6 | *Witnessing to all* |

### THURSDAY

| | | | |
|---|---|---|---|
| *Good Figs and bad* | Jer. 24 | 1 Pet. 4:7–19* | *The End at Hand* |
| *Seventy Years' Exile* | Jer. 25:1–14* | 1 Pet. 5* | *A Word to Elders* |

### FRIDAY

| | | | |
|---|---|---|---|
| *Jeremiah arrested* | Jer. 26:1–9 | 2 Pet. 1:1–11* | *'Add diligence'* |
| *Tried and acquitted* | Jer. 26:10–24 | 2 Pet. 1:12–21* | *A personal Testimony* |

### SATURDAY

| | | | |
|---|---|---|---|
| *A Word to the Exiles* | Jer. 29:1, 4–14* | 2 Pet. 2* | *False Teachers* |
| *The Exile God's Act* | Jer. 30:10–22* | 2 Pet. 3* | *Waiting for the End* |

# FIFTH BEFORE EASTER
## SECOND IN LENT

*REMIAH 31–36*                                              *JAMES AND JUDE*

### MONDAY

| | | |
|---|---|---|
| Renewal of Israel | Jer. 31:1–9* | Jas. 1:1–11 | Singleness of Mind |
| Comfort for Rachel | Jer. 31:15–22 | Jas. 1:12–21 | Temptations; Gifts |

### TUESDAY

| | | |
|---|---|---|
| A Time for planting | Jer. 31:23–30 | Jas. 1:22–27 | Doers and Hearers |
| A new Covenant | Jer. 31:31–40 | Jas. 2:1–13 | The Royal Law |

### WEDNESDAY

| | | |
|---|---|---|
| A Prisoner buys Land | Jer. 32:1–15* | Jas. 2:14–26 | Faith and Works |
| Jeremiah's Prayer | Jer. 32:16–27* | Jas. 3:1–12 | Ruling the Tongue |

### THURSDAY

| | | |
|---|---|---|
| God's Promise | Jer. 32:36–44* | Jas. 3:13–18* | Peaceableness |
| A broken Covenant | Jer. 34:8–22* | Jas. 4:1–12* | Ruling the Passions |

### FRIDAY

| | | |
|---|---|---|
| The Rechabites | Jer. 35* | Jas. 4:13—5:6* | The Vain, the Rich |
| Jeremiah's Book | Jer. 36:1–8 | Jas. 5:7–20* | Patience and Prayer |

### SATURDAY

| | | |
|---|---|---|
| The Book destroyed | Jer. 36:9–26 | Jude 1–16* | The unending Battle |
| A new Book | Jer. 36:27–32 | Jude 17–25* | Warnings; Ascription |

# FOURTH BEFORE EASTER
## THIRD IN LENT

*JEREMIAH 37–45*                                                    *MARK 1–4*

### MONDAY

| | | |
|---|---|---|
| Warnings to Zedekiah | Jer. 37:1–10* | Mark 1:1–13 | The Baptism of Jesus |
| Arrest | Jer. 37:11–21* | Mark 1:14–20 | The Time fulfilled |

### TUESDAY

| | | |
|---|---|---|
| In a Dungeon | Jer. 38:1–13* | Mark 1:21–39 | A Sabbath Day |
| A secret Meeting | Jer. 38:14–28* | Mark 1:40–45* | A Healing |

### WEDNESDAY

| | | |
|---|---|---|
| Jerusalem falls | Jer. 39:1–14 | Mark 2:1–12* | Healing, forgiving |
| Promise to a Helper | Jer. 39:15–18* | Mark 2:13–17* | Meal with Publicans |

### THURSDAY

| | | |
|---|---|---|
| Gedaliah | Jer. 40 | Mark 2:18–28* | Fasting and Sabbath |
| Murder of Gedaliah | Jer. 41 | Mark 3:1–6 | A Sabbath Healing |

### FRIDAY

| | | |
|---|---|---|
| Jeremiah's Counsel | Jer. 42:1–16 | Mark 3:7–19 | Crowds; the Twelve |
| Flight to Egypt | Jer. 43 | Mark 3:20–35 | Binding Satan |

### SATURDAY

| | | |
|---|---|---|
| Jeremiah in Egypt | Jer. 44:1–3, 15–23* | Mark 4:1–20* | The Sower |
| A Promise to Baruch | Jer. 45 | Mark 4:21–34* | Other Parables |

## THIRD BEFORE EASTER
## FOURTH IN LENT

*THE END OF JERUSALEM*                                      *MARK 4–8*

### MONDAY

| The Day of Wrath | Zeph. 1:10–18* | Mark 4:35–41 | Stilling a Storm |
| The Wrath of God | Nah. 1:1–10* | Mark 5:1–20 | A Demoniac |

### TUESDAY

| Fighting in Nineveh | Nah. 2:1–12 | Mark 5:21–43 | Jairus's Daughter |
| Woe on the City | Nah. 3:1–3, 12–19* | Mark 6:1–6 | Unbelief in Nazareth |

### WEDNESDAY

| The Chaldeans | Hab. 1:5–14* | Mark 6:7–13 | Twelve sent out |
| Faith and Idolatry | Hab. 2:1–4, 19f | Mark 6:14–29 | The Death of John |

### THURSDAY

| 'Yet will I rejoice' | Hab. 3:1–4, 16–19* | Mark 6:30–44* | The Five Thousand |
| Edom the Jackal | Obad. 6–18 | Mark 6:45–56* | Walking on Water |

### FRIDAY

| A Vision | Ezek. 1:1–14 | Mark 7:1–23* | Clean and unclean |
| A Voice | Ezek. 1:15—2:2 | Mark 7:24–37* | Two Miracles |

### SATURDAY

| His Commission | Ezek. 2:3—3:11 | Mark 8:1–10* | The Four Thousand |
| Sent to the Exiles | Ezek. 3:12–27* | Mark 8:11–26* | Blindness |

## SECOND BEFORE EASTER
## FIFTH IN LENT

*EZEKIEL 5–32*                                             *MARK 8–10*

### MONDAY

| Doom on Jerusalem | Ezek. 5:5–12* | Mark 8:27–33 | Peter's Confession |
| Sin in the Temple | Ezek. 8:1–12 | Mark 8:34—9:1 | The Disciples' Cross |

### TUESDAY

| The Faithful sealed | Ezek. 9 | Mark 9:2–8 | The Transfiguration |
| The Glory departs | Ezek. 10:1–4, 9–19 | Mark 9:9–13 | On the Resurrection |

### WEDNESDAY

| Restoration | Ezek. 11:14–25 | Mark 9:14–29* | An epileptic Boy |
| Divine Judgement | Ezek. 14:12–23* | Mark 9:30–37* | Greatness |

### THURSDAY

| Responsibility | Ezek. 18:1–9, 30–32 | Mark 9:38–50* | Various Sayings |
| Bereavement—a Sign | Ezek. 24:15–27* | Mark 10:1–16* | Marriage; Childhood |

### FRIDAY

| Doom on Tyre | Ezek. 26:1–14* | Mark 10:17–22* | The rich young Ruler |
| Tyre the fine Ship | Ezek. 27:1–9, 26–36 | Mark 10:23–31* | Money |

### SATURDAY

| The Humbling of Tyre | Ezek. 28:1–10* | Mark 10:32–45 | James and John |
| Pharaoh in the Pit | Ezek. 32:17–32* | Mark 10:46–52 | Bartimaeus |

# NEXT BEFORE EASTER: PALM SUNDAY
*HOLY WEEK*

## MONDAY
| | | | |
|---|---|---|---|
| 'My servant' | Isa. 42:1–9 | Eph. 2:11–22 | *Christ our Peace* |
| 'How long, O Lord?' | Ps. 13 | Mark 11:12–19 | *The Temple cleansed* |
| God's Promises | Ezek. 36:22–28 | Heb. 10:19–25 | *'Be therefore bold'* |

## TUESDAY
| | | | |
|---|---|---|---|
| A Light to the Gentiles | Isa. 49:1–13 | Rom. 5:6–11 | *Reconciled* |
| 'In thee, O Lord' | Ps. 31:1–5 | Mark 11:20—12:44† | *Questions* |
| God's Vineyard | Isa. 5:1–7 | 1 Pet. 2:18–25 | *Christ's Example* |

## WEDNESDAY
| | | | |
|---|---|---|---|
| 'He is near' | Isa. 50:4–9 | Heb. 5:5–10 | *Made perfect* |
| 'Vindicate me, O God' | Ps. 43 | Mark 14:1–11 | *Anointed and sold* |
| The brass Serpent | Num. 21:4–9 | John 3:11–21 | *Lifted up* |

## THURSDAY
| | | | |
|---|---|---|---|
| The new Covenant | Jer. 31:31–34 | Heb. 8:1–6 | *A better Covenant* |
| 'O God, thou art my God' | Ps. 63:1–4 | Mark 14:12–72 | *Upper Room, Garden* |
| 'He was afflicted' | Isa. 63:7–9 | John 13 | *Jesus and his Disciples* |

## GOOD FRIDAY
| | | | |
|---|---|---|---|
| A Ransom for many | Isa. 52:13—53:12 | Heb. 10:4–18 | *The true Sacrifice* |
| 'My God, my God' | Ps. 22 | John 18:1—19:16 | *Arrest and Trials* |
| 'Is it nothing?' | Lam. 1:7–12 | John 19:17–42 | *Friday Evening* |

## SATURDAY
| | | | |
|---|---|---|---|
| The Resurrection | Dan. 12:1–4 | 1 Pet. 3:17–22 | *Spirits in Prison* |
| 'Preserve me, O God' | Ps. 16 | Matt. 27:57–66 | *Burial; the Guard* |
| The Dry Bones | Ezek. 37:1–14 | Rom. 6:1–11 | *Buried with Him* |

# EASTER WEEK
## MONDAY
| | | | |
|---|---|---|---|
| The Red Sea | Exod. 14:15–31* | John 21:1–14 | *By the Lake* |
| God's Purchase | Exod. 15:13–21 | Mark 16:1–8 | *Sunday Morning* |

## TUESDAY
| | | | |
|---|---|---|---|
| Death in Shunem | 2 Kings 4:8–17* | John 21:15–25 | *Jesus and Peter* |
| Resurrection | 2 Kings 4:18–37* | Mark 16:9–20* | *Jesus' Commission* |

## WEDNESDAY
| | | | |
|---|---|---|---|
| Death swallowed up | Isa. 25:1–9 | Luke 24:1–12* | *Sunday Morning* |
| 'Thy dead live' | Isa. 26:13–19 | Matt. 28:1–15* | *Sunday Morning* |

## THURSDAY
| | | | |
|---|---|---|---|
| Everlasting Love | Jer. 31:1–9* | Luke 24:13–35 | *Emmaus* |
| Jacob redeemed | Jer. 31:10–16 | Matt. 28:16–20 | *All Nations* |

## FRIDAY
| | | | |
|---|---|---|---|
| God, not Man | Hos. 11:1–9 | Luke 24:36–53 | *Command & Promise* |
| The Walls rebuilt | Mic. 7:7–12* | Acts 7:54–60* | *Stephen* |

## SATURDAY
| | | | |
|---|---|---|---|
| 'The nations see' | Mic. 7:14–20 | 1 Cor. 15:1–10* | *Paul's Story* |
| Promise to Jerusalem | Zech. 8:1–8* | Acts 9:1–9* | *Paul* |

† Mark 13, Fourth Sunday before Christmas.

# NEXT AFTER EASTER

*EZEKIEL 33–48*                                                           *ACTS 1–5*

### MONDAY

| | | |
|---|---|---|
| *A Prophet a Watchman* | Ezek. 33:1–9 | Acts 1:1–14 | *The Ascension* |
| *The Way of the Lord* | Ezek. 33:10–20 | Acts 1:15–26* | *Matthias* |

### TUESDAY

| | | |
|---|---|---|
| *The Good Shepherd* | Ezek. 34:1–12 | Acts 2:1–13 | *Pentecost* |
| *The Shepherd David* | Ezek. 34:20–31 | Acts 2:14–36 | *Peter's Sermon* |

### WEDNESDAY

| | | |
|---|---|---|
| *'For my name'* | Ezek. 36:16–28* | Acts 2:37–47 | *The Church grows* |
| *The Dry Bones* | Ezek. 37:1–14 | Acts 3* | *A lame Man* |

### THURSDAY

| | | |
|---|---|---|
| *Judah and Ephraim* | Ezek. 37:15–28* | Acts 4:1–12 | *Peter and John tried* |
| *The Nations* | Ezek. 38:14–23* | Acts 4:13–31 | *Threats and Release* |

### FRIDAY

| | | |
|---|---|---|
| *Israel to know God* | Ezek. 39:17–29* | Acts 4:32—5:11* | *Sharing of Goods* |
| *The Glory returns* | Ezek.40:1–4;43:1–5* | Acts 5:12–16* | *The Church grows* |

### SATURDAY

| | | |
|---|---|---|
| *Purity in the House* | Ezek. 44:1–14* | Acts 5:17–26* | *Arrest and Escape* |
| *Healing Waters* | Ezek. 47:1–12 | Acts 5:27–42* | *Trial and Discharge* |

# SECOND AFTER EASTER

*ISAIAH 40–45*                                                           *ACTS 6–8*

### MONDAY

| | | |
|---|---|---|
| *The Lord's Return* | Isa. 40:1–11 | Acts 6:1–7 | *Deacons* |
| *God and Creation* | Isa. 40:12–26 | Acts 6:8–15 | *Stephen on Trial* |

### TUESDAY

| | | |
|---|---|---|
| *God and Man* | Isa. 40:27–31 | Acts 7:1–8* | *His Defence: Abraham;* |
| *God will help* | Isa. 41:8–20* | Acts 7:9–16* | *Joseph;* |

### WEDNESDAY

| | | |
|---|---|---|
| *God's Chosen One* | Isa. 42:1–9 | Acts 7:17–22* | *Moses' Birth;* |
| *Deaf and blind* | Isa. 42:10–19* | Acts 7:23–34* | *His Call;* |

### THURSDAY

| | | |
|---|---|---|
| *God's Witnesses* | Isa. 43:1–13 | Acts 7:35–43* | *His Rejection;* |
| *Rivers in the Desert* | Isa. 43:14–21* | Acts 7:44–53* | *The Spirit* |

### FRIDAY

| | | |
|---|---|---|
| *King and Redeemer* | Isa. 44:1–8* | Acts 7:54—8:3 | *Stephen's Death* |
| *Idolatry is Folly* | Isa. 44:9–20* | Acts 8:4–13 | *Philip in Samaria* |

### SATURDAY

| | | |
|---|---|---|
| *God the Redeemer* | Isa. 44:21–28* | Acts 8:14–25 | *The Spirit; Simon* |
| *Cyrus, God's Anointed* | Isa. 45:1–8 | Acts 8:26–40 | *The Ethiopian* |

# THIRD AFTER EASTER

*ISAIAH 45–52*                                                              *ACTS 9–12*

### MONDAY

| | | | |
|---|---|---|---|
| God hides himself | Isa. 45:9–17* | Acts 9:1–9 | Saul's Conversion |
| No other God | Isa. 45:18–25* | Acts 9:10–25 | Saul and Ananias |

### TUESDAY

| | | | |
|---|---|---|---|
| Salvation is near | Isa. 46:3–13* | Acts 9:26–31* | Barnabas and Saul |
| Babylon humbled | Isa. 47:5–14* | Acts 9:32–43 | Peter at Joppa |

### WEDNESDAY

| | | | |
|---|---|---|---|
| Israel to be purged | Isa. 48:1–11* | Acts 10:1–16 | Peter's Vision |
| Flee from Babylon | Isa. 48:12–22* | Acts 10:17–29 | Peter at Caesarea |

### THURSDAY

| | | | |
|---|---|---|---|
| Light to the Nations | Isa. 49:1–13 | Acts 10:30–43 | Peter and Cornelius |
| God's Love for Zion | Isa. 49:14–23 | Acts 10:44–48* | The Spirit; Baptism |

### FRIDAY

| | | | |
|---|---|---|---|
| The Faithful Servant | Isa. 50:4–9 | Acts 11:1–18* | Peter on Gentiles |
| Salvation for ever | Isa. 51:1–8 | Acts 11:19–30* | Beginning at Antioch |

### SATURDAY

| | | | |
|---|---|---|---|
| A Prayer; its Answer | Isa. 51:9–16 | Acts 12:1–11* | Peter's Escape |
| Publishing Salvation | Isa. 52:1–12 | Acts 12:12–25* | Peter's Farewell |

# FOURTH AFTER EASTER

*THE RETURN*                                                              *ACTS 13–18*

### MONDAY

| | | | |
|---|---|---|---|
| The Servant (1) | Isa. 52:13—53:3 | Acts 13:1–12* | First Journey: Cyprus; |
| The Servant (2) | Isa. 53:4–12 | Acts 13:13–41* | Antioch in Pisidia; |

### TUESDAY

| | | | |
|---|---|---|---|
| A Covenant of Peace | Isa. 54:1–10 | Acts 13:42–52* | Unbelief of the Jews; |
| New Foundations | Isa. 54:11–17 | Acts 14:1–7* | Iconium; |

### WEDNESDAY

| | | | |
|---|---|---|---|
| David the Witness | Isa. 55:1–5 | Acts 14:8–28* | Lystra, Derbe, Return |
| The Word of God | Isa. 55:6–13 | Acts 15:1–21 | A Council on the Law |

### THURSDAY

| | | | |
|---|---|---|---|
| No House for God | Hag. 1:1–11* | Acts 15:22–35* | A Letter to Antioch |
| Glory to come | Hag. 1:12—2:9* | Acts 15:36—16:15 | The Second Journey: |

### FRIDAY

| | | | |
|---|---|---|---|
| God's Return | Zech. 1:7–17* | Acts 16:16–40 | Philippi; |
| The Small Things | Zech. 4* | Acts 17:1–15 | Thessalonica, Beroea; |

### SATURDAY

| | | | |
|---|---|---|---|
| Joshua crowned | Zech. 6:9–15* | Acts 17:16–34 | Athens; |
| The City of Truth | Zech. 8:1–8* | Acts 18:1–22 | Corinth, Return |

# FIFTH AFTER EASTER

*THE JEWISH STATE(1)*                                          *ACTS 19–21*

## MONDAY

| | | | |
|---|---|---|---|
| *Maimed Sacrifices* | Mal. 1:6–14* | Acts 18:23—19:7 | *The Third Journey:* |
| *The Lord's Coming* | Mal. 2:17—3:6 | Acts 19:8–22* | *Ephesus;* |

## TUESDAY

| | | | |
|---|---|---|---|
| *Elijah and the Day* | Mal. 3:13—4:6 | Acts 19:23–41 | *A Riot;* |
| *A Swarm of Locusts* | Joel 1:1–7, 13–20* | Acts 20:1–16* | *Greece; Troas;* |

## WEDNESDAY

| | | | |
|---|---|---|---|
| *'Rend your hearts'* | Joel 2:1–13* | Acts 20:17–38* | *Elders of Ephesus;* |
| *'Fear not, O land'* | Joel 2:15–25 | Acts 21:1–16 | *To Jerusalem* |

## THURSDAY: ASCENSION DAY

| | | | |
|---|---|---|---|
| *Elijah's Ascension* | 2 Kings 2:1–15 | Acts 1:1–11 | *The Ascension of Jesus* |
| *'Clap your hands'* | Ps. 47 | Luke 24:44–53 | *God's Promise* |
| *New Heavens and Earth* | Isa. 65:17–25 | Acts 1:12–26 | *After the Ascension* |

## FRIDAY

| | | | |
|---|---|---|---|
| *Aaron's Priesthood* | Exod. 30:1–10* | Heb. 9:1–14 | *The true High Priest* |
| *A Pattern in Heaven* | Exod. 25:1–9 | Heb. 9:19–28* | *The true Sanctuary* |

## SATURDAY

| | | | |
|---|---|---|---|
| *The new Covenant* | Jer. 31:31–34 | Heb. 10:4–13* | *The true Sacrifice* |
| *Along the Way* | Exod. 13:17–22* | Heb. 10:19–25 | *The new Way* |

# SIXTH AFTER EASTER
# SUNDAY AFTER ASCENSION DAY

*THE JEWISH STATE (2)*                                          *ACTS 21–28*

## MONDAY

| | | | |
|---|---|---|---|
| *'For all peoples'* | Isa. 56:1–8 | Acts 21:17–26 | *Paul in the Temple* |
| *The Holiness of God* | Isa. 57:14–18* | Acts 21:27–40* | *A Riot* |

## TUESDAY

| | | | |
|---|---|---|---|
| *True fasting* | Isa. 58:1–12* | Acts 22:1–21* | *Paul's Speech* |
| *'God shall arise'* | Isa. 60:1–9 | Acts 22:22—23:11 | *Before the Sanhedrin* |

## WEDNESDAY

| | | | |
|---|---|---|---|
| *Your God your Glory* | Isa. 60:13–22* | Acts 23:12–35* | *To Caesarea* |
| *Anointed to preach* | Isa. 61:1–7* | Acts 24* | *Felix* |

## THURSDAY

| | | | |
|---|---|---|---|
| *A City not forsaken* | Isa. 62 | Acts 25* | *Festus and Agrippa* |
| *Grapes of Wrath* | Isa. 63:1–6* | Acts 26* | *Paul's Speech* |

## FRIDAY

| | | | |
|---|---|---|---|
| *A Prayer in Darkness* | Isa. 63:7–19* | Acts 27:1–26 | *To Crete* |
| *'Come down'* | Isa. 64 | Acts 27:27–44 | *Shipwreck* |

## SATURDAY

| | | | |
|---|---|---|---|
| *New Heavens and Earth* | Isa. 65:17–25 | Acts 28:1–16 | *Malta and Rome* |
| *A Purging* | Isa. 66:1, 2, 18–24 | Acts 28:17–31 | *Rome* |

# PENTECOST

*THE SPIRIT*

### MONDAY

| | | | |
|---|---|---|---|
| Bezalel | Exod. 31:1–11* | Luke 1:26–38 | Born of the Spirit |
| Joshua | Num. 27:12–23* | Rom. 8:1–11* | Indwelling Spirit |

### TUESDAY

| | | | |
|---|---|---|---|
| David | 2 Sam. 23:1–5* | Luke 2:22–32 | Known by the Spirit |
| Elijah | 2 Kings 2:1–15* | Rom. 8:12–17* | Spirit of Sonship |

### WEDNESDAY

| | | | |
|---|---|---|---|
| Spirit and Justice | Mic. 3:1–8* | Luke 3:15–22 | Spirit-baptized |
| Spirit and Lord | Isa. 11:1–5 | Rom. 8:18–27* | He frees; he prays |

### THURSDAY

| | | | |
|---|---|---|---|
| Spirit and Servant | Isa. 61:1–4 | Luke 4:16–21 | Spirit-anointed |
| Spirit and Servant | Isa. 42:1–9 | 1 Cor. 12:1–13* | One Spirit |

### FRIDAY

| | | | |
|---|---|---|---|
| The Spirit within | Ezek. 2:1–6* | John 3:1–8 | Born of the Spirit |
| A new Spirit | Ezek. 36:22–28 | Gal. 5:16–25* | Fruit of the Spirit |

### SATURDAY

| | | | |
|---|---|---|---|
| The Dry Bones | Ezek. 37:1–14 | John 16:5–15 | The Spirit of Truth |
| 'Not by might' | Zech. 4:1–10 | Heb. 9:11–14* | Eternal Spirit |

# NEXT AFTER PENTECOST
# TRINITY SUNDAY

*THE TRANSCENDENCE OF GOD*      *THE UPPER ROOM*

### MONDAY

| | | | |
|---|---|---|---|
| God as Creator | Gen. 1:1–8 | John 13:1–20 | The Foot-washing |
| God the incomparable | Isa. 40:12–26* | John 13:21–30* | Judas |

### TUESDAY

| | | | |
|---|---|---|---|
| 'Seek the Lord' | Amos 5:6–9* | John 13:31–38* | The Glory of the Son |
| 'I am that I am' | Exod. 3:1–15 | John 14:1–14 | Going to the Father |

### WEDNESDAY

| | | | |
|---|---|---|---|
| Moses' Vision | Exod. 33:12–23 | John 14:15–31* | His Gift: the Spirit |
| Divine Imperative | Deut. 5:1–21* | John 15:1–17 | The Church in Christ |

### THURSDAY

| | | | |
|---|---|---|---|
| 'The word nigh thee' | Deut. 30:11–20* | John 15:18–27* | Church and World |
| The Giver of all | 1 Chron. 29:10–20 | John 16:1–15* | Spirit and Church |

### FRIDAY

| | | | |
|---|---|---|---|
| Solomon's Prayer | 1 Kings 8:22–30* | John 16:16–33* | Coming and going |
| Ezekiel's Vision | Ezek. 1:1–14* | John 17:1–5 | Prayer for himself |

### SATURDAY

| | | | |
|---|---|---|---|
| Out of the Whirlwind | Job 38:1–11 | John 17:6–19 | For the Apostles |
| Creature and Creator | Job 38:19–38 | John 17:20–26 | 'Nor for these only' |

## SECOND AFTER PENTECOST

GENESIS 12–24            GALATIANS

### MONDAY

| | | | |
|---|---|---|---|
| The Call of Abraham | Gen. 12:1–10 | Gal. 1:1–10 | One Gospel |
| Abraham and Lot | Gen. 13* | Gal. 1:11–24* | Visit to Jerusalem |

### TUESDAY

| | | | |
|---|---|---|---|
| Melchizedek | Gen. 14:8–24* | Gal. 2:1–10* | A Second Visit |
| A Covenant | Gen. 15:1, 5–18* | Gal. 2:11–21 | Peter in Antioch |

### WEDNESDAY

| | | | |
|---|---|---|---|
| Circumcision | Gen. 17:1–19* | Gal. 3:1–5 | Appeal to Experience |
| Visitors to Abraham | Gen. 18:1–15 | Gal. 3:6–22 | Promise and Law |

### THURSDAY

| | | | |
|---|---|---|---|
| Abraham intercedes | Gen. 18:16–33 | Gal. 3:23—4:7* | No longer Slaves |
| Sodom destroyed | Gen. 19:1–3, 12–28* | Gal. 4:8–20 | His Work among them |

### FRIDAY

| | | | |
|---|---|---|---|
| Sarah and Hagar | Gen. 21:1–21* | Gal. 4:21—5:1* | Sarah and Hagar |
| Sacrifice of Isaac | Gen. 22:1–19 | Gal. 5:2–12* | Circumcision |

### SATURDAY

| | | | |
|---|---|---|---|
| Rebekah | Gen. 24:1–4, 10–34 | Gal. 5:13–26 | Living by the Spirit |
| Rebekah and Isaac | Gen. 24:50–67 | Gal. 6* | Last Words |

## THIRD AFTER PENTECOST

GENESIS 25–33            THESSALONIANS

### MONDAY

| | | | |
|---|---|---|---|
| Esau's Birthright | Gen. 25:8–11, 21–34* | 1 Thess. 1* | Thanksgiving |
| Esau's Blessing | Gen. 27:1–29 | 1 Thess. 2:1–12 | His Visit to them |

### TUESDAY

| | | | |
|---|---|---|---|
| Jacob's Flight | Gen. 27:30—28:5 | 1 Thess. 2:13–20* | Their Faithfulness |
| Jacob at Bethel | Gen. 28:10–22 | 1 Thess. 3* | News through Timothy |

### WEDNESDAY

| | | | |
|---|---|---|---|
| Jacob at Paddan-aram | Gen. 29:1–14 | 1 Thess. 4:1–12* | Purity and Love |
| Leah and Rachel | Gen. 29:15–30 | 1 Thess. 4:13–18 | Hope for the Dead |

### THURSDAY

| | | | |
|---|---|---|---|
| Jacob and Laban | Gen. 30:25–43* | 1 Thess. 5:1–11 | A Call to wake up |
| Jacob's Return | Gen. 31:1–21* | 1 Thess. 5:12–28 | A Call to work |

### FRIDAY

| | | | |
|---|---|---|---|
| Parting from Laban | Gen. 31:22–46* | 2 Thess. 1* | Comfort in Trouble |
| Jacob's Fear of Esau | Gen. 32:3–21* | 2 Thess. 2:1–12 | The End not yet |

### SATURDAY

| | | | |
|---|---|---|---|
| Jacob at Jabbok | Gen. 32:22–32 | 2 Thess. 2:13–17 | A Call to stand firm |
| Jacob and Esau | Gen. 33:1–17* | 2 Thess. 3 | Quiet Work |

# FOURTH AFTER PENTECOST

*GENESIS 37–50*                                    *1 CORINTHIANS 1–8*

### MONDAY

| | | | |
|---|---|---|---|
| *Joseph's Brothers* | Gen. 37:1–24 | 1 Cor. 1:1–9 | *Introduction* |
| *Sold into Egypt* | Gen. 37:25–36 | 1 Cor. 1:10–17 | *Against Parties* |

### TUESDAY

| | | | |
|---|---|---|---|
| *Joseph in Egypt* | Gen. 39* | 1 Cor. 1:18–31 | *'God also is wise'* |
| *Butler and Baker* | Gen. 40* | 1 Cor. 2 | *The Mind of Christ* |

### WEDNESDAY

| | | | |
|---|---|---|---|
| *Pharaoh's Dreams* | Gen. 41:1–16, 25–40 | 1 Cor. 3:1–15 | *Christ the Foundation* |
| *The Brothers' Visit* | Gen. 41:53—42:26 | 1 Cor. 3:16–23 | *'All things are yours'* |

### THURSDAY

| | | | |
|---|---|---|---|
| *Their Return* | Gen. 42:29—43:14* | 1 Cor. 4* | *Only God can judge* |
| *Joseph's Greeting* | Gen. 43:15–34* | 1 Cor. 5:1—6:8* | *Proceedings* |

### FRIDAY

| | | | |
|---|---|---|---|
| *The Recognition* | Gen. 45:1–15 | 1 Cor. 6:9–20* | *Members of Christ* |
| *Jacob and Joseph* | Gen. 45:16—46:7 | 1 Cor. 7:1–24* | *Advice to the married* |

### SATURDAY

| | | | |
|---|---|---|---|
| *Joseph's Sons* | Gen. 48:1–19* | 1 Cor. 7:25–40* | *The unmarried* |
| *Death of Jacob* | Gen. 49:28—50:21* | 1 Cor. 8* | *Food offered to Idols* |

# FIFTH AFTER PENTECOST

*EXODUS 1–15*                                    *1 CORINTHIANS 9–14*

### MONDAY

| | | | |
|---|---|---|---|
| *Persecution in Egypt* | Exod. 1:8–14, 22* | 1 Cor. 9:1–18* | *An Apostle's Rights* |
| *Preparation of Moses* | Exod. 2:1–22 | 1 Cor. 9:19–27* | *Paul the Athlete* |

### TUESDAY

| | | | |
|---|---|---|---|
| *The Burning Bush* | Exod. 3:1–12 | 1 Cor. 10:1–22* | *Against Idolatry* |
| *Moses' Commission* | Exod. 3:13–22* | 1 Cor. 10:23—11:1* | *Considering others* |

### WEDNESDAY

| | | | |
|---|---|---|---|
| *The Help of Aaron* | Exod. 4:10–16* | 1 Cor. 11:2–22* | *Rules for Meetings* |
| *Moses and Pharaoh* | Exod. 5:1–12* | 1 Cor. 11:23–34* | *The Lord's Supper* |

### THURSDAY

| | | | |
|---|---|---|---|
| *Darkness in Egypt* | Exod. 10:21–29* | 1 Cor. 12:1–11 | *Many Gifts, one Spirit* |
| *Instructions* | Exod. 12:1–14* | 1 Cor. 12:12–31 | *Members and Body* |

### FRIDAY

| | | | |
|---|---|---|---|
| *The Passover* | Exod. 12:21–28 | 1 Cor. 13 | *The best Gift* |
| *The last Plague* | Exod. 12:29–42 | 1 Cor. 14:1–12 | *Prophecy and Tongues* |

### SATURDAY

| | | | |
|---|---|---|---|
| *The Red Sea* | Exod. 14:8–27 | 1 Cor. 14:13–25 | *Prophecy* |
| *Thanksgiving* | Exod. 15:1–11, 20, 21 | 1 Cor. 14:26–40 | *Rules for Worship* |

## SIXTH AFTER PENTECOST

*EXODUS 16–32*                    *1 COR. 15, 16, & 2 COR. 10–13*

### MONDAY

| | | | |
|---|---|---|---|
| Manna | Exod. 15:27—16:15 | 1 Cor. 15:1–11 | The Gospel |
| Manna and Sabbath | Exod. 16:22–36* | 1 Cor. 15:12–19 | Our Resurrection |

### TUESDAY

| | | | |
|---|---|---|---|
| Rephidim: Water | Exod. 17:1–7* | 1 Cor. 15:20–34 | Christ must reign |
| Battle with Amalek | Exod. 17:8–16* | 1 Cor. 15:35–50 | The Resurrection Body |

### WEDNESDAY

| | | | |
|---|---|---|---|
| Sharing the Work | Exod. 18:13–24* | 1 Cor. 15:51–58 | 'Therefore be stedfast' |
| The People's Promise | Exod. 19:1–9 | 1 Cor. 16* | Personal Messages |

### THURSDAY

| | | | |
|---|---|---|---|
| Moses on the Mount | Exod. 19:10–25 | 2 Cor. 10* | Boasting in the Lord |
| The Commandments | Exod. 20:1–20 | 2 Cor. 11:1–15* | 'I am not inferior' |

### FRIDAY

| | | | |
|---|---|---|---|
| Justice; the Land | Exod. 23:1–11 | 2 Cor. 11:16–33* | Boasting in himself |
| A Covenant of Blood | Exod. 24:1–11 | 2 Cor. 12:1–10 | A Vision and a Thorn |

### SATURDAY

| | | | |
|---|---|---|---|
| The Golden Calf | Exod. 32:1–14* | 2 Cor. 12:11—13:4* | A third Visit |
| Moses intercedes | Exod. 32:15–35* | 2 Cor. 13:5–14* | Farewell and Blessing |

## SEVENTH AFTER PENTECOST

*EXODUS 33–36, LEVITICUS*                    *2 CORINTHIANS 1–9*

### MONDAY

| | | | |
|---|---|---|---|
| The Glory of God | Exod. 33:7–23 | 2 Cor. 1:1–14 | God of all Comfort |
| The Face of Moses | Exod. 34:29–35 | 2 Cor. 1:15—2:4* | His Change of Plan |

### TUESDAY

| | | | |
|---|---|---|---|
| Bezalel's Gift | Exod. 35:20—36:1 | 2 Cor. 2:5–17 | From Life to Life |
| Burnt Offerings | Lev. 1:1–9 | 2 Cor. 3:1–6 | Sufficiency from God |

### WEDNESDAY

| | | | |
|---|---|---|---|
| The Scapegoat | Lev. 16:1–10* | 2 Cor. 3:7–18 | From Glory to Glory |
| Holiness | Lev. 19:1–18 | 2 Cor. 4 | Temporal and eternal |

### THURSDAY

| | | | |
|---|---|---|---|
| Sabbath and Passover | Lev. 23:1–14* | 2 Cor. 5 | Ambassadors for Christ |
| Pentecost | Lev. 23:15–22* | 2 Cor. 6:1–13* | A Plea for a Response |

### FRIDAY

| | | | |
|---|---|---|---|
| The Day of Atonement | Lev. 23:23–32* | 2 Cor. 6:14—7:1* | 'Come out!' |
| Tabernacles | Lev. 23:33–44* | 2 Cor. 7:2–16* | Titus's good News |

### SATURDAY

| | | | |
|---|---|---|---|
| Sabbath-year; Jubilee | Lev. 25:1–12* | 2 Cor. 8* | What to give |
| Redemption | Lev. 25:47–55 | 2 Cor. 9* | How to give |

# EIGHTH AFTER PENTECOST

*NUMBERS*                                             *MATTHEW 1–7*

### MONDAY

| | | |
|---|---|---|
| Cloud and Fire | Num. 9:15–23 | Matt. 1:18–25* | The miraculous Birth |
| Seventy Elders | Num. 11:4–17, 24–29 | Matt. 2* | Signs at the Birth |

### TUESDAY

| | | |
|---|---|---|
| Aaron and Miriam | Num. 12* | Matt. 3* | The Baptism of Jesus |
| The Sending of Spies | Num. 13:1f., 17–24 | Matt. 4:1–11* | The Temptation |

### WEDNESDAY

| | | |
|---|---|---|
| Their Return | Num. 13:25—14:10 | Matt. 4:12–25* | Beginning in Galilee |
| Sin and Punishment | Num. 14:11–25* | Matt. 5:1–16 | Blessedness |

### THURSDAY

| | | |
|---|---|---|
| Kadesh: Moses' Sin | Num. 20:1–13* | Matt. 5:17–37 | Law, old and new |
| The brass Serpent | Num. 21:4–9* | Matt. 5:38–48 | Retaliation and Love |

### FRIDAY

| | | |
|---|---|---|
| Sihon and Og | Num. 21:21–35* | Matt. 6:1–18 | The three good Works |
| Balak and Balaam | Num. 22:2–15, 21–35 | Matt. 6:19–34 | The Single Eye |

### SATURDAY

| | | |
|---|---|---|
| Balaam's Prophecy | Num. 22:36—23:12 | Matt. 7:1–12* | Judging, asking |
| Moses and Joshua | Num. 27:12–23* | Matt. 7:13–29 | Gates and Houses |

# NINTH AFTER PENTECOST

*DEUTERONOMY 1–10*                                   *MATTHEW 8–10*

### MONDAY

| | | |
|---|---|---|
| The last Month | Deut. 1:1–8 | Matt. 8:1–17* | Miracles of Healing |
| The Nearness of God | Deut. 4:1–13* | Matt. 8:18–22* | Cost of Discipleship |

### TUESDAY

| | | |
|---|---|---|
| A Voice out of Fire | Deut. 4:14–24* | Matt. 8:23—9:8* | The Power of Jesus |
| 'The Lord is God' | Deut. 4:25–35* | Matt. 9:9–17* | The Call of Matthew |

### WEDNESDAY

| | | |
|---|---|---|
| Ten Commandments | Deut. 5:1–21* | Matt. 9:18–26* | Two Healings |
| The People's Fear | Deut. 5:22–33* | Matt. 9:27–34* | The Blind, the Dumb |

### THURSDAY

| | | |
|---|---|---|
| 'Hear, O Israel' | Deut. 6:1–12 | Matt. 9:35–38 | The Harvest |
| Teaching their Sons | Deut. 6:20–25* | Matt. 10:1–8 | Called and sent |

### FRIDAY

| | | |
|---|---|---|
| Remembering | Deut. 8:1–10 | Matt. 10:9–15 | Where to preach |
| Humility before God | Deut. 8:11–18 | Matt. 10:16–25 | Sheep among Wolves |

### SATURDAY

| | | |
|---|---|---|
| He has no Favourites | Deut. 9:1–5 | Matt. 10:26–33 | Whom to fear |
| 'He is thy praise' | Deut. 10:12–22 | Matt. 10:34—11:1 | No Peace on Earth |

## TENTH AFTER PENTECOST

*DEUTERONOMY 11–34*                                      *MATTHEW 11–13*

### MONDAY

| | | | |
|---|---|---|---|
| *The Promised Land* | Deut. 11:1–12 | Matt. 11:2–6* | *John's Question* |
| *One Sanctuary* | Deut. 12:1–11* | Matt. 11:7–19 | *Jesus on John* |

### TUESDAY

| | | | |
|---|---|---|---|
| *The Test of Prophecy* | Deut. 13:1–5* | Matt. 11:20–30 | *Woes and Blessings* |
| *Lending and giving* | Deut. 15:1–11* | Matt. 12:1–8* | *Sabbath in the Corn* |

### WEDNESDAY

| | | | |
|---|---|---|---|
| *Promise of a Prophet* | Deut. 18:9–18 | Matt. 12:9–21* | *Healings* |
| *Firstfruits* | Deut. 26:1–11 | Matt. 12:22–32* | *Beelzebub* |

### THURSDAY

| | | | |
|---|---|---|---|
| *A Command, a Choice* | Deut. 30:11–20 | Matt. 12:33–50 | *Signs* |
| *Moses and Joshua* | Deut. 31:1–8* | Matt. 13:1–9* | *The Sower* |

### FRIDAY

| | | | |
|---|---|---|---|
| *The Song of Moses* | Deut. 32:1–12* | Matt. 13:10–23* | *The Use of Parables* |
| *The Rock* | Deut. 32:15, 29–39* | Matt. 13:24–33 | *Weeds, Seed, Leaven* |

### SATURDAY

| | | | |
|---|---|---|---|
| *Moses on Pisgah* | Deut. 32:44–52 | Matt. 13:34–43 | *Jesus' Parables* |
| *The Death of Moses* | Deut. 34 | Matt. 13:44–58 | *More Parables* |

## ELEVENTH AFTER PENTECOST

*JOSHUA*                                                 *MATTHEW 14–18*

### MONDAY

| | | | |
|---|---|---|---|
| *Promise to Joshua* | Josh. 1:1–11 | Matt. 14:1–12* | *The Death of John* |
| *Rahab and the Spies* | Josh. 2:1–21 | Matt. 14:13–36* | *'He had compassion'* |

### TUESDAY

| | | | |
|---|---|---|---|
| *Crossing Jordan* | Josh. 3:1, 9–17 | Matt. 15:1–20* | *What defiles* |
| *Memorial Stones* | Josh. 4:1–11* | Matt. 15:21–28* | *The Greek Woman* |

### WEDNESDAY

| | | | |
|---|---|---|---|
| *Jericho encompassed* | Josh. 5:13—6:11 | Matt. 15:29–39* | *Healing and feeding* |
| *Jericho taken* | Josh. 6:12–23 | Matt. 16:1–12 | *Hypocrisy* |

### THURSDAY

| | | | |
|---|---|---|---|
| *Defeat at Ai* | Josh. 7:1–13* | Matt. 16:13–28 | *Peter's Confession* |
| *Punishment of Achan* | Josh. 7:16–26* | Matt. 17:1–13* | *The Transfiguration* |

### FRIDAY

| | | | |
|---|---|---|---|
| *The Capture of Ai* | Josh. 8:10–22* | Matt. 17:14–27 | *An epileptic Boy* |
| *The Gibeonites* | Josh. 9:3–21* | Matt. 18:1–14 | *Little Ones* |

### SATURDAY

| | | | |
|---|---|---|---|
| *God's Mercies* | Josh. 24:1–13* | Matt. 18:15–20 | *Life in the Church* |
| *The People's Promise* | Josh. 24:14–25 | Matt. 18:21–35 | *The two Debtors* |

# TWELFTH AFTER PENTECOST

*JUDGES*                                                    *MATTHEW 19–24*

### MONDAY

| | | | |
|---|---|---|---|
| *Rebellion; a Saviour* | **Judg. 2:11–23\*** | **Matt. 19:1–15** | *Journey from Galilee* |
| *Deborah and Sisera* | **Judg. 4:1–21\*** | **Matt. 19:16—20:16** | *Love of Money* |

### TUESDAY

| | | | |
|---|---|---|---|
| *The Song of Deborah (1)* | **Judg. 5:1–12** | **Matt. 20:17–28\*** | *A Ransom for many* |
| *The Song of Deborah (2)* | **Judg. 5:19–31** | **Matt. 20:29—21:17** | *Triumphal Entry* |

### WEDNESDAY

| | | | |
|---|---|---|---|
| *The Call of Gideon* | **Judg. 6:1, 11–32** | **Matt. 21:18–32** | *The Priests dispute* |
| *The Defeat of Midian* | **Judg. 7:1–22** | **Matt. 21:33–46\*** | *The Vineyard-farmers* |

### THURSDAY

| | | | |
|---|---|---|---|
| *Jephtha* | **Judg. 11:1–6, 29–40\*** | **Matt. 22:1–22** | *The Marriage-feast* |
| *The Birth of Samson* | **Judges 13\*** | **Matt. 22:23–46\*** | *Questions* |

### FRIDAY

| | | | |
|---|---|---|---|
| *Samson and Delilah* | **Judg. 16:4–22** | **Matt. 23:1–12\*** | *The Pharisees* |
| *The Death of Samson* | **Judg. 16:23–31** | **Matt. 23:13–39** | *The Woes* |

### SATURDAY

| | | | |
|---|---|---|---|
| *Micah and the Levite* | **Judg. 17\*** | **Matt. 24:1–28\*** | *Great Tribulation* |
| *The Founding of Dan* | **Judg.18:1–20,27f.\*** | **Matt. 24:29–51\*†** | *Coming of the Judge* |

# THIRTEENTH AFTER PENTECOST

*1 SAMUEL 1–15*                                             *MATTHEW 26–28*

### MONDAY

| | | | |
|---|---|---|---|
| *Birth of Samuel* | **1 Sam. 1:1–20** | **Matt. 26:1–16\*** | *Anointing at Bethany* |
| *His Dedication* | **1 Sam. 1:21—2:11** | **Matt. 26:17–29\*** | *The Last Supper* |

### TUESDAY

| | | | |
|---|---|---|---|
| *Samuel at Shiloh* | **1 Sam. 2:12–21\*** | **Matt. 26:30–46\*** | *The Agony* |
| *The Lord speaks* | **1 Sam. 3:1–19** | **Matt. 26:47–56\*** | *The Arrest* |

### WEDNESDAY

| | | | |
|---|---|---|---|
| *The Ark captured* | **1 Sam. 4:1–18** | **Matt. 26:57–75\*** | *Caiaphas's House* |
| *The Ark returned* | **1 Sam. 5:1—6:16** | **Matt. 27:1–10\*** | *Judas's Repentance* |

### THURSDAY

| | | | |
|---|---|---|---|
| *Saul comes to Samuel* | **1 Sam. 9:1–14** | **Matt. 27:11–26** | *Jesus before Pilate* |
| *Saul anointed* | **1 Sam. 9:15—10:1\*** | **Matt. 27:27–45** | *The Crucifixion* |

### FRIDAY

| | | | |
|---|---|---|---|
| *Jonathan's Prowess* | **1 Sam. 14:1–15\*** | **Matt. 27:46–56** | *The Death of Jesus* |
| *His Disobedience* | **1 Sam. 14:24–46\*** | **Matt. 27:57–66** | *The Burial* |

### SATURDAY

| | | | |
|---|---|---|---|
| *Defeat of Amalek* | **1 Sam. 15:1–11\*** | **Matt. 28:1–10** | *The Empty Tomb* |
| *Rejection of Saul* | **1 Sam. 15:12–33\*** | **Matt. 28:11–20** | *The Risen Lord* |

† Matthew 25, Fourth Sunday before Christmas.

# FOURTEENTH AFTER PENTECOST

*1 SAMUEL 16–31*                                                    *ROMANS 1–6*

### MONDAY

| | | | |
|---|---|---|---|
| *Anointing of David* | 1 Sam. 16:1–13 | Rom. 1:1–17 | *God's Righteousness* |
| *Saul's Madness* | 1 Sam. 16:14–23 | Rom. 1:18–32* | *Human Wisdom a Snare* |

### TUESDAY

| | | | |
|---|---|---|---|
| *Goliath (1)* | 1 Sam. 17:1–25* | Rom. 2:1–16* | *Greek and Jew* |
| *Goliath (2)* | 1 Sam. 17:26–50* | Rom. 2:17–29 | *The Law a broken Reed* |

### WEDNESDAY

| | | | |
|---|---|---|---|
| *Saul's Jealousy* | 1 Sam. 18:1–16 | Rom. 3:1–20* | *No Man righteous* |
| *David's Escape* | 1 Sam. 19:1–17* | Rom. 3:21–31 | *But God justifies* |

### THURSDAY

| | | | |
|---|---|---|---|
| *Jonathan's Farewell* | 1 Sam. 20:17–39 | Rom. 4:1–12 | *Abraham's Faith* |
| *David spares Saul* | 1 Sam. 24 | Rom. 4:13–25* | *An Example to us* |

### FRIDAY

| | | | |
|---|---|---|---|
| *Abigail (1)* | 1 Sam. 25:1–20* | Rom. 5:1–11 | *Reconciled with God* |
| *Abigail (2)* | 1 Sam. 25:23–33, 35–42* | Rom. 5:12–21* | *Adam and Christ* |

### SATURDAY

| | | | |
|---|---|---|---|
| *The Witch of Endor* | 1 Sam. 28:3–25* | Rom. 6:1–14 | *Buried and raised* |
| *The Death of Saul* | 1 Sam. 31 | Rom. 6:15–23* | *Example from Slavery* |

# FIFTEENTH AFTER PENTECOST

*2 SAMUEL 1–12*                                                    *ROMANS 7–11*

### MONDAY

| | | | |
|---|---|---|---|
| *David hears the News* | 2 Sam. 1:1–16 | Rom. 7:1–6* | *Example from Marriage* |
| *David's Lament* | 2 Sam. 1:17–27 | Rom. 7:7–25* | *How Sin works* |

### TUESDAY

| | | | |
|---|---|---|---|
| *David in Hebron* | 2 Sam. 2:1–11* | Rom. 8:1–11 | *Law of the Spirit* |
| *David in Jerusalem* | 2 Sam. 5:1–10* | Rom. 8:12–17 | *Spirit of Sonship* |

### WEDNESDAY

| | | | |
|---|---|---|---|
| *The Philistines* | 2 Sam. 5:17–25* | Rom. 8:18–30 | *Spirit of Hope* |
| *The Ark in Jerusalem* | 2 Sam. 6:1–19 | Rom. 8:31–39 | *The Love of God* |

### THURSDAY

| | | | |
|---|---|---|---|
| *The Promise to David* | 2 Sam. 7:1–13* | Rom. 9:1–13* | *Rejection of Israel* |
| *David's Prayer* | 2 Sam. 7:18–29* | Rom. 9:14–29* | *God is sovereign* |

### FRIDAY

| | | | |
|---|---|---|---|
| *Mephibosheth* | 2 Sam. 9* | Rom. 9:30—10:10* | *Man is responsible* |
| *Bathsheba* | 2 Sam. 11:1–17 | Rom. 10:11–21* | *God's Offer* |

### SATURDAY

| | | | |
|---|---|---|---|
| *Nathan* | 2 Sam. 12:1–10 | Rom. 11:1–24 | *Rejection not final* |
| *Repentant, punished* | 2 Sam. 12:13–25 | Rom. 11:25–36 | *The Mystery of God* |

## SIXTEENTH AFTER PENTECOST

*2 SAMUEL 15—1 KINGS 1*                                    *ROMANS 12–16*

### MONDAY

| *Absalom's Rebellion* | 2 Sam. 15:1–15 | Rom. 12:1–8 | *One Body in Christ* |
| *David's Flight* | 2 Sam. 15:19–37 | Rom. 12:9–21 | *Practical Religion* |

### TUESDAY

| *Ziba, Shimei* | 2 Sam. 16:1–14 | Rom. 13:1–7* | *'The powers that be'* |
| *Hushai, Ahithophel* | 2 Sam. 17:1–23 | Rom. 13:8–14 | *Love, and wake up!* |

### WEDNESDAY

| *Death of Absalom* | 2 Sam. 18:1–18 | Rom. 14:1–12* | *Weak Consciences* |
| *David's Grief* | 2 Sam. 18:19–33 | Rom. 14:13–23* | *No Quarrels on Food* |

### THURSDAY

| *Joab's Rebuke* | 2 Sam. 19:1–8* | Rom. 15:1–6 | *The Example of Jesus* |
| *David's Return* | 2 Sam. 19:15–39* | Rom. 15:7–13* | *Jew and Gentile* |

### FRIDAY

| *David's last Words* | 2 Sam. 23:1–7* | Rom. 15:14–21 | *Paul's Travels* |
| *David's mighty Men* | 2 Sam. 23:8–23* | Rom. 15:22–33 | *His Plans* |

### SATURDAY

| *Adonijah's Plot* | 1 Kings 1:5–31* | Rom. 16:1–16* | *Personal Messages* |
| *King Solomon* | 1 Kings 1:38–53* | Rom. 16:17–27* | *Last Words* |


## SEVENTEENTH AFTER PENTECOST

*1 KINGS 3–12*                                    *PHIL., COL., PHILEM.*

### MONDAY

| *Solomon's Dream* | 1 Kings 3:3–15 | Phil. 1:1–26* | *Greetings from Prison* |
| *Solomon's Glory* | 1 Kings 4:20–34* | Phil. 1:27—2:13 | *The Mind of Christ* |

### TUESDAY

| *Solomon and Hiram* | 1 Kings 5:1–12* | Phil. 2:14–30* | *Paul's Care* |
| *The Lord's House* | 1 Kings 6:1–14* | Phil. 3:1–16 | *The Goal and the Prize* |

### WEDNESDAY

| *The Ark in the House* | 1 Kings 8:1–11 | Phil. 3:17—4:1* | *A Colony of Heaven* |
| *Solomon's Blessing* | 1 Kings 8:12–21* | Phil. 4:2–23* | *Last Words* |

### THURSDAY

| *Solomon's Prayer* | 1 Kings 8:22–30 | Col. 1:1–20 | *Christ in Creation* |
| *The Dedication* | 1 Kings 8:54–66 | Col. 1:21—2:7 | *God's Will a Mystery* |

### FRIDAY

| *Queen of Sheba* | 1 Kings 10:1–13, 21 f. | Col. 2:8—3:4 | *Life hid in Christ* |
| *Solomon's Sins* | 1 Kings 11:1–13* | Col. 3:5–17 | *He is all, and in all* |

### SATURDAY

| *Ahijah and Jeroboam* | 1 Kings 11:26–40* | Col. 3:18—4:18* | *Last Words* |
| *Rehoboam's Folly* | 1 Kings 11:43—12:16 | Philemon* | *A runaway Slave* |

# EIGHTEENTH AFTER PENTECOST

*1 KINGS 12–22*                                                                 *EPHESIANS*

### MONDAY

| | | | |
|---|---|---|---|
| *Idolatry in Israel* | 1 Kings 12:25–33* | Eph. 1:1–14 | *God's Will a Mystery* |
| *Ahab and Elijah* | 1 Kings 16:29—17:7* | Eph. 1:15–23 | *God's Work in Christ* |

### TUESDAY

| | | | |
|---|---|---|---|
| *Widow of Zarephath* | 1 Kings 17:8–24* | Eph. 2:1–10 | *Created in Christ* |
| *Elijah sent to Ahab* | 1 Kings 18:1–16 | Eph. 2:11–22 | *The one new Man* |

### WEDNESDAY

| | | | |
|---|---|---|---|
| *The Failure of Baal* | 1 Kings 18:17–29 | Eph. 3:1–13 | *Paul's Mission* |
| *The Lord's Triumph* | 1 Kings 18:30–46 | Eph. 3:14–21 | *His Prayer for them* |

### THURSDAY

| | | | |
|---|---|---|---|
| *Elijah on Horeb* | 1 Kings 19 | Eph. 4:1–16* | *One Spirit* |
| *A Prophet on Ahab* | 1 Kings 20:23–43* | Eph. 4:17–32* | *A new Nature* |

### FRIDAY

| | | | |
|---|---|---|---|
| *The Murder of Naboth* | 1 Kings 21:1–16 | Eph. 5:1–14* | *Imitators of God* |
| *Elijah on Ahab* | 1 Kings 21:17–29 | Eph. 5:15–20* | *A Faith that sings* |

### SATURDAY

| | | | |
|---|---|---|---|
| *Prophecy of Micaiah* | 1 Kings 22:1–28* | Eph. 5:21—6:9* | *A Faith that works* |
| *The Death of Ahab* | 1 Kings 22:29–40* | Eph. 6:10–24* | *A Faith that fights* |

# NINETEENTH AFTER PENTECOST

*2 KINGS 2–13*                                                                 *LUKE 1–4*

### MONDAY

| | | | |
|---|---|---|---|
| *Ascension of Elijah* | 2 Kings 2:1–14 | Luke 1:1–25* | *Promise to Zechariah* |
| *The Defeat of Moab* | 2 Kings 3:4–24* | Luke 1:26–38* | *The Promise to Mary* |

### TUESDAY

| | | | |
|---|---|---|---|
| *The Shunamite Woman* | 2 Kings 4:1–17 | Luke 1:39–56* | *Mary and Elizabeth* |
| *A Resurrection* | 2 Kings 4:18–37 | Luke 1:57–66* | *The Birth of John* |

### WEDNESDAY

| | | | |
|---|---|---|---|
| *Naaman healed* | 2 Kings 5:1–19 | Luke 1:67–80* | *Thanksgiving* |
| *Chariots of Fire* | 2 Kings 6:8–23 | Luke 2:1–7* | *The Birth of Jesus* |

### THURSDAY

| | | | |
|---|---|---|---|
| *Samaria besieged* | 2 Kings 6:24—7:2* | Luke 2:8–20 | *The Shepherds* |
| *Samaria delivered* | 2 Kings 7:3–20* | Luke 2:21–40 | *The Presentation* |

### FRIDAY

| | | | |
|---|---|---|---|
| *Elisha and Jehu* | 2 Kings 9:1–13 | Luke 2:41–52 | *The Boy Jesus* |
| *Joram and Jezebel* | 2 Kings 9:14–37* | Luke 3:1–14 | *John the Baptist* |

### SATURDAY

| | | | |
|---|---|---|---|
| *Jehu and Baalites* | 2 Kings 10:15–28* | Luke 3:15–22 | *The Baptism of Jesus* |
| *The Death of Elisha* | 2 Kings 13:14–21* | Luke 4:1–13 | *The Temptation* |

# TWENTIETH AFTER PENTECOST

*KINGS 16–25*                                              *LUKE 4–7*

### MONDAY

| | | |
|---|---|---|
| Ahaz and Assyria | 2 Kings 16:1–11* | Luke 4:14–30 | *Nazareth: Rejection* |
| The Fall of Samaria | 2 Kings 17:1–14* | Luke 4:31–44* | *Healing and praying* |

### TUESDAY

| | | |
|---|---|---|
| Hezekiah | 2 Kings 18:1–8 | Luke 5:1–11 | *The Catch of Fish* |
| Sennacherib's Threat | 2 Kings 18:13–25 | Luke 5:12–26* | *Two Healings* |

### WEDNESDAY

| | | |
|---|---|---|
| Isaiah's Prophecy | 2 Kings 19:1–19 | Luke 5:27–39* | *The Call of Levi* |
| End of Sennacherib | 2 Kings 19:20–37 | Luke 6:1–11* | *Lord of the Sabbath* |

### THURSDAY

| | | |
|---|---|---|
| Josiah and the Book | 2 Kings 22:3–20 | Luke 6:12–26* | *The Twelve; Teaching* |
| Josiah's Reformation | 2 Kings 23:1–20 | Luke 6:27–38 | *The Love of Enemies* |

### FRIDAY

| | | |
|---|---|---|
| The Passover | 2 Kings 23:21–30* | Luke 6:39–49* | *Judging and doing* |
| Nebuchadnezzar | 2 Kings 24:8–17* | Luke 7:1–17 | *Two Miracles* |

### SATURDAY

| | | |
|---|---|---|
| Zedekiah; Exile | 2 Kings 24:18—25:12* | Luke 7:18–35 | *John the Baptist* |
| The Remnant | 2 Kings 25:22–30* | Luke 7:36–50 | *Woman with Ointment* |

# TWENTY-FIRST AFTER PENTECOST

*EZRA–NEHEMIAH*                                            *LUKE 8–10*

### MONDAY

| | | |
|---|---|---|
| Cyrus's Proclamation | Ezra 1* | Luke 8:1–18* | *The Sower* |
| Altar and Temple | Ezra 3* | Luke 8:19–25* | *A Storm stilled* |

### TUESDAY

| | | |
|---|---|---|
| Arrival of Ezra | Ezra 7:1, 6–10* | Luke 8:26–39* | *The Gerasene Demoniac* |
| Ezra's own Account | Ezra 8:15–32* | Luke 8:40–56* | *Two Healings* |

### WEDNESDAY

| | | |
|---|---|---|
| The Walls in Ruin | Neh. 1 | Luke 9:1–9 | *The Twelve sent out* |
| Arrival of Nehemiah | Neh. 2 | Luke 9:10–17* | *The Crowds fed* |

### THURSDAY

| | | |
|---|---|---|
| Work and Opposition | Neh. 4:6–23 | Luke 9:18–27 | *Peter's Confession* |
| Usury stopped | Neh. 5 | Luke 9:28–36 | *The Transfiguration* |

### FRIDAY

| | | |
|---|---|---|
| The Walls finished | Neh. 6:1–15 | Luke 9:37–50* | *The End in Galilee* |
| Reading the Law | Neh. 8:1–3, 5–18 | Luke 9:51–62 | *Journey to Jerusalem* |

### SATURDAY

| | | |
|---|---|---|
| Dedication | Neh. 12:27–31, 37–43* | Luke 10:1–24 | *Seventy sent out* |
| Nehemiah's Reforms | Neh. 13:15–31* | Luke 10:25–42 | *The Good Samaritan* |

## TWENTY-SECOND AFTER PENTECOST

*DANIEL 1-6*                                                 *LUKE 11-14*

### MONDAY

| Daniel in Captivity | Dan. 1 | Luke 11:1-13 | On Prayer |
| The King's Dream | Dan. 2:1-12 | Luke 11:14-26* | Beelzebub |

### TUESDAY

| Daniel prays | Dan. 2:13-24 | Luke 11:27-36* | Signs |
| Daniel interprets | Dan. 2:25-46 | Luke 11:37-54* | Pharisees; Lawyers |

### WEDNESDAY

| The Image of Gold | Dan. 3:1-18 | Luke 12:1-21 | Whom to fear |
| Saved from Fire | Dan. 3:19-30 | Luke 12:22-34* | Anxiety |

### THURSDAY

| A Dream of a Tree | Dan. 4:1-18* | Luke 12:35-48 | Faithful Servants |
| Nebuchadnezzar mad | Dan. 4:19-34* | Luke 12:49-59 | No Peace on Earth |

### FRIDAY

| Writing on the Wall | Dan. 5:1-12* | Luke 13:1-17 | 'Repent or perish' |
| Daniel interprets | Dan. 5:13-31* | Luke 13:18-35* | 'Are many saved?' |

### SATURDAY

| Plot against Daniel | Dan. 6:1-14* | Luke 14:1-14 | On Humility |
| Saved from Lions | Dan. 6:15-28* | Luke 14:15-35* | The Cost of following |


## TWENTY-THIRD AFTER PENTECOST

*RUTH, JONAH, ESTHER*                                        *LUKE 15-19*

### MONDAY

| Ruth and Naomi | Ruth 1 | Luke 15:1-10 | Seeking the lost |
| Kindness of Boaz | Ruth 2:1-17 | Luke 15:11-32 | The Two Sons |

### TUESDAY

| Ruth goes to Boaz | Ruth 3 | Luke 16:1-13 | The Dishonest Steward |
| Boaz marries Ruth | Ruth 4:1-17 | Luke 16:14-31 | A certain rich Man |

### WEDNESDAY

| Jonah's Flight | Jonah 1:1-16* | Luke 17:1-10* | Offences |
| Jonah's Return | Jonah 1:17—2:10* | Luke 17:11-19* | Ten Lepers |

### THURSDAY

| Nineveh converted | Jonah 3 | Luke 17:20-37 | Kingdom and Day |
| Jonah rebuked | Jonah 4 | Luke 18:1-14* | Two Stories of Faith |

### FRIDAY

| The King's Choice | Esth. 2:5-23* | Luke 18:15-30* | The rich young Ruler |
| Haman and the Jews | Esth. 3* | Luke 18:31-43* | Bartimaeus |

### SATURDAY

| Esther's Boldness | Esth. 4:1—5:8* | Luke 19:1-10 | Zacchaeus |
| Downfall of Haman | Esth. 6:1—7:10* | Luke 19:11-28* | The Pounds |

# TWENTY-FOURTH AFTER PENTECOST

*JOB*                                                              *LUKE 20–24*

### MONDAY

| | | |
|---|---|---|
| *The good Man tested* | **Job 1** | **Luke 19:29—20:8*** *Arrival in Jerusalem* |
| *A second Test* | **Job 2*** | **Luke 20:9–47*** *Jesus and the Leaders* |

### TUESDAY

| | | |
|---|---|---|
| *Job's Complaint* | **Job 3:1–17** | **Luke 21:1–19*** *Warnings of the End* |
| *A 'Comforter'* | **Job 4:1–17** | **Luke 21:20–38** *'Therefore watch!'* |

### WEDNESDAY

| | | |
|---|---|---|
| *One of Job's Replies* | **Job 13:1–15** | **Luke 22:1–23** *The Last Supper* |
| *Man's Transience* | **Job 14:1–13*** | **Luke 22:24–46** *After Supper* |

### THURSDAY

| | | |
|---|---|---|
| *Hope of a Redeemer* | **Job 19:14–27*** | **Luke 22:47–71*** *Arrest and Trial* |
| *A Cry for Justice* | **Job 31:13–37*** | **Luke 23:1–25** *Condemnation* |

### FRIDAY

| | | |
|---|---|---|
| *God's Answer* | **Job 38:1–11** | **Luke 23:26–49*** *Crucifixion* |
| *Breadth of the Earth* | **Job 38:18–38*** | **Luke 23:50—24:12*** *The Women* |

### SATURDAY

| | | |
|---|---|---|
| *Job's Vision of God* | **Job 42:1–6** | **Luke 24:13–35** *The Walk to Emmaus* |
| *His Vindication* | **Job 42:7–17*** | **Luke 24:36–53** *Command and Promise* |

If there are any weeks coming between the week of the twenty-fourth Sunday after Pentecost and the beginning of Advent, the passages provided for Extra Weeks are read in order, excluding any that have been read earlier the same year (see the Table on p. 186).

# FIRST EXTRA WEEK

*PROVERBS*                                                        *TIMOTHY, TITUS*

### MONDAY

| | | |
|---|---|---|
| *Wisdom invites Men* | **Prov. 1:20–33*** | **1 Tim. 1:1–17** *The Task in Ephesus* |
| *Wisdom in Creation* | **Prov. 3:11–20** | **1 Tim. 1:18—2:15*** *Public Worship* |

### TUESDAY

| | | |
|---|---|---|
| *The Principal Thing* | **Prov. 4:1–9*** | **1 Tim. 3** *The House of God* |
| *The Marks of Wisdom* | **Prov. 6:6–19** | **1 Tim. 4** *Timothy's Task* |

### WEDNESDAY

| | | |
|---|---|---|
| *The Call of Wisdom* | **Prov. 8:1–17** | **1 Tim. 5:1—6:2** *Dealing with People* |
| *Wisdom is eternal* | **Prov. 8:22–36** | **1 Tim. 6:3–21*** *Final Warnings* |

### THURSDAY

| | | |
|---|---|---|
| *The House of Wisdom* | **Prov. 9:1–10*** | **2 Tim. 1*** *Greeting from Prison* |
| *Fools and Sluggards* | **Prov. 26:1–16*** | **2 Tim. 2*** *A Soldier of Christ* |

### FRIDAY

| | | |
|---|---|---|
| *Various* | **Prov. 27:6–22*** | **2 Tim. 3** *Evil Days ahead* |
| *The Words of Agur* | **Prov. 30:1–9** | **2 Tim. 4*** *His Farewell* |

### SATURDAY

| | | |
|---|---|---|
| *Some Numbers* | **Prov. 30:15–31*** | **Tit. 1:1—2:10*** *Life in the Church* |
| *The good Wife* | **Prov. 31:10–31** | **Tit. 2:11—3:15** *The blessed Hope* |

## SECOND EXTRA WEEK

*VARIOUS*                                                    *JESUS' MEETINGS*

### MONDAY

| | | | |
|---|---|---|---|
| *Where is Wisdom?* | Job 28:1–12 | Mark 1:16–20 | *The first Disciples* |
| *The Fear of the Lord* | Job 28:12–28 | Mark 5:1–20* | *The Gerasene Demoniac* |

### TUESDAY

| | | | |
|---|---|---|---|
| *Duet: Man and Maid* | Song 1:9—2:7* | Mark 7:24–30* | *An impatient Mother* |
| *Village Wedding* | Song 3:6–11 | Mark 9:14–29* | *An impatient Father* |

### WEDNESDAY

| | | | |
|---|---|---|---|
| *The lost Lover* | Song 5:2–8* | Mark 10:17–22* | *The rich young Ruler* |
| *The Woman speaks* | Song 7:10—8:7* | Luke 7:1–10 | *The good Centurion* |

### THURSDAY

| | | | |
|---|---|---|---|
| *Jerusalem desolate* | Lam. 2:5–12* | Luke 7:36–50 | *Woman with Ointment* |
| *A Prayer for Help* | Lam. 2:13–22 | Luke 19:1–10 | *Zacchaeus* |

### FRIDAY

| | | | |
|---|---|---|---|
| *Solomon's Experience* | Eccl. 1 | Luke 23:32–43* | *The penitent Thief* |
| *Times and Seasons* | Eccl. 3:1–15* | John 3:1–15 | *Nicodemus* |

### SATURDAY

| | | | |
|---|---|---|---|
| *One Event to all* | Eccl. 9:1–16* | John 4:46–54* | *A certain Nobleman* |
| *Advice to the young* | Eccl. 11:9—12:8 | John 7:53—8:11 | *An Adulteress* |

## THIRD EXTRA WEEK

*CHRONICLES*                          *THE CREED IN THE EPISTLES*

### MONDAY

| | | | |
|---|---|---|---|
| *David succeeds Saul* | 1 Chron. 10:1—11:3 | Col. 1:9–20 | *Father and Son* |
| *A Leader* | 1 Chron. 12:16–23, 38–40 | Phil. 2:1–11 | *'was made man'* |

### TUESDAY

| | | | |
|---|---|---|---|
| *David's Legacy* | 1 Chron. 28:1–10 | 1 Pet. 2:18–25 | *'was crucified'* |
| *Plans for the Temple* | 1 Chron. 28:11–21 | 1 Cor. 15:12–20 | *'He rose again'* |

### WEDNESDAY

| | | | |
|---|---|---|---|
| *The People's Offering* | 1 Chron. 29:1–9 | Col. 3:1–11 | *'on the right hand'* |
| *Solomon anointed* | 1 Chron. 29:10–25 | 1 Thess. 5:1–11 | *'He shall come again'* |

### THURSDAY

| | | | |
|---|---|---|---|
| *The Ark in the Temple* | 2 Chron. 5* | Rom. 8:1–11* | *The Holy Spirit* |
| *Judah in Battle* | 2 Chron. 13:1–17* | 1 Cor. 3:10–23* | *The Catholic Church* |

### FRIDAY

| | | | |
|---|---|---|---|
| *Athaliah, Jehoiada* | 2 Chron. 22:10—23:15* | Heb. 12:1, 2, 18–24* | *The Saints* |
| *Zechariah martyred* | 2 Chron. 24:15–25* | Rom. 5:1–11* | *Forgiveness of Sins* |

### SATURDAY

| | | | |
|---|---|---|---|
| *Uzziah* | 2 Chron. 26:1–5, 16–21* | 1 Cor. 15:51–58* | *The Resurrection* |
| *Hezekiah's Worship* | 2 Chron. 29:20–30* | Rev. 21:23—22:5* | *The World to come* |

# FOURTH EXTRA WEEK

*GOD'S LOVE FOR ALL*

### MONDAY

| | | | |
|---|---|---|---|
| *Promise to Abraham* | Gen. 12:1–9 | Matt. 28:16–20 | *Jesus' Commission* |
| *Promise to Jacob* | Gen. 28:10–22* | Mark 14:3–9* | *Throughout the World* |

### TUESDAY

| | | | |
|---|---|---|---|
| *The Earth to know God* | Isa. 11:1–9 | John 10:7–16 | *'Other sheep I have'* |
| *Assyria, Egypt, Israel* | Isa. 19:23–25* | John 12:20–32* | *'I will draw all men'* |

### WEDNESDAY

| | | | |
|---|---|---|---|
| *Light to Gentiles* | Isa. 42:1–9* | Acts 1:1–11 | *The Ends of the Earth* |
| *Witnesses to all* | Isa. 43:1–13* | Acts 2:29–39* | *'All that are far off'* |

### THURSDAY

| | | | |
|---|---|---|---|
| *The Ends of the Earth* | Isa. 49:1–6 | Rom. 11:25–36 | *Mercy on all* |
| *'I will gather'* | Isa. 56:1–8 | 1 Cor. 15:20–25* | *In Christ all live* |

### FRIDAY

| | | | |
|---|---|---|---|
| *To teach the Nations* | Ezek. 36:16–28* | Eph. 1:1–10 | *To sum up All Things* |
| *The Lord of all* | Amos 9:1–7* | Col. 1:9–23* | *In all Creation* |

### SATURDAY

| | | | |
|---|---|---|---|
| *Many Nations* | Mic. 4:1–5 | Rev. 5:1–10 | *Men of every Tribe* |
| *Gentile Worship* | Mal. 1:6–11 | Rev. 7:9–17* | *A great Multitude* |

# ADDITIONAL READINGS
# FROM THE APOCRYPHA

*(These Readings may be used instead of the Readings from the Old Testament in any
of the Extra Weeks except the first)*

*MACCABEES, WISDOM*            *ECCLESIASTICUS*

### MONDAY

| | | | |
|---|---|---|---|
| *Antiochus Epiphanes* | 1 Macc. 1:1–15 | Ecclus. 2 | *Seek the Lord* |
| *His Persecution* | 1 Macc. 1:41–64 | Ecclus. 4:11–28 | *Wisdom and her Sons* |

### TUESDAY

| | | | |
|---|---|---|---|
| *Mattathias rebels* | 1 Macc. 2:1–28 | Ecclus. 7:26–36 | *Duties* |
| *Keeping the Sabbath* | 1 Macc. 2:29–48 | Ecclus. 22:27—23:15 | *Ruling the Mouth* |

### WEDNESDAY

| | | | |
|---|---|---|---|
| *Judas Maccabeus* | 1 Macc. 3:1–26 | Ecclus. 25:1–11 | *Happiness* |
| *Cleansing the Temple* | 1 Macc. 4:36–61 | Ecclus. 28:1–12 | *Forgiveness* |

### THURSDAY

| | | | |
|---|---|---|---|
| *'Love righteousness'* | Wisd. 1 | Ecclus. 29:1–13 | *Neighbourliness* |
| *The Wicked* | Wisd. 2:1–20 | Ecclus. 35:1–11 | *Offerings* |

### FRIDAY

| | | | |
|---|---|---|---|
| *Immortality* | Wisd. 2:21—3:9 | Ecclus. 36:1–17 | *Missionary Canticle* |
| *Wisdom* | Wisd. 7:15—8:1 | Ecclus. 38:24–34 | *The Workmen* |

### SATURDAY

| | | | |
|---|---|---|---|
| *Prayer for Wisdom* | Wisd. 9 | Ecclus. 44:1–15 | *Hymn of the Fathers* |
| *Repentance* | Wisd. 11:21—12:2 | Ecclus. 51:1–12 | *Ben Sira's Prayer* |

PRINTED IN GREAT BRITAIN
AT THE UNIVERSITY PRESS, OXFORD
BY VIVIAN RIDLER
PRINTER TO THE UNIVERSITY